Barcelona

A CITY GUIDE

by
George Semler

SOMERSET LIMITED

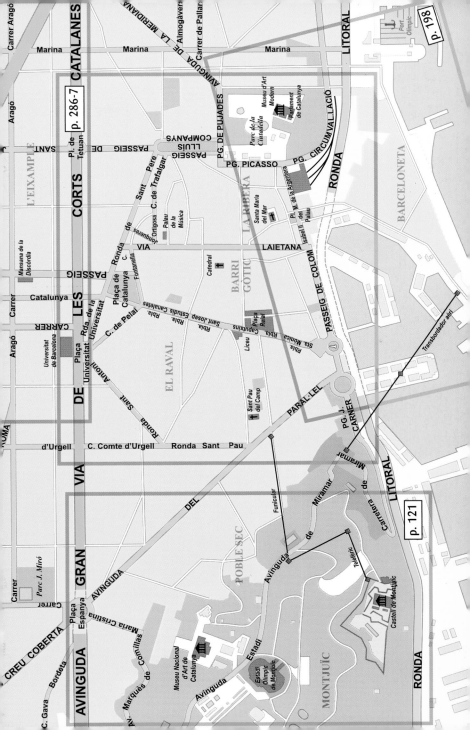

Layout & design: *Regina Rácz*
Photographs: *Mihail Moldoveanu, Annabel Barber, Thomas Howells,
Christine Scharf, Dorota Wasik, Peter Frew,*
*©MNAC (Calaveras/Mérida/Sagristà), Hungart (p. 48, Pablo Picasso: 'El
Paseo de Colón'; p. 132, Pablo Picasso: 'Picasso y Junyer llegan a París'),
courtesy of Lluís Domènech Girbau (p. 91),
courtesy of Carmen Güell (p. 104)*
Editor: *Annabel Barber*
Ground plans & colour drawings: *Imre Bába*
Line drawings: *Michael Mansell RIBA*
Maps: *Dimap Bt.*

Acknowledgements:
*With thanks to Lucie Hayes Semler, Lluís Domènech Girbau,
Mónika Papp, James Townsend Pi-Sunyer*

This is the first edition of **Visible Cities Barcelona**:
corrections, comments and views will be welcomed.

Other titles in the Visible Cities series:
Visible Cities Budapest
Visible Cities Dubrovnik
Visible Cities Krakow
Visible Cities Vienna
Further titles are in preparation.

Cover illustration: *Detail from the roof of La Pedrera, Digital Vision*
Previous page and chapter headers: *The Catalan shield,
from a house on the Rambla*

George Semler (*pictured on p. 209*), a Barcelona resident since 1975, has
written books and articles on cultural aspects of Spain, Morocco, Cuba and
France for publications ranging from *Saveur* magazine to the *International
Herald Tribune* and the *Los Angeles Times*. He is presently completing a book
about the Pyrenees.

ISBN 963 206 323 6
ISSN 1587-6403

CONTENTS

INTRODUCTION

Capital of Catalonia and traditionally Spain's most cosmopolitan metropolis, Barcelona is one of the most visually exciting cities in Europe. The medieval romance of its Gothic Quarter and the feast of architecture from Roman and Romanesque to Art Nouveau - including the fantasmagoric creations of Antoni Gaudí - all come together in a glorious compendium. The aura and influence of Picasso and Miró permeate this steamy port city - but it is not only its love-affair with the avant garde that makes it what it is. Catalonia's national poet, Jacint Verdaguer, described Barcelona as soaring on 'the wings of art and industry'. He was right: the two are never far apart. A strong medieval merchant tradition has left its mark, and the spirit of the 19th-century textile barons who formed the ruling elite has refused to die, despite bloody uprisings and a civil war. Barcelona is prosperous and commercially astute, a vibrant crossroads between western Europe and the Mediterranean. The city today is thriving as never before, relentlessly alive and artistically omnivorous.

Don't expect to learn much about Spain in Barcelona. This is the least Spanish of all the country's cities, more Mediterranean than Iberian, and historically and linguistically closer to Marseilles than Madrid. Plenty of Catalans feel only nominally part of Spain, seeing themselves as a nation without a state, an entity apart, where southern passion and northern common sense come together in a unique brew of artistic daring and business acumen, a peculiar mixture of the conservative and the revolutionary.

CATALAN

A full-fledged Romance language directly descended from Provençal French, Catalan was first suppressed in 1715 after the War of the Spanish Succession. A late 19th-century reflourishing of Catalan culture revived it as a literary language with a fixed orthography. The military dictatorship of Primo de Rivera (1923-1931) again officially banned Catalan, though the Second Spanish Republic (1931-1936) conceded ample autonomy to Catalonia, including full linguistic normalization.

View out to sea across the sprawling city, from the esplanade at Gaudí's Parc Güell.

The centralist Franco regime (1939-1975) repressed Catalan more vigorously than ever, though after Franco's death the language made a powerful comeback. All Catalans understand and speak Castilian Spanish, though many feel more at home in their own language. Debate currently rages as to how best to safeguard Catalan's survival while ensuring full competence in Spanish, Spain's one common tongue.

PRONUNCIATION

ç: like the 's' in 'sin'
j: like the 'zh' in 'treasure'
ll: like the soft 'ly' in 'valiant'

l.l: like the 'll' in 'dalliance'
tx: like the 'ch' in 'cheek'
x: like the 'sh' in 'shell'

MAJOR BARCELONA DISTRICTS

El Barri Gòtic (Gothic Quarter): The ancient center, a warren of narrow alleys. Key sights include the cathedral (*p. 49*) and the Plaça del Rei (*p. 155*).

La Ribera: Barcelona's waterfront district, once home to its seafarers and artisans. Includes the church of Santa Maria del Mar (*p. 70*) and Carrer Montcada with the Picasso Museum (*p. 131*).

El Raval: This district of former convents was once notoriously seamy. It still can be. Things to see include the ancient church of Sant Pau del Camp (*p. 77*), the medieval Hospital de la Santa Creu (*p. 191*), Gaudí's Palau Güell (*p. 103*), and the MACBA contemporary art museum (*p. 130*).

L'Eixample: A late 19th-century geometric grid. This is the best place to see Modernist architecture, including the Sagrada Família (*p. 63*) and La Pedrera (*p. 60*).

Gràcia: Named for the Santa Maria de Jesús de Gràcia convent destroyed in 1714 and rebuilt in this outlying village, Gràcia became a 19th-century factory town and working-class enclave. Casa Vicens, Gaudí's first house, and works by his right-hand man, Francesc Berenguer, are highlights. (*p. 219*).

Pedralbes & Sarrià: Once an outlying village, now a leafy, lively residential neighborhood, best known for its exquisite medieval convent (*p. 207*).

Montjuïc: Hill overlooking the city, quarried for the stone that built it, and now home to its major art gallery, MNAC (*p. 123*), and the Miró museum (*p. 123*).

Barceloneta: Picturesque early fishing district situated between the Port Olímpic and the Marina, with excellent rice and seafood restaurants and sandy beaches (*p. 199ff.*).

Rambla de Catalunya.

TEN THINGS TO DO IN BARCELONA

Some ideas for getting the most out of the city - above and beyond the major sights described on pp. 31-74.

1. Glimpse the relationship between Modernism and its patrons in the solemn madness of Palau Güell (*p. 103*).

2. Dazzle ears and eyes alike at the Modernist tour de force Palau de la Música Catalana (*p. 143*).

3. Watch generations team up to build *castells* (human towers), a dramatic and moving spectacle (*p. 140*).

4. Spend an evening grazing through taverns and tapas in La Ribera (*p. 177*).

5. See one of Europe's most beautiful medieval cloisters, the Monestir de Pedralbes (*p. 208*).

6. Dine at Casa Calvet, the Gaudí-designed former offices of a textile baron (*p. 244*).

7. Try a paella or a bouillabaisse-like *arroz caldoso* overlooking the Mediterranean in Barceloneta (*p. 199*).

8. Visit the MNAC for a tour of Catalan art, from Romanesque to modern (*p. 123*).

9. Drink coffee in the patio of a medieval palace, the Museu Tèxtil (*p. 134*).

10. Stroll down the other Rambla - Rambla de Catalunya in the stylish Eixample (*p. 231*).

HISTORIA NACIONAL
DE CATALUNYA

PER A. ROVIRA I VIRGILI

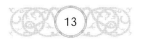
HISTORY

Barcelona's history up to its triumphal Olympic Games of 1992 was a checkered saga of brilliant moments interspersed with promises broken and promise unfulfilled. That a city once the capital of a medieval Mediterranean empire, now administrative seat of a region with more inhabitants than Denmark or Norway, should end up struggling for the right to maintain its own language and culture is one of Europe's greatest and, until recently, least understood dramas.

An aboriginal Iberian people called the Laietani were the first known settlers of the hills between the mouths of the Llobregat and Besòs rivers. One of their settlements, on the promontory now known as Montjuïc, was called Barkena. That this was inscribed on Iberian coins unearthed recently in archeological digs debunks the romantic theory that the Carthaginian general Hamilcar Barca, father of Hannibal, had founded the city around 237 BC, and the even more fanciful legend that the city was founded by Hercules.

When a Roman colony was established as Colonia Favencia Julia Augusta Paterna Barcino, part of Hispania Citerior, Barcino (pronounced _bark_-eeno) was a nod to the local toponym and identity: and indeed identity has been Barcelona's battle-cry ever since. The initial walls of that Roman town - originally little more than a way-station between Empúries to the north and the regional capital at Tarraco, now Tarragona - were built in the 1st century during the Pax Romana, when Rome's supremacy in the Mediterranean was uncontested. Three hundred years later that supremacy was beginning to falter, and despite the construction of the massive defensive walls still partially visible today, Barcelona fell to the Visigoths. Their king, Ataülf (reigned 410-415), set up court at Barcelona, and the city enjoyed a period of prosperity until the Visigoths transferred their capital to Toledo in the mid 6th century. Then, in 717, the Moors roared through Barcelona on their northward conquering steamroller. The city remained under Muslim rule until delivered by Charlemagne's armies in 801. In less than a century the city had been ruled by Visigoths, Moors and Franks.

Sant Jordi (St George), patron saint of Catalonia, as depicted on the cover of a history book. Jordi was adopted as patron after allegedly saving a local princess from the jaws of a dragon. His image adorns the city everywhere, and his feast day (April 23rd) is a major event.

The guilds of medieval Barcelona, each with its patron saint. The top echelon of Barcelona artisans was respresented in the city's early parliament.

MEDIEVAL BARCELONA: THE SOVEREIGN COUNTS

The Visigoths had had a vision of a united Christian Iberia. The Moors had wanted to conquer the entire peninsula and unite it under Allah. It is to the Franks that Catalonia owes its separate identity and status. In the 9th century the region became the Marca Hispanica (Spanish March), the southernmost edge of the sprawling Carolingian Empire, designed as a buffer zone against the Moorish Al-Andalus, which began at the Massif del Garraf just south of Barcelona. Eventually Catalonia would fall through the cracks between the over-extended Franks to the north and the Moorish empire to the south.

The Franks divided the Marca into geographical entities ruled by counts, of whom Sunifred and later his son Guifré el Pilós (Wilfred the Hairy) emerged as the strongest. As the authority of the Frankish kings gradually weakened, so that of the Marca's sovereign counts grew stronger. When Guifré died in 897 he passed his title on to his son as a hereditary right rather than by designation of the Frankish king, another step in the development of Catalan sovereignty. A century later, when Al-Mansur, Moorish regent of Cordoba, sacked Barcelona, Sovereign Count Borrell II requested help from the Franks; he received none, and thus ended any vestigial feudal allegiance. As of 988, Catalonia was on its own: a loose federation of counties, with Barcelona as its capital.

Over the next four generations of sovereign counts, Barcelona and Catalonia consolidated authority over the former Marca and expanded into southern France. In 1137, Ramon Berenguer IV, through his marriage to the infant daughter of King Ramiro II of Aragon, united Catalonia with the peninsular and landlocked House of Aragon: a fateful alliance that aided the rise of Catalonia in the Mediterranean but eventually led to Catalonia's political eclipse after Aragon's union with the Spanish crowns of Castile and León (*see p. 17*).

MEDITERRANEAN EMPIRE & EARLY DEMOCRACY

Jaume I el Conqueridor (1208-1276) is one of the greatest figures in Catalan history. Captured by the French at the age of 5 when his father Pere I was killed in battle, he returned to Catalonia and was proclaimed king, ruling from the year 1225 until his death 50 years later. It was during his reign that Catalonia's Mediterranean expansion was largely achieved and its maritime code of law, the *Llibre del consolat de mar*, was compiled. Jaume even dictated his own

autobiography, the *Llibre dels faits* ('Book of Deeds'). Described as tall, handsome and sensitive, El Conqueridor was the paradigmatic Catalan hero. He conquered Majorca in 1229, later adding Ibiza and Valencia to Catalonia's Mediterranean empire. During his reign Barcelona grew rapidly. New walls were erected - the second set - encircling the Sant Pere and Ribera areas. Elections of municipal representatives led to the

King Jaume I (d. 1276), architect of Catalonia's medieval maritime empire.

PHOTO: MUSEU NACIONAL D'ART DE CATALUNYA

Mural showing Sovereign Count Jaume I's military encampment on Majorca. He took the island from the Moors in 1229.

establishment of the Consell de Cent in 1265, which rivals Westminster as Europe's earliest parliament. The Consell, two-thirds patricians and one-third wealthy merchants and artisans, advised the municipal magistrates who governed the city up until the Bourbon conquest of Barcelona in 1714. It was another sovereign count, Pere II el Gran, who set up a governing body, the Corts de Barcelona, in 1283. These Corts became known as the Generalitat from the 14th century; the Generalitat still governs Catalonia today.

The empire continued to grow. Pere III (1336-1387) controlled Majorca and the Balearic Islands, the region of Roussillon in southern France (still known as 'Catalunya Nord' by Catalan nationalists) as far north as Montpellier, as well as Sicily and Sardinia. Even Athens was a colony of the Crown of Aragon from 1311 to 1381 as Catalonia gradually acquired stepping stones across the Mediterranean to the rich trading fields of gold and spices beyond. The Barcelona shipyards added relentlessly to a Catalan navy and merchant fleet, said to be so vast that 'not even a fish dared swim the Mediterranean without the colors of the *senyera*' (Catalonia's red and gold striped flag). Skilled artisans and consummate traders, Barcelona merchants imported raw materials from around the Mediterranean and exported manufactured goods, primarily textiles, as well as iron and steel weaponry from the Pyrenees.

FERDINAND & ISABELLA AND THE UNION WITH CASTILE

As the might of the Ottoman Empire grew in the eastern Mediterranean, coupled with the supremacy of Venice, Barcelona's fortunes began to wane. The final years of the 14th century were times of pestilence and pogroms. The plague of 1348 wiped out a third of Barcelona's population of 25,000, while in 1391 a wave of anti-Semitic violence, sparked by bad harvests and famine, began in Seville and swept the Iberian Pensinsula, effectively eliminating Barcelona's Jewish community. In 1410 Martí I, the last sovereign count, died without an heir. The crown passed to his nephew Ferdinand de Trastamara. The age of the sovereign counts was over. From this point on, Catalonia's fate depended largely on a series of dynastic successions and marriages.

The most famous dynastic marriage of all was that of Ferdinand II, who married Isabella of Castile in 1469, forming the formidable tandem known as the

Reyes Católicos, the Catholic monarchs. The marriage brought about the unification of the crowns of Castile and León with that of Aragon, which included Catalonia. The last monarchs to rule, albeit part-time, from Barcelona's royal palace in the Plaça del Rei (*see p. 155*), Ferdinand and Isabella managed in a single year (1492) to unify Spain by taking Granada from the Moors; to expel all non-Christians from the Iberian peninsula; to establish the Inquisition; and

Isabella of Castile (1451-1504), whose marriage to Ferdinand of Aragon united the two provinces, centralizing Spanish government and taking influence away from Catalonia.

to discover America. During his 64-year reign, Ferdinand unified the Spanish crowns and converted Spain into an Atlantic sea power, shifting influence away from Catalonia and the Mediterranean.

Under Carlos I (1516-56), generally known as Holy Roman Emperor Charles V, Barcelona was no longer used as one of the itinerant royal courts, although the Generalitat, Catalonia's autonomous government, remained in place. Charles V, grandson of Ferdinand and Isabella and of the Holy Roman Emperor Maximilian I, inherited the thrones of Spain, the Habsburg Netherlands, and most of Central Europe, as well as Spain's holdings in the New World. He spent his reign in relentless pursuit of universal empire. Portrayed as an athletic and forceful figure, said to have spoken French to men, Italian to women, German to his horse and Spanish to God, he retired, at the age of 56, to the monastery of Yuste, after a lifetime of wars and largely unrealized imperial ambitions. His son Felipe II, charged with administrating the vast but rapidly crumbling empire, made Madrid his capital in 1561, leaving Barcelona even farther from the center of the imperial stage. Even as a minor player, though, Catalonia was still crucial to the plot. Before he died Charles V had sworn an oath of allegiance to honor and defend Catalonia's constitution. This oath set the stage for the pivotal events of the War of the Spanish Succession.

THE WAR OF THE SPANISH SUCCESSION

When Carlos II, the last Spanish Habsburg monarch, died without an heir in 1700, two principal pretenders to his throne emerged. Catalonia was bound to Archduke Karl of Austria through the pledge made by his great-great-great grandfather Charles V. Philip of Anjou, grandson of Louis XIV, was the opposition favorite. All of Europe took sides in the developing Habsburg-Bourbon struggle for continental power. Archduke Karl, with the help of England, invaded Spain and in 1704 established himself as Carlos III in Barcelona with the support of Catalan nationalists. But seven years later his brother Joseph, Holy Roman Emperor and Archduke of Austria, died without an heir. Karl was elected to succeed him. England, fearing Habsburg hegemony in Europe, instantly withdrew her support for his claim to the Spanish throne. The move left Barcelona kingless, defenseless, and still committed to resisting Philip. From August 1713 to the final battle on September 11th, 1714 - a day

Map of 18th-century Barcelona, a fortified city between the sea and the Collserola Hills, dominated by the cathedral and the port.

of tragi-heroic defeat now celebrated as Catalonia's national day - Philip laid siege to the city. Two-thirds of Barcelona's houses were destroyed or damaged, and many more were later torn down to make fields of fire for the Ciutadella fortress constructed by the French and Castilian forces on the city's north-eastern approach. Dominated by the Montjuïc stronghold guarding the entrance to the harbor on one side and the Ciutadella batteries on the other, 18th-century Barcelona was governed by occupation Bourbon troops, while all vestiges of home rule disappeared. Philip ascended the Spanish throne as Felipe V.

And yet after 1714, although Catalonia had officially lost her identity and institutions, Barcelona obstinately continued to prosper and grow, thanks to its commercial instincts and its textiles industry. The early 19th century brought the Peninsular War, fought between Spain and France. Between 1808 and 1813 Napoleonic troops took Barcelona and converted it into the capital of the Imperial Department of Montserrat - a brief return to the Carolingian Marca. It was only brief, however. In 1815 Napoleon was defeated at Waterloo, and Catalonia - willingly or unwillingly - was returned to the House of Bourbon.

INDUSTRIALIZATION & THE ARTS:
THE NINETEENTH CENTURY

The 19th century was Barcelona's boomtime. Catalan industry flourished; so much so that by the end of the century two thirds of all manufactured goods in Spain came from the mills and factories of Catalonia - mainly from Barcelona itself. Catalan-made goods dominated the markets of the whole peninsula. And to keep it that way Barcelona's industrialists became fiercely protectionist, as indeed were the workers themselves, who wanted secure employment. But factory hours were punishing and conditions hard. The burgeoning industries created great wealth; they also created a working class that was too numerous for the cramped medieval quarters that housed them. Barcelona became a more populous city than Madrid, but for the most part people were living in penury and squalor. Appalling conditions made the working class highly vocal: the entire century was marred by strikes and public demonstrations - but the workers were not organized or radicalized enough to have a unified voice or

Ceramic tiles depicting the execution of Catalan dissidents following Napoleon's conquest of Catalonia during the Peninsular War of 1808-1813.

The Battle of Tetuan (1863) as painted by Marià Fortuny. Catalonia often fought unwillingly in the 19th century's colonial wars in Morocco and Cuba, wars that she felt were Spanish, not Catalan, business.

coherent demands. For the most part the demonstrations degenerated into anarchic riots, which were then quelled by armed force. In 1842 and 1843, for example, the artillery battery at Montjuïc put down a workers' revolt with a 13-hour barrage of missiles.

The second half of the 19th century saw a reassertion of Catalonia's belief in her local identity and in her projection abroad, mainly driven by the wealthy bourgeoisie. This bourgeois elite was broadly liberal in political outlook. They were also largely Catalanist, and supported the revolution of 1868, led by General Prim, a Catalan-born soldier, which ejected the Bourbon queen Isabella II from the throne and set Amadeus of Savoy up in her stead. Amadeus was a weak monarch, but that fact worked in Barcelona's favor. He abdicated in 1873, and Spain joyfully proclaimed herself a republic. Catalonia also proclaimed herself independent, but the republic was to be short-lived. The Bourbons were restored in 1874. During the intervening years, however, weak leadership from Madrid meant that Catalonia had gained more say in her own affairs. One of the ways Barcelona expressed this was to throw off its medieval corset forever. The city finally burst out of its walls, creating a geometric grid of carefully planned streets and graceful - if monotonous - urban vistas. The walls, which Barcelonese had come to see as a symbol of repression, were no more, and the Eixample avenues, which Madrid had feared as a symbol of Barcelona's metropolitan might, had come into being, all named for territory which Catalonia had ruled in her medieval heyday: Valencia, Corsica, Majorca, Roussillon... Barcelona was spreading its wings as a city with the power and the will - and the money - to shape its own destiny. The World Exhibition of 1888 marked the beginning of the city's modern cosmopolitanism, while the *Renaixença*, a rebirth of Catalan national feeling, bloomed in literature and the arts, as well as in the colorful and formally lavish Modernist architecture that filled *fin de siècle* Barcelona.

THE EARLY TWENTIETH CENTURY: THE CIVIL WAR & FRANCO

1898, at the dawn of the new century, was a fateful year for Spain. She lost her remaining colonies, Cuba and the Philippines, and endured a humiliating naval defeat at the hands of the United States. But demoralization and soul-searching in Madrid opened windows for Barcelona. A number of Catalan political parties gained ground and Catalanism became more of an ideological cause and less just the pipe-dream of the intelligentsia. Catalan confidence and sense of identity were growing ever stronger. Electoral successes for Catalanist parties in the early 20th century led to the establishment of the Mancomunitat (Commonwealth) de

Catalunya, an autonomous Catalan representational parliament within the Bourbon monarchy of King Alfonso XIII. But there were tensions bubbling below the surface. The plight of the working classes had not been addressed, and in 1902 a general strike paralyzed the entire city for a week. In 1909 came the *Setmana Tràgica* (Tragic Week). A protest against the sending of troops (mainly from Barcelona) to fight a war in Morocco that few Catalans supported escalated into several days of bloody

Bust of Francesc Macià by Josep Maria Subirachs, the sculptor currently working on the Sagrada Família. Macià was a major early 20th-century force in favor of an independent Catalonia.

street violence. The reaction from central government was to put down the riot with such brutality that the tide began to turn. Barcelona's workers, who until now had felt little sympathy for the liberal, nationalist posturing of their employers, now began to feel a flicker of Catalanist sentiment.

The Mancomunitat lasted from 1914 until 1924. In 1923 Francesc Macià, a romantic idealist filled with Catalanist fervor, formed a party that not only aimed to give Catalonia a voice; it aimed to make it an independent state. For the working classes this was a step too far. Macià failed to unite all of Barcelona behind his standard - though the reason was more economic than ideological. During the First World War Spain had remained neutral and Barcelona's factories had had a field day, with orders pouring in from all over the continent. The result had been a period of full employment and decent living wages. When the war ceased the orders dried up, and factories found themselves having to cut pay and lay off workers. A period of strikes and violent civil unrest followed, and Madrid became seriously alarmed. In a twin bid to silence the Catalanist separatists and to pacify the workers, General Miguel Primo de Rivera seized power and turned Spain into a military dictatorship. With the acquiescence of the king, Primo de Rivera introduced martial law, and ruled Spain with an iron fist. If Barcelona society had ever shown signs of coming together, Primo de Rivera's paternalist, autocratic stance wedged it firmly apart again. He appeased the working classes by granting them full employment and affordable food. He antagonized Barcelona's bourgeoisie by banning the use of Catalan in schools, and showing marked preference for the conservative and the rural over the liberal and urban. His regime ended in 1930, and in 1931, after a major republican electoral victory, Alfonso XIII abdicated, leading to the proclamation of the Second Spanish Republic. This Republic, within which the Generalitat de Catalunya once again governed in Barcelona, found itself struggling against the determined opposition of the right as well as the radicalization of the workers' movement on the left. The two sides effectively polarized Spanish society and set the stage for conflict. The national elections of 1936 were won by the Popular Front, a coalition of republicans, Socialists, Communists, and syndicalists, who supported Catalan autonomy. Violent opposition was mounted by the anti-liberal, anti-secular National Front, as well as by the Falange, an organization which was anti-Marxist and anti-capitalist at the same time, believed in Spanish unity, a Spanish imperial mission, and had explicit sympathies with Mussolini's Italy. When in July 1936 Primo de Rivera's former finance minister was assassinated in revenge for a political murder by the Falange, a military uprising ensued, which escalated into civil war. One of the leaders of that uprising was a Galician general by the name of Francisco Franco.

Short in stature, with a high-pitched voice and a strong provincial accent, Franco was driven by a loathing of Communists and a thirst for personal prestige. Alfonso XIII had been best man at his wedding; he was a man who needed to be important. His political imagination was also very limited. A society regulated by monarchy, church and army was the only kind of society he understood. When the Spanish Civil War ended in 1939, Franco emerged as leader of Spain, and embarked on four decades of absolute personal power. Though broadly pro-Hitler in his sympathies, he managed to avoid taking Spain into the Second World War: the price Spain paid was international isolation after the overthrow of Nazism, and though Franco could make the claim to have saved Spain from Communism, he also saved it from democracy and normal social and economic development for almost 40 years. His regime was particularly hard

Propaganda posters from the Civil War. The 'Russian monster' was the bugbear used to mobilize the right. Workers on the left, forced to work from dawn to dusk to feed their enemies, are exhorted to continue working from dawn to dusk to annihilate those enemies.

on Catalonia. Once again, as during the War of the Spanish Succession, Barcelona had backed the losing side, and this time the crackdown on Catalan culture and identity was even more totalitarian. Lluís Companys, the Generalitat's president at the end of the Civil War, was returned from Nazi-occupied France and executed in 1940. During the Civil War bands of Communist workers had rampaged through Barcelona's streets murdering nuns and setting churches on fire. Alongside the clergy, it was Barcelona's middle class who had had the most to lose from Communism, and they may have seen Franco as their deliverer. They were wrong. Franco was a Spanish nationalist, and set out with the aim to rid Spain of its regional distinctions. His Madrid-centered policies stressing national unity placed Catalan culture under repressive pressure. Bans on the use of the Catalan language (children were punished in school, usually corporeally, for any utterance in the forbidden tongue), were combined with the constant ideological presence of the unifying, centralist *Movimiento Nacional*. It pervaded all areas of life, from the media, to publishing, to education, to street names. Telephone conversations were cut off by operators if conducted in the wrong language; birth certificates were legal in Spanish only, so that a fifth-generation Jordi was required to become a Castilian Jorge.

BARCELONA TODAY

One legacy Franco left behind him - certainly unintentionally - was a homogenous Catalan society, united under the aegis of its flag, its language and its culture. Resentment of the Generalísimo's crude attempt to eradicate the region's distinct heritage ran (and still runs) deep, and the result was solidarity from all sides. When Franco died on November 20th, 1975, Catalans saw hope for a return to less centralized government, more autonomous rights and privileges, and an end to internal exile, and were elated to see the last of a dictator who had signed execution orders on family and friends. Since then, thanks in large part to the courage and popularity of another Bourbon, King Juan Carlos I, whom many predicted would be dubbed 'Juan the Short' for the anticipated brevity of his reign, Catalonia has lived through a Golden Age of national reformation. Although Franco had groomed Prince Juan Carlos as his successor, Juan Carlos carefully concealed his democratic ideas from his mentor, and soon after succeeding to the throne, boldly undertook the drafting of a

'Barcelona, make yourself beautiful!' The slogan adopted at the time of the 1992 Olympiad is still much in use today, as the city's all-over face-lift continues.

constitution and the formation of a modern democratic government. The king was instrumental in quelling the attempted military coup of February 23rd 1981, led by a lieutenant colonel described by the press as 'nostalgic' for the Franco regime. In perhaps the finest hour of modern monarchical leadership, the young king, in a nationally televised address, called the military to order in defense of the constitution, thus dismantling the conspiracy. With the 1977 return of Josep Tarradellas, president-in-exile of the Generalitat, Catalonia's local government was restored.

Barcelona is now rapidly becoming one of Europe's most modern urban showcases. The walls presently checking the city's expansion are the very Collserola Hills that separate it from the Catalan hinterland. The success of the 1992 Olympic Games provided impetus for improving communications and restoring buildings. The sooty Barcelona of 1975, once dubbed the 'gray city' for the layers of grime covering its façades, has exploded onto the world scene with unprecedented energy as its third millennium picks up steam, proud of its cosmopolitan past and excited about its Catalan and internationalist future.

Orwell on Barcelona

'...When one came straight from England the aspect of Barcelona was something startling and overwhelming. It was the first time that I had ever been in a town where the working class was in the saddle. Practically every building of any size had been seized by the workers and was draped with red flags...; every wall was scrawled with the hammer and sickle; almost every church had been gutted and its images burnt. ...Every shop and café had an inscription saying that it had been collectivised....

Down the Ramblas...the loud-speakers were bellowing revolutionary songs all day and far into the night. And it was the aspect of the crowds that was the queerest thing of all. In outward appearance it was a town in which the wealthy classes had practically ceased to exist.... Practically everyone wore rough working-class clothes, or blue overalls or some variant of militia uniform. All this was queer and moving. There was much in this that I did not understand; in some ways I did not not even like it, but I recognized it immediately as a state of affairs worth fighting for. Also, I believed that things were as they appeared, that this was really a workers' state and that the entire bourgeoisie had either fled, been killed or voluntarily come over to the workers' side; I did not realise that great numbers of well-to-do bourgeois were simply lying low and disguising themselves as proletarians for the time being.

...Above all, there was a belief in the revolution and the future, a feeling of having suddenly emerged into an era of equality and freedom. Human beings were trying to behave as human beings and not as cogs in the capitalist machine. In the barbers' shops were Anarchist notices...solemnly explaining that barbers were no longer slaves.'

From *Homage to Catalonia*.

Second-hand book stall selling Orwelliana in the Plaça George Orwell.

A HANDFUL OF DATES

801	Barcelona freed from Moorish rule.
988	Catalonia becomes an independent federal region.
1229	Jaume I conquers Majorca, the first of Catalonia's colonies.
1283	The Corts de Barcelona, forerunner of the Generalitat, is convened to govern Catalonia.
1469	Ferdinand II marries Isabella of Castile. Royal power begins to shift away from Catalonia.
1561	Felipe II makes Madrid his capital. Barcelona loses influence.
1714	War of the Spanish Succession is won by the Bourbon contender Philip (Felipe V), whom Barcelona did not support. Barcelona completely subjugated.
1873-4	Catalonia briefly proclaims herself a republic.
1914	The Mancomunitat, Catalonia's representative body, is set up.
1931	Second Spanish Republic. The Generalitat governs Catalonia once more.
1936-9	Spanish Civil War. Beginning of the Franco regime.
1975	Franco dies. Catalonia begins to reassert her identity.
1992	Barcelona hosts the Olympic Games. Catalan confidence at its height.

Font de les Canaletes at the top of the Rambla. Drink once from the magic spring, and be fated always to return to Barcelona.

PART II

GUIDE TO THE CITY

MAJOR SIGHTS

THE RAMBLA

Barcelona's Rambla is a tumultuous, all-purpose pedestrian promenade, sidewalk café, press and flower kiosk and outdoor theater. Full of life and fun, or noise and crowds - it depends on your mood at the time. But whether you fall in love with the Rambla or not, it has to be experienced at least once, and it more than repays time spent exploring it in detail.

Some 50 meters wide, with vehicle traffic on either side, the Rambla descends for just over a kilometer from Plaça Catalunya to the harbor. Its name derives from the Arabic word for sand, *rmel*, and it began as an *arroyo*, a watercourse, dry except during rainy seasons when it drained the Collserola Hills that rise behind the city to the northwest. Barcelona's 13th-century city walls overlooked the left side of this sandy crease: little by little over the centuries it became a hive

The Rambla as it once was: a sandy stretch of hawkers and vendors outside the city walls.

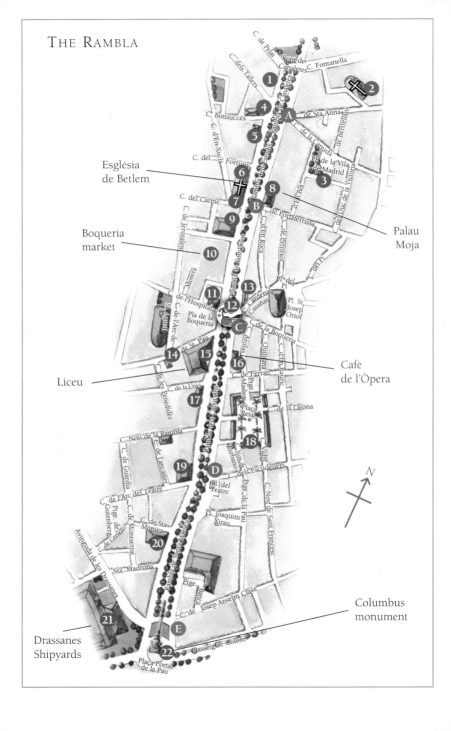

THE RAMBLA

Església
de Betlem

Boqueria
market

Palau
Moja

Cafè
de l'Òpera

Liceu

Columbus
monument

Drassanes
Shipyards

of extramural activity, attracting butchers, costermongers, journeyman workers, thieves and quacks, pickpockets and preachers: humanity, in other words, of every stripe and spot. By the time those walls were torn down in the late 17th century, the Rambla had become essential to the life of the city and was left open as a thoroughfare and promenade.

The Ramblas are often cited in the plural because there are five sections, each corresponding to one of the five medieval gates through the city walls: La Porta de Santa Anna **A**; La Portaferrissa **B**; La Porta de la Boqueria **C**; La Porta dels Ollers (potters) **D**; and the Porta de la Drassana opposite the medieval shipyards, Les Drassanes, now known as Portal de la Pau (Portal of Peace) **E**.

THE UPPER RAMBLA: A STROLLING TOUR

At the head of the Rambla, ever diminishing groups of well-dressed senior gentlemen can usually be spotted discussing (venting spleen over, to be exact) the perennial misfortunes of Barcelona's soccer club-cum-soap-opera, FC Barcelona. This sight was especially common during the Franco regime when

there were no politics to be discussed and certainly nothing to be done about them, so all indignation and harangue was limited to the world of sport and surfaced here at this Rambla version of London's Speaker's Corner.

A few steps down on the right is the Font de les Canaletes, **1** another Barcelona nerve center, famous for what was once known to be the best water available in the city, carried down in small canals or *canaletes* from the source of the River Llobregat high in the Pyrenees. Now the fountain's

Well-groomed elderly gentlemen and their cigars still congregate on the upper Rambla.

four brass faucets dispense water that is merely magic, as the bronze plaque embedded in the pavement explains: anyone who drinks from this fountain is doomed to fall in love with Barcelona and will always return, no matter how far they may stray. Rallying point for the celebration of FC Barcelona's infrequent soccer triumphs, the fountain's municipal coat of arms encrusted in the bronze spigots and painted above as well has the cross of Sant Jordi (St George) in the upper left and lower right quadrants, with the gold and red *quatre barres*, the four bars of the Catalan banner at the upper right and lower left. The *quatre barres*, according to legend, was created with the blood of Guifré el Pilós (Wilfred the Hairy): as Catalonia's sovereign count lay dying, fiefless and unemblazoned, in 897, after battling for the Franks against the Moors, he lamented his failure to establish a coat of arms for his native demesne. The Frankish leader Charles II, grandson of Charlemagne, dipped his fingers into Guifré's wound and painted four crimson stripes on his plain gilded shield: 'What better insignia than that of your own noble blood?'

About halfway to the second press kiosk, you will probably encounter your first of the many painted and costumed human sculptures and street performers

Tomb of Miquel de Boera, captain of the Spanish fleet, in the church of Santa Anna.

that line the Rambla. A throwback to the saltimbanques and jesters that once entertained the crowds along the medieval thoroughfare, there may be as many as two dozen acts and events spread up and down the Rambla on a given day, interspersed with the *trileros* playing the (always rigged) 'which pod has the pea' shell game, along with musicians and buskers of every denomination.

On the left is the Hotel Continental, where George Orwell stayed in 1937 while recovering from a bullet wound that miraculously passed through his throat without hitting anything vital. (In fact, in 1937, the Continental was in the next building uphill, but the management is the same and the story stands on its merits.) Orwell's *Homage to Catalonia* recounts his adventures and misadventures fighting for Republican Spain and the internecine fighting that he barely escaped with his life.

Back across the Rambla at what was once the Portal de Santa Anna entrance through the city walls, now the junction of Rambla de les Canaletes and Rambla dels Estudis, two streets fork out. The one on the left leads down 100 yards to the diminutive Santa Anna Church (at No. 29 on the left) ❷, one of Barcelona's two earliest pre-Romanesque churches, in a cobbled courtyard shared with a florist. It contains the magnificent 16th-century tomb of Miquel de Boera, who served as captain of the Spanish fleet under Holy Roman Emperor Charles V, and led Spanish troops to victory against French invasion in Roussillon in 1543.

The right-hand fork, Carrer Canuda, leads down past the Ateneu Barcelonès, the city's cultural club and library, to the Plaça de la Vila de Madrid ❸. This square is one of the few gestures of Barcelona-Madrid friendship you will find in Catalonia, and may in fact be suspect as the square's name refers pointedly to Madrid's lowly status as - until very recently - a cathedral-less *vila* or town as opposed to Barcelona's ancient glory as a full-fledged city, senior to the Spanish capital by a thousand years. The Madrid *maja* on the pedestal is dressed in typical folkloric festive dress, behind the two cities' respective escutcheons.

Barcelona's seniority is reiterated in the Roman roadway and tombs down in the grassy park below the ochre structure and walkway. As the plaque explains, this sepulchral road is flanked with tombs from the 2nd and 3rd centuries, on either side of the way into the northern decumanus - the north-south axis of all Roman towns, literally ten (*decu*) hands (*manus*) wide - gate of Barcino to the right of the cathedral.

Back out on the Rambla, on the far side, is the Farmacia Antiga Dr Masó Arumí at the corner of Carrer del Bonsuccés ❹. Originally founded in 1850, as

The Teatre Poliorama, famous for its clock giving the official time, and for its tower, from where George Orwell surveyed street fighting during the Civil War.

the stone scroll over the corner will tell you, the pharmacy's Noucentista (post-Modernist) façade was redesigned in 1917 by Ismael Smith (*see p. 118*). The sculpture centering the upper façade, a Rubens-esque baby enfolded by a snake drinking from the chalice in the baby's hand, seems to combine the story of Hercules, mythological founder of Barcelona and strangler of snakes, with the serpent and chalice symbol of pharmacy and medicine.

The next section of the Rambla is the Rambla dels Estudis, so-named for the medieval university that stood here until Felipe V, prime villain of Catalan history (*see pp. 18-19*), banished the university to Cervera, 100 kilometers west of town, following the 1714 siege that ended the War of the Spanish Succession. Cafè Viena at No. 115 on the right is a venerable Rambla landmark, with spectacular painted panels on either side of the door, an enclosed rectangular bar, and narrow shelf around the wall. Note the ceiling paintings of flying putti overhead and the elevated piano balcony in the rear of the café, occasionally played in the evenings and open to any and all piano-playing customers. Next to the Cafè Viena is the Reial Acadèmia de Ciències i Arts de Barcelona **5**, since

1906 home of the Teatre Poliorama, built in 1883 by Josep Domènech i Estapà, a specialist in an eclectic and monumental pre-Modernist architectural style. The ornate façade is centered by a clock that has been Barcelona's official city chronometer since 1891. The winged angels are allegories for art and science, while the towers atop the building, observatories for astronomy and meteorology, are another George Orwell landmark. In *Homage to Catalonia*, Orwell wrote (in chapter 10) '*Immediately opposite, there was a cinematograph called the Poliorama, with a museum above it, and at the top, high above the general level of the roofs, a small observatory with twin domes. Those domes commanded the street*'. Orwell spent several nights in the spring of 1937 manning the domes and keeping an eye on members of a rival faction within the Republican movement who were barricaded into the Cafè Moka across the street.

Further down on the right is the Tabacos de Filipinas building ⑥ (at No. 109), now the elegant new Hotel 1898. This grand Rambla edifice was built in 1880 by the same architect (Josep Oriol Mestres) who restored the Liceu opera house after its first fire in 1861. The Tabacos de Filipinas company was founded by Antonio López y López (1817-1883). From a poor background in Cantabria, López went to Cuba to seek his fortune and returned a wealthy man and committed colonialist. He became one of the most important shipping magnates in Barcelona history, founded the Tabacos de Filipinas and the Banco Hispano Colonial, and lent the Spanish government 25 million pesetas to help them resist the Cuban independence movement. He was rewarded by being created Marquis of Comillas, the humble village of his origin. The diamond-faced stone wall next door to the old Tabacos building is the Església de Betlem ⑦, a medieval foundation with a Baroque façade added by the Jesuits in the late 18th century. The much-restored interior is undistinguished (largely because it was destroyed by mob violence during the Civil War), but the intensely sculpted façade features St Ignatius Loyola, founder of the Jesuit order, and San Francisco de Borja, in similar poses between Solomonic columns to the left and right of the door. Francisco de Borja carries a skull and Bible, symbols of his rejection of secular authority. Over the corner of Carrer d'en Xuclà is San Francisco de Santa Cruz, a nobleman who gave up his worldly goods to follow the Jesuits.

On the other side of the Rambla, through the rackety bird market, is the opening into Carrer Portaferrissa. The building on the left is the Palau Moja ⑧, once the home of Antonio López y López, Marqués de Comillas. In addition to his business activities, López was a patron of the arts, particularly of the priest-

Captive canaries longing to be given a home and space to stretch their wings.

HEMBRAS DE CANARIO

poet Jacint Verdaguer (*see p. 184*). López's daughter Isabel married Eusebi Güell, patron of Gaudí (*see p. 104*) in the Palau Moja's family chapel. Writing about the house in later years, López's grandson called it '*the prototype mansion of the ancien régime. Built in the middle of the 18th century, it was an enormous palace of large narrow salons and dark corridors, with windows giving onto interior patios. On most days correctness and order prevailed over luxury. The servants wore black jackets and white gloves, the doors to all the grand salons were shut, and each reception room was lit by only a single gas taper. On special occasions the aspect of the house changed completely. The salons were thrown open and the enormous chandeliers converted the dismal mansion into a palace*'. Any polite request to consult the second-floor Palau Moja library (ask at the reception desk at Carrer Portaferrissa No. 9) will score a visitor's pass, which will allow you to admire the creaky wooden floors, the ballroom with its cut-glass chandelier resembling an explosion of ice and its Francesc Pla mural paintings around the walls, and the elaborately sculpted mahogany mantelpiece on the way into the library. The exterior Pla murals over the Carrer Portaferrissa façade remain one of Barcelona's mysteries. Even an 1870 *Diario de Barcelona* article was unable to decipher the six images of what, beginning on the left, appear to be Roman soldiers who carry away a woman in the second drawing, the next two apparently of women involved in undecipherable events, the fifth a woman begging a soldier and the last, on the right, a woman holding a baby up by the foot. Biblical scenes including the Slaughter of the Innocents and the Judgement of Solomon have been proposed, though none of them are entirely convincing.

Across Carrer Portaferrissa from Palau Moja is a fountain backed by ceramic tiles portraying the 13th-century city walls and the medieval Rambla, featuring stands selling poultry, a hunter with game (probably for sale), and typical Rambla activities not too different from what is going on just over your shoulder. The inscription on the tiles explains that the Porta Ferrica (Iron Door) was one of the doorways through the 13th-century walls, so-called for an iron bar mounted on it, used as the standard measure of length for traders and merchants in Barcelona.

Back out on the Rambla, the Mercat de les Flors - the next section down - is one of the most romantic and certainly the most fragrant. Here the Rambla seems to narrow and dally, the human traffic gently crushed into the center of the flow by the encroaching flower stalls on either side. At the time of their establishment here in 1853, these stalls were the only place in Barcelona where flowers were sold, and each kiosk was known for its *tertulia*, or group of friends and usual suspects. The florists were famous for their beauty and Barcelona's foremost Modernist painter Ramon Casas (*see p. 116*) snagged his best model and eventual wife from behind the counter of one these stalls.

Further down on the right is the Palau de la Virreina at Rambla No. 99 **9**. Built by Spain's Viceroy in Peru, Manuel Amat i Junyent, and completed in

Flower-sellers setting up their stall in the early morning.

1778, the palace has always been named after Amat's widow, La Virreina, Francisca Maria Fivaller. The Viceroy had married his teenage bride after she was abandoned at the altar of the nearby Betlem church by his own nephew. La Virreina, descended from Barcelona's first democratic municipal representative, Joan Fivaller (*see p. 161*), was an important city benefactress for over half a century.

The Palau de la Virreina, discretely indented from the surrounding alignment of façades, is a typical example of Barcelona's late 18th-century aristocratic architecture. Now the seat of the Institut de Cultura, La Virreina is always boiling with art exhibits, lectures, and poetry readings.

La Boqueria produce market **10**, generally agreed to have been named for the medieval sale of goat meat (*boc*) at the nearby Pla de la Boqueria, is a cornucopia of the senses, filled with the steady hum of trade. Many of the city's finest chefs are among the early shoppers, looking for the best and freshest ingredients with which to concoct memorable dining. The main entrance to the market is spectacular - wildly chromatic, thick with people and produce - adorned with a welcoming ceramic and stained-glass Modernist arch announcing the Mercat de Sant Josep. The smoothly massive Ionic columns around the perimeter of the market show the lines and design of the original Plaça de Sant Josep constructed between 1836 and 1840 by Francesc Daniel Molina (also architect of the Neoclassical Plaça Reial, *see p. 45*). Built on the site of the convent of the Carmelites Descalços de Sant Josep, who had been summarily 'excloistered' during the anti-clerical *desamortització* (disentailment) of 1835, Molina's John Nash-inspired square was almost immediately occupied by butchers' shops and produce stands, though the steel hangar roof covering the entire market was not completed until 1870.

The Boqueria is the best place for fresh game in hunting season.

THE BOQUERIA MARKET

For market lovers the Boqueria accompanies Gaudí's Sagrada Família among the city's main sights and delights. The vegetable, fruit and wild mushroom display at the entrance is already more colorful than any painting, while the chilly circular fish and seafood theater in the heart of the market provides a complete course in oceanography and ichthyology, as well as a mid-city blast of iodine and salt sea freshness. Just short of the fish display, a left turn will take you past the brilliantly illuminated **Peña** fruit and vegetables stand into one of the Boqueria's prettiest corners. Past the neo-Modernist **Verdures Ramona** island, with its undulating stained glass fruit stand, across from the Genaro seafood counter, is a living, three-dimensional Van Gogh painting featuring ropes of peppers from all over the world, along with nuts, vegetables, exquisite new potatoes, and every manner of dry goods impeccably arranged. **Jesús y Carmen** is the official title of this stand (#579-581), though all of this information is concealed by the painstakingly-placed produce. Not far away, near the Kiosko Universal restaurant counter, the **Avinova Serramitjana** stand (#689) is the place, in hunting season, to have a look at the redleg partridge, woodcock, duck and hare. **Petràs, Fruits del bosc** (fruits of the forest), at the back of the market, (#869-870) is a fascinating and educational look at wild mushrooms, spices and herbs from Catalonia and around the world. Morels, chanterelles, *rovellons*, *camagrocs*, truffles, *ous de reig* (king's testicles), *pets de llop* (wolf farts) - you name it, Llorenç Petràs will have it if it has surfaced anywhere on the planet. A Barcelona and Boqueria institution, Petràs takes careful care of Barcelona's greatest chefs, for whom wild mushrooms and truffles are primordial ingredients. The Petràs wild mushroom cookbook is in its eighth edition and promises to be a runaway bestseller forever. For more cookbooks and general information on the Boqueria and Barcelona's 48 Mercats Municipals, all open produce markets similar to, if smaller than, the Boqueria, look for the **Punt d'Informació** in aisle #7 at stand # 435, near the **Bar Boqueria** - which, by the way, serves superb *tortilla de patata* (potato omelet). For the most celebrated eating in the market, find your way to **Pinotxo**, just inside the main entrance. The place is easily identifiable for the effigy of the wooden-nosed puppet sitting over the corner above the bar. Here you report in to Juanito Bayén (*pictured above*). If the dozen bar stools are filled (which is usually the case), Juanito will give you a flute or two of his house cava while you wait. The longer the wait, the happier and hungrier you will become, surrounded by this raging epicurean cathedral.

THE LOWER RAMBLA

The lower section of the Rambla stretches from the Boqueria down to the port. On your right, at the corner of Carrer de la Petxina, is the Christian Escribà Pastisseria ⓫, originally the Antigua Casa Figueras, Fábrica de Pastas

Alimenticias, founded in 1820, as the mosaic lettering says. This exuberantly Modernist café and pastry emporium was refurbished in 1902. The comprehensive Modernist discourse here includes ceramic mosaics, stained glass, wrought iron, a stippled profusion of color, and a stone sculpture over the corner portraying a peasant woman with Dutch

Modernist decoration on the Casa Figueras.

clogs wearing a dirndl and carrying sheaves of wheat and a rake, a reference to the grain harvest. The aromas inside are as dazzling as the façade.

In the centre of the Rambla at this point is a colorful mosaic by Joan Miró (*see p. 123*) ⓬. It was unveiled in 1976 as part of the artist's project to fill the streets of his native Barcelona with as much of his work as he could. On the other side is the once garish, now fading chinoiserie of the Casa Bruno Quadros ⓭. This former umbrella shop is described as eclectic by critics and chroniclers of Barcelona's art and architecture; the most famous of all the city's architecture critics, Cirici i Pellicer, dismissively describes the amalgam of fans, parasols, and a

Chinoiserie dragon on the Casa Quadros.

Ramon Casas mermaids - human as far as their ankles - adorn the Fonda Espanya.

lantern-wielding Chinese dragon as neo-Egyptian. It must have been the stylized lotus-flower motifs of the wrought-iron balconies that gave him the idea. Reformed by Josep Vilaseca in 1885 for a store specializing in oriental goods, the Caixa de Sabadell has been here since 1980: possibly the world's most bizarre bank building.

From the right hand side of the Rambla, duck down Carrer de Sant Pau to No. 9-11, the spectacular Modernist hotel La Fonda Espanya **14**, by Lluís Domènech i Montaner (*see p. 91*), built in 1903. Oddly, for a city obsessed with its Modernist treasures, the present-day hotel has been allowed to deteriorate to a barely-decent-enough-for-youth-groups status, and actually staying here, for the moment anyway, is above and beyond (even) the call of curiosity. The toast of the town a century ago, recipient of the 1903 prize for the best architectural creation of the year, this down-at-the-heels gem still merits a careful exploration. To the left of the lobby a door takes you through into the breakfast room, which is dominated by an enormous alabaster fireplace by Eusebi Arnau, the most acclaimed sculptor of his day. Cats warm themselves on the hearth, an old man stretches his gnarled hands towards the source of heat, and a mother sits with her baby. The whole conglomeration is a typical neo-Romantic amalgam of sinuous lines and sentimentality. On the chimney breast stands the coat of arms of royal Spain: the double-headed eagle of the Holy Roman Empire, and the Order of the Golden Fleece hanging below it, a chivalric order founded by Philip the Good of Burgundy in 1429, and which survived in Spain until Alfonso XIII's abdication in 1931. To the right of the lobby, behind the reception desk, is the restaurant, nearly always empty, but richly endowed with decoration. Beyond that is the famous aquarium dining room, with mermaid murals by Ramon Casas (*see p. 116*), and a wooden lattice-work dado with convex ceramic tiles in its interstices decorated with the coats of arms of the provinces of Spain.

Back on the Rambla, on your immediate right, stands Barcelona's opera house, the Gran Teatre del Liceu **15**, which continues to be a gala hub for the city's bourgeoisie, a place where fur coats can be seen until early June. (*For more on the Liceu, see p. 141*). On the other side of the Rambla is the venerable Cafè de l'Òpera **16**, a fundamental Rambla rendezvous point for well over 100 years. The original Thonet chairs, the 19th-century mirrors with acid engravings of female opera figures, the magical acid-engraved back door, and the well-worn feel of the place contribute to the old-world charm of this historic spot.

This section of the Rambla is almost palpably thick with memories of the past - both the glory and the gory. It is difficult not to be struck by the curious combination of elegance and ribaldry at this crossroads between the traditionally tawdry lower Rambla, the pomp and flash of the Liceu, and the flower market just uphill. Pla de la Boqueria was also known in medieval times as Pla de l'Os ('Place of the Bone') for the executed criminals left hanging here as a warning to potential miscreants. It has been one of Barcelona's busiest intersections since the early middle ages, when it was a four-way crossroads for travelers coming into town from Girona and France to the north, from Montjuïc, from the old city nucleus to the east, and from Sants and the Llobregat valley to the west (a road then known as the Via Morisca, or Moorish way, as it proceeded to and from Al-Andalus, the Moorish empire on the Iberian Peninsula): this hub of humanity still vibrates with the energy of untold millions of souls long departed.

Another Rambla landmark is the Hotel Internacional, with its founding date of 1894 proudly atop the façade. In 1994 the Liceu was destroyed in a fire, and Catalan soprano Montserrat Caballé watched her beloved opera house go up in smoke from the hotel's balcony over the Pla de la Boqueria. The Hotel Oriente **17**, with its brace of angels playing fanfare over the door (reminders of the 16th-century Sant Àngel Màrtir convent that once occupied this space) was once Barcelona's finest. It is still famous for lodging Hans Christian Andersen in 1864, as well as the grandfather of King Juan Carlos I, Alfonso XIII, and later luminaries including Errol Flynn, the matryred bullfighter Manolete, and soprano Maria Callas. Though less than splendid inside today, a trip upstairs to the breakfast room offers a look down into the former convent cloister, now the grandly chandeliered ballroom, where generations of textile manufacturers' daughters were formally launched in society.

Plaça Reial **18** lies just down past Carrer Ferran to the left. Built in 1848 on the site of a former Capuchin monastery, this Neoclassical square, designed by Francesc Daniel Molina, would have been the sister ship of the Plaça de Sant Josep, now filled with the Boqueria market. For all its symmetry, the palm trees from the Balearic Islands, transplanted to and thriving in Barcelona, provide the first hint that this square is subtly different from other stately Neoclassical squares around Spain. Denizens of Barcelona's underworld and vagabonds wandering through long patches of bad luck have made the benches home while tourists, attracted to the winter sun on the north side of the square, pack into the

The Plaça Reial, which for all its elegant symmetry has a pungently bohemian underbelly.

third-rate restaurants serving pre-fab paella, sangría, and worse. Nevertheless, the apartments behind the ochre façades are becoming fashionable spaces for Barcelona and world celebrities ranging from Nobel Prize-winning novelist Gabriél García Márquez to Barcelona architect and urban planner Oriol Bohigas (co-designer of the Hotel Claris), and Pasqual Maragall, the city's former mayor. Plaça Reial's best restaurant is La Taxidermista. Its central fountain, *Les Tres Gràcies* - The Three Graces, Aglaia (Adornment), Euphrosyne (Joy), and Thalia (Bloom) - stands between two Gaudí lamp posts designed in 1878 when the great Modernist was a mere 26 years old. The spiky branches of the lamp and the winged helmet couldn't be less Gaudí-esque, though the open-mouthed, screaming serpents reassure us that the real Gaudí is in there somewhere. Looking back out to the Rambla, find the two pairs of putti silhouetted against the sky at either side of the entrance, supporting royal crowns and the coats of arms of León and Castile, in honor of Isabella II, Spain's queen from 1833 to 1868. Underneath are medallions commemorating Iberia's great mariners, explorers, and conquistadors: Cortés, Pizarro, Magellan, Elkano and Cisneros.

Back on the Rambla, on the left, you will come to the Teatre Principal **19**, with its four cut-out ticket windows, another work by Francesc Daniel Molina. Barcelona's earliest theater stood on this site, dating back to 1568. The statue opposite commemorates the 19th-century playwright Frederic Soler, king of modern Catalan theater. He is invariably not-so-regally crowned with a pigeon or its leavings.

This part of the Rambla, from here to the port, has traditionally been a prime habitat for streetwalkers, transvestites, pimps, portraitists, tarot card readers, and the overflow from the Barrio Chino's most scrofulous corners in along Carrer Arc del Teatre. The Centre d'Art de Santa Mònica **20**, a modern art gallery and bookstore attached to the 1618 convent of the Agustins Descalços de Santa Mònica, is the last building on the right at the bottom of the Rambla. Opposite it is an ornamental drinking fountain, one of only a few surviving public fountains donated to the city for the World Exhibition of 1888 by the British philanthropist Richard Wallace, of London's Wallace Collection fame.

Les Drassanes Reials **21**, the medieval shipyards which now house the Maritime Museum, are across the Rambla on the edge of Plaça del Portal de la Pau. The shipyards are not only an excellent surviving example of late 14th-century Catalan Gothic architecture; they can also claim to be the best-preserved medieval shipyards in the world, topping even Venice's Arsenale. In their heyday

BARRIO CHINO

Barcelona's infamous Barrio Chino (Barri Xinès in Catalan) stretches from Carrer de l'Hospital down to the Avinguda del Paral.lel. Despite its name, it is neither a typical Chinatown nor in any way related to matters sinological. The term '*chino*' was coined as a reference to foreigners in general, as the area was traditionally home to people from other parts of Spain or from abroad. Indeed it is still very much a cosmopolitan redoubt, with immigrants flowing in from North Africa and the Middle East. During the late 19th and early 20th centuries, the area developed an exotic allure as a sanctuary for prostitution, petty crime and a general loucheness easily associated with transgression of every kind. Barcelona's version of the Moulin Rouge, La Molina (presently closed), overlooks the southern edge of this free-for-all, while the

Police presence on the lower Rambla, and a Wallace fountain (see opposite).

notorious Baghdad Café, reputed to have the most pornographic floor show in the world, still operates successfully at the south end of Carrer Nou de la Rambla. Other standard hangouts such as the Marsella at Carrer Sant Pau 65, the London Bar at Nou de la Rambla 34, or the Pastis at Carrer de Santa Mònica 4, gather energy from the Barrio Chino's adrenaline rush. Jean Genet's novel *La Marge* colorfully describes the district, and its legions of pimps, prostitutes, transvestites, pickpockets, thieves and gypsies. Today the Raval in general and the Barrio Chino in particular have been cleared out and gentrified with museums, cultural centers, art galleries, shops, and even the palm tree-lined Rambla del Raval, which slices broadly down from Carrer de l'Hospital to Carrer de Sant Pau. The area is not nearly as dangerous as it once was. In fact, the ubiquitous police presence may even make it safer than the Rambla or other parts of the old town - but you can never be sure. There are still pockets of streetwalkers, drug pushers and thieves along the appropriately named Carrer d'en Robador ('Robber Street') and Carrer de Sant Ramon. It's best to walk warily.

Lateral wall of the Drassanes, showing the 14th-century fortifications.

the Drassanes built the ships of Catalonia's Mediterranean fleet and launched them directly down their slipways into the sea (today's embankment that leaves the Drassanes beached is a relatively new construction). The shipyards marked the waterside edge of 14th-century Barcelona. Walk round the outside of them, and on the Avinguda del Paral.lel side you will see a completely intact section of the 14th to 15th-century city walls. (*For information on the Maritime Museum, see p. 138*)

The Columbus Monument ㉒ towers 80 meters over the foot of the Rambla as if it were the city's proudest possession. Columbus, however, has his back to the city, a fact which might be seen as significant. Catalonia and 'The Discoverer' have never been the best of allies. Ferdinand and Isabella sponsored Columbus's voyage; in fact the Drassanes shipyards constructed two of the ships in Columbus's fleet. Columbus discovered America, and brought the glad tidings back to the itinerant royal court in Barcelona - and then the Spanish crown excluded Catalonia from New World trade, confining her to the Mediterranean.

© HUNGART

The Lower Rambla and Columbus Monument as seen through the eyes of Pablo Picasso (1917).

Standing on high atop his iron pedestal, Columbus seems to be looking out towards the new world he discovered. In fact he is pointing out at the very Mediterranean which had always been and was to remain Barcelona's destiny. For a panoramic view over port and Rambla, take the elevator to the top of the column.

THE CATHEDRAL
Catedral de la Seu
Pla de la Seu. Open daily 7.45am-1.30pm & 4pm-7.45pm.

Barcelona's cathedral is officially dedicated to the Holy Cross; its spire is crowned with a statue of St Helen, mother of Constantine, who discovered the remains of the True Cross in Jerusalem. The local cult of Santa Eulàlia (*see p. 50*), whose tomb the cathedral contains, is much stronger, however: she is the cathedral's unofficial patron. There has been a church on this site since the 3rd century, the

earliest days of Christianity. The present building was constructed between 1298 and 1450, with the neo-Gothic façade and lantern spire added later (1892-1913). Both were the work of Josep Oriol Mestres, the architect of the Liceu opera house (*see p. 141*). The two octagonal belltowers are late 14th-century. One tolled to announce each ecclesiastical office, from matins to compline; the other, also the city clocktower, tolled to call citizens to prayer and to announce curfew, when the city gates were closed at night.

Barcelona cathedral, reputedly the darkest in the world.

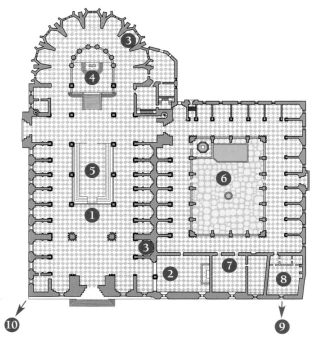

1 IMAGES OF SANTA EULÀLIA
2 THE LEPANTO CHAPEL
3 THE MARTORELL ALTARPIECES
4 TOMB OF SANTA EULÀLIA
5 THE CHOIR STALLS

6 THE CLOISTER
7 CATHEDRAL MUSEUM
8 CAPELLA DE SANTA LLÚCIA
9 CASA DE L'ARDIACA
10 CASA DE LA PIA ALMOINA

INSIDE THE CATHEDRAL

1 IMAGES OF SANTA EULÀLIA: Barcelona claims Santa Eulàlia as its very own saint: a virtuous virgin born to wealthy parents in Sarrià, tortured and put to death by Dacian, Roman governor of Tarragona, for refusing to renounce her Christian faith. Four scenes showing her final torture and martyrdom are sculpted in high relief on the choir screen. Moving left to right, the first scene shows her in front of Dacian, who attempted to break her faith with flattery, bribery, and ultimately torture. Her left hand is on her heart; her right hand points obdurately at a cross in the distance.

Santa Eulàlia, with X-shaped cross and palm of martyrdom.

In the next scene Eulàlia is tied to a post and being whipped by Dacian's henchmen. In the third scene she is shown having fainted from her wounds, and finally we see her being lashed to the saltire cross upon which she was crucified, in Barcelona's Plaça del Pedró, in AD 303. A freak fall of snow is said to have covered her virgin body until Christians rescued it and secretly buried it nearby.

2 THE LEPANTO CHAPEL: This chapel, in the far right corner as you come in the main door, contains the Sant Crist de Lepant, a 15th-century painted wood sculpture of a dark-skinned Christ. It is said that the sculpture was fixed to the bowsprit of the Spanish flagship at the naval battle fought between the Holy League and Ottoman Turkey in the Gulf of Patras off Lepanto (now Nafpaktos, Greece) in 1571 (a life-size model of that ship is housed in the Maritime Museum). The Holy League was an alliance of Spain, Venice, Genoa and the Papal States. Its fleet was commanded by John of Austria, half brother of Felipe II. The Ottoman force, led by Ali Pasha, had never yet been defeated; they were routed at Lepanto. Ali Pasha's severed head was displayed from the mast of his own galleon, and victory was declared for Christendom, with a death tally of around 7,000. The Ottomans lost twice that number. One participant in the conflict was the 24-year-old Miguel de Cervantes, the future author of *Don Quijote*, who sustained wounds that cost him the use of his left hand. The victory at Lepanto was possibly Spain's last truly fine hour. Felipe II was not as successful at sea as his half-brother: after the defeat of his famous Armada in the English Channel in 1588, Spain began to lose power, and gradually her colonies fell away, all the way down to the final 1898 Spanish-American War, in which her remaining possessions, Cuba and the Philippines, were lost to the United States.

3 THE MARTORELL ALTARPIECES: Bernat Martorell is one of Catalonia's great medieval masters. His style is intensely narrative, full of detail and pictorial information. His altarpiece of SS. Cosmas and Damian is adjacent to the Lepanto Chapel. The chapel of St Benedict, in the ambulatory, has his altarpiece of the Transfiguration (1452). In the centre stands Christ with his disciples and Moses and Elijah. Flanking this are images of the Transfiguration, plus representations of the Wedding at Cana and the Feeding of the Five Thousand.

4 THE TOMB OF SANTA EULÀLIA: Eulàlia was originally interred in the church of Santa Maria del Mar. Her body was moved to the newly-constructed cathedral crypt in 1339, where it remains to this day, in an elaborate tomb of Italian alabaster supported on eight columns, and decorated with scenes from her life. Eulàlia's cult is still very much alive, and her tomb an object of veneration.

5 THE CHOIR STALLS: These beautiful 15th-century stalls with their carved misericords are notable for the painted escutcheons on their backrests. In 1519 a convocation of crowned heads of Europe met here to discuss defending the continent against the Ottoman menace. Each delegate was a member of the Order of the Golden Fleece, a chivalric order founded by Philip of Burgundy in 1429, and the escutcheons denote where each prince or duke sat during the conference.

AROUND THE CATHEDRAL

6 THE CLOISTER: A door in the south aisle leads out into the tranquil, palm-shaded cloister centered by a tropical garden and pool with 13 pure white geese, one for each of the 13 tortures suffered by Santa Eulàlia before her crucifixion. Legend has it that these geese are descendants of the flock from Rome's Capitoline Hill.

7 THE MUSEUM: The collection contains works by medieval master Jaume Huguet (*see p. 124*), as well as the cathedral's most prized possession, a Pietà by Bartolomé Bermejo (1490), in which a bespectacled St Jerome, news reporter-like, takes in every detail of events for his Vulgate Bible.

8 CAPELLA DE SANTA LLÚCIA: This small, separate chapel is dedicated to St Lucy or Santa Lucia. In order to avoid an offer of marriage, Lucy is

The tranquil cathedral cloister.

darkness. It now marks the beginning of the Christmas season.

9 CASA DE L'ARDIACA (ARCHDEACON'S HOUSE): This lovely little courtyard opposite the Santa Llúcia chapel comes into its own on the day of Corpus Christi (in June; the first Thursday after Trinity), with one of the most athletic dancing eggs (*l'ou com balla*) in Barcelona. The tradition is to place an egg on top of the jets of water from the city's fountains: the water acts as a natural juggler. Floral arrangements are also an important part of Corpus Christi - the one here is particularly

said to have mutilated herself by tearing out her eyes, which she then presented to her suitor on a platter, a scene graphically depicted over the altar. St Lucy is patron saint of the blind and partially-sighted, of seamstresses and of spiritual enlightenment. A pair of eyes on a tray is her traditional attribute. Her feast day, December 13th, the longest day in the old calendar, was celebrated as a festival of light, after which the northern hemisphere began its slow climb out of winter

Capella de Santa Llúcia, dedicated to the patron saint of light, whose feast day opens the yuletide season.

Roman bastion on the Plaça Nova side
of Casa de l'Ardiaca.

spectacular. Casa de l'Ardiaca now houses the municipal archives (upstairs). The marble letterbox by the front entrance was designed in 1895 by Lluís Domènech i Montaner (*see p. 91*) for the Lawyers' Association. It is said that the swallows are intended as symbols of the swiftness of natural justice, while the turtles stand for the plodding pace of the human administrative process.

10 CASA DE LA PIA ALMOINA - MUSEU DIOCESÀ (DIOCESAN MUSEUM): Formerly a house of charity, which dispensed 300 free meals a day to the

city's hungry, this is now a museum, housing a permanent collection of religious sculptures and a miscellany of liturgical objects. It also stages temporary exhibitions. The building itself, though much restored, is a good place to see vestiges of Roman Barcino. The vestibule has an excellent relief map/scale model of the garrison town. Roman stones are visible in the interior. Particularly interesting are the remains of the only surviving octagonal tower of the 82 that ringed the 4th-century colony. *Open Mon-Sat 10am-2pm & 5pm-8pm; Sun 11am-2pm.*

Human statue in Plaça Nova, with the Casa de la Pia Almoina in the background.

MODERNIST BARCELONA:
THE EIXAMPLE

The Eixample (pronounced 'ay-shampla'), which means 'widening' in Catalan, is easily identifiable on any city map as the broad, regular grid between Plaça de Catalunya and the jumbled streets of the formerly outlying villages of Gràcia, Sarrià, Sants and Horta. Though, in spots, it is too large and noisy for enjoyable exploration, it boasts most of the city's best Modernist buildings. Despite its symmetry, it is curiously confusing, and even baffles Barcelona natives, so don't be embarrassed to resort frequently to a map (*see p. 284*).

The Eixample was a planned project which came about when Barcelona's medieval walls were dismantled in 1860. The city immediately began a major expansion financed by industrial prosperity, wealthy *indianos* (repatriated colonials) returning from the New World, and by provincial aristocrats selling their rural holdings in favor urban life and the promise of manufacturing wealth. Though Barcelona had chosen a design by Antoni Rovira i Trias (*see p. 222*), Madrid insisted on a plan by Ildefons Cerdà, with the result that much of his plan was deliberately subverted by Eixample residents and owners. Most of the Eixample's buildings went up between 1860 and 1890, in a sober, unexceptional architectural style. Near the end of the 19th century, Barcelona's industrialists began to buy properties in the fashionable streets around Passeig de Gràcia, the so-called 'Quadrat d'Or' or golden quadrangle. Having bought them they then hired Modernist architects to remodel them, vying with each other in exuberance. The Manzana de la Discòrdia is the most dramatic example.

THE MANZANA DE LA DISCORDIA
Passeig de Gràcia (between Aragó and Consell de Cent)

Oddly enough for the prime expression of an architectural style so identified with Catalonia, the pun behind the Manzana de la Discordia only works in Spanish. *Manzana* means both 'city block' and 'apple' in Castilian; La Manzana de la Discordia compares this architectural jostling for attention with the classical myth of the Apple of Discord, the prize Paris was charged to bestow upon his favorite goddess. He chose Aphrodite, who helped him to abduct Helen, and all hell broke loose. This, then, is the 'city block of discord', where the three greatest figures of Barcelona Modernism - Domènech i Montaner, Puig i Cadafalch, and

Gaudí - go head to head with three very different, and very important, buildings: Casa Lleó Morera, Casa Amatller, and Casa Batlló.

NB: Modernism is described in more detail on p. 83. More information on Gaudí and Modernism's other major architects can be found on pp. 91-111.

CASA BATLLÓ
Passeig de Gràcia 43.
For visits, consult the Ruta del Modernisme,
Casa Amatller, Passeig de Gràcia 41. Tel: 93/488-0139.

Exotic and other-worldly, with its rainbow coloring, mascaron balconies and stippled façade, flecks of which catch the sunlight like sequins, Casa Batlló is Gaudí at his most original. As with much of Gaudí's work, there is something faintly sinister about it as well. Gaudí said that he aimed to create a 'vision of paradise', though milk and honey seem to have been replaced with something much less easy to digest. The entire construct is imbued with nationalist symbolism. The undulating roof represents a humpbacked dragon. The turret is placed in such a way that it punctures the roof-line: St George's lance, topped with a cross, piercing the monster's side. The ghoulish balconies seem wrought from the bones of the dragon's victims. Gaudí is said to have directed the composition of the façade from the middle of the road, calling individual instructions to workmen on

Passeig de Gràcia paving stones, designed by Antoni Gaudí.

scaffolding. Casa Batlló was a remodeling of an existing building, but Gaudí's idea of remodeling went beyond simply adding superficial decorative elements to an existing base structure. He completely altered the house from within. When Senyora Batlló fretted that there would be no room for her daughter's piano, Gaudí reassured her that a solution would be found. When the house was completed, and sure enough the piano didn't fit, Gaudí was called upon to provide the promised solution: 'Ask your daughter to take up the violin'. Completed in 1906, the house won a prize the following year, despite mixed public reaction. All the money that Gaudí made on this project was put towards the building of the Sagrada Família.

CASA AMATLLER
Passeig de Gràcia 41. Closed to the public, but an office on site dispenses tickets for the tour Ruta del Modernisme (see p. 99).

(see p. 99).

Once again, this was a remodeling job, completed in 1900 by Josep Puig i Cadafalch for Antoni Amatller i Costa, whose money came from the family chocolate business. In private his interests were artistic, encompassing archeology, applied art and music. He was also a keen amateur photographer. Puig i Cadafalch's remodeling is eclectic in spirit, borrowing from the neo-Gothic and

Romantic schools, as well as including a Flemish step-gabled roof. The sculptures on the façade are by Eusebi Arnau, Modernism's most celebrated sculptor. Playful animals are shown indulging in Amatller's own pursuits and hobbies. Two rabbits pour liquid chocolate; a pig turns a clay pot. St George and the dragon are locked in combat on the main entrance. The demure 'Princesa' above is thought to be modeled on Amatller's daughter. The shop in the entranceway sells a selection of 'Amatller chocolate', still made to this day, though not by the same family.

CASA LLEÓ MORERA
Passeig de Gràcia 35. Closed to the public.

The town house that originally stood on this site was extensively remodeled in 1902-1906 by Palau de la Música architect Domènech i Montaner. It was built for Albert Lleó i Morera, and his family, and its avowed aim is to be new and daring: the result is a supreme example both of Catalan Modernism and of the architect's own individual 'floral' style. Look carefully at the wealth of sculpted decoration swarming across the pinnacled façade, and you will notice that what looks at first like abstract molding is in fact hundreds of delicate flower motifs. Other decorative elements include female figures using the modern inventions of the age: the telephone, the light bulb, the photographic camera, and the gramophone. The main circular balcony makes flamboyant use of the street-corner chamfer.

Casa Batlló, by Gaudí

LA PEDRERA
(Casa Milà)
Passeig de Gràcia 92. Open 10am-8pm every day.
Guided tours at 6pm Mon-Fri; 11am Sat-Sun. Tel: 93/484-5995.

Casa Milà is one of Gaudí's most controversial buildings. It was unveiled in 1910 to the consternation of local residents. Instantly it was dubbed 'La Pedrera', the 'quarry', and the name stuck. Senyora de Milà herself wailed that it looked like a cave for bats and serpents, not a house for human habitation.

Seemingly defying all architectural rules, the exterior has no straight lines. Five levels of undulating balconies are capped with a froth of seaweed-like wrought iron, the work of Josep Maria Jujol (*see p. 94*). The structure has no supporting walls; all the weight is borne by a fretwork of beams and pillars. Gaudí boasted that this made it supremely flexible, convertible for any purpose, as its partition walls can be moved at will. Unlike the houses of the Manzana de la Discordia, La Pedrera was built from scratch on an empty lot, giving Gaudí *carte blanche* to indulge his imagination. The resulting building cost four times the budget, plunging the Milà family into near-ruin.

To appreciate Gaudí from an engineering rather than simply a visual perspective, visit the **Espai Gaudí** in the attic. This has a display of drawings and models explaining Gaudí's theory and practice. On the fourth floor is the **Pis de la Pedrera**, an apartment-museum that gives a fascinating glimpse into the domestic life of families who once lived here. People - not bats or serpents - still live in the other apartments.

THE ROOF & 'LA PEDRERA DE NIT'

The most famous motifs from La Pedrera are from the roof, where the chimney pots and cowls over the ventilation shafts have been variously interpreted as veiled Scheherazades, Berber nomads, or helmeted warriors. They were nicknamed *espantabruixes* ('witch-scarers') when the building was first unveiled. From mid-June to mid-September, enjoy *La Pedrera de Nit* ('La Pedrera by night'), when the roof opens on Friday and Saturday nights for live music, drinks, and romantic stargazing. Not something that the ascetic Gaudí would ever have dreamed of.

Seaweed-like wrought iron on the balconies of La Pedrera, the work of Jujol (see p. 94).

THE SAGRADA FAMÍLIA

(Temple Expiatori de la Sagrada Família;
Expiatory Temple of the Holy Family)
Plaça de la Sagrada Família
Open Sept-Mar 9am-6pm every day; Apr-Aug 9am-8pm every day.
Guided tours daily at 11.30am, 1pm, 4pm, & 5.30pm.

George Orwell famously described the Sagrada Família as 'the ugliest building in the world' and expressed regret that the anarchists had failed to blow it up in 1936. Salvador Dalí described all of Modernism as 'creative bad taste'. Even Catalonia's own favorite chronicler, Josep Pla, once wrote that Gaudí's church reminded him of an 'immense pile of chicken guts'. Times and tastes do change, however, and what was fashionable in late 19th-century Barcelona and became hideous to critics in the 1940s and 50s has now, once again, become iconic.

Still under construction over 120 years after it was begun, the Sagrada Família is Barcelona's most emblematic building. Sprouting from the Barcelona soil like a metropolitan version of the Montserrat massif, Catalonia's holy mountain to the west of the city, it was conceived as a three-dimensional representation of the Christian religion. The current lateral façades will one day be dwarfed by the main Glory Façade, the central spire of which - the Tower of the Savior - will be crowned by a polychrome ceramic cross and soar to a height of 170 meters, just 1 meter shorter ('The work of man must not surpass that of God': Antoni Gaudí) than the Montjuïc promontory guarding the harbor.

WORK IN PROGRESS

The Sagrada Família was begun in 1882, a grand and solemn undertaking to 'wake faint hearts to faith', as inscribed on a parchment laid with the first stone. Following disagreements with the project's founding bishops, architect Francesc Villar was dismissed, and in 1883 Gaudí was appointed. He worked on the project until his death in 1926. When asked when he aimed to have the church completed, Gaudí refused to commit himself, stating simply 'My client is not in a hurry'. It's just as well: the Sagrada Família is still estimated to be 19 or 20 years from completion, despite burgeoning budgets and ever-speedier modern construction techniques. Gaudí's church, like the great cathedral churches of the middle ages, is not for the impatient.

Francesc Villar's original concept was neo-Gothic. The Gaudí touch began with Art Nouveau floral capitals in the crypt, and then, in 1893, came the sea-change: Gaudí embarked on the Nativity Façade of a radically different and ambitious project, intended to impress the visitor with the full power of scriptural revelation. For the last 15 years of his life, Gaudí lived in the church grounds. His life was cut short in 1926 when he was run over by a trolley car and, initially unidentified, died in the medieval Hospital de la Santa Creu (*see p. 191*) shortly before his 74th birthday. He had lived to see just one tower completed, that of St Barnabas, on the eastern side of the Nativity Façade.

Gaudí planned three façades: those of the Nativity and the Passion are currently complete. An even larger Glory Façade will front the main entrance on Carrer Mallorca. Four belltowers will rise over each of the three façades, making a total of twelve, one for each of the apostles. Around the central Tower of the Savior will be four larger belltowers, representing the four evangelists. Another tower in honor of the Virgin will be placed at the west edge of the apse.

The developing Sagrada Família pierces the skyline amid a forest of cranes.

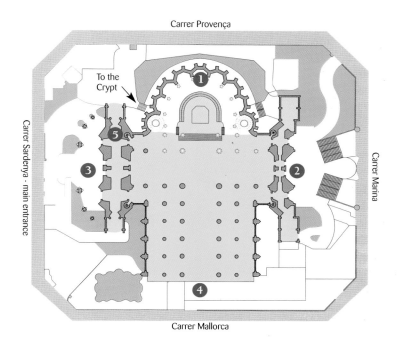

Carrer Provença

Carrer Sardenya - main entrance

Carrer Marina

To the Crypt

Carrer Mallorca

1 THE APSE (BY VILLAR & GAUDÍ)
2 THE NATIVITY FAÇADE (BY GAUDÍ)
3 THE PASSION FAÇADE (BY SUBIRACHS)

4 FUTURE MAIN ENTRANCE & GLORY FAÇADE
5 SOUVENIR SHOP

TOUR OF THE CHURCH

1 THE APSE

The oldest part of the church, constructed by Villar. At first glance it looks like a typical 19th-century interpretation of Norman Gothic: solidly built and rather dull. Look closer, though, and you will find unmistakably Gaudíesque additions,

notably the exterior gargoyles, in the shape of sea-creatures, lizards, serpents and shells. Gaudí is buried in the crypt below.

2 THE NATIVITY FAÇADE

This is the most complete example of Gaudí's work. Soaring skyward in

The Massacre of the Innocents, from Gaudí's Nativity Façade.

intricate levels of carving and sculpture, the Nativity Façade is partly made of stone from Montserrat, Catalonia's favorite place of pilgrimage and home to its protector, La Moreneta, the Black Virgin.

The façade has three doorways, representing the Christian virtues of Faith on the right, Hope on the left, and Charity (the greatest of the three) in the center. The symbolism of the **Portal of Charity** explores the fundamental mystery of Christianity: why does God the Creator become, through Christ, a part of his own creation? The answer, as given in scripture, is that 'God so loved the world that He gave His only begotten Son' to save man from sin and grant

him everlasting life. The serpent, crushed by the central column bearing Matthew's genealogy of Jesus, is surrounded by an iron fence, representing man's enslavement by selfishness and evil. The apple in the snake's mouth refers to the banishment from Eden.

Above the column is a portrayal of the Nativity itself. Above this is the Annunciation, with the Coronation of the Virgin represented above that. The evergreen cypress tree is a symbol of eternity, while the white doves in its branches are souls cleansed by the love of Christ and drawn up to eternal life.

On the **Portal of Faith** to the right, above flora and fauna from the Holy Land, we see scenes of Christ's youth: Jesus preaching at the age of 13, for example. The left-hand **Portal of Hope** begins at the bottom with flora and fauna from the Nile. Then comes the massacre of the Innocents and the flight of the Holy Family into Egypt.

❸ THE PASSION FAÇADE
The Passion Façade is not by Gaudí, though it is based on a Gaudí sketch of how he intended it to look. It is the work of contemporary sculptor **Josep**

Maria Subirachs, who was chosen in 1986 to execute Gaudí's plans. The sculptural style is markedly different from the Nativity Façade, unsurprising perhaps, given the two artists' different attitudes to their subject. Gaudí was a fervent believer; Subirachs a self-confessed atheist (though his views are rumored to have mellowed somewhat over the years he has been involved in the Sagrada Família project). Though Subirachs has never tried to imitate Gaudí, he does not distance himself from him entirely, and twice pays homage to him in the Passion Façade: Gaudí appears over the left side of the main entrance making notes or drawings; and the Roman soldiers are helmeted like Gaudí's chimney cowls from the roof of La Pedrera (*see picture below*).

The Passion Façade features sculpted scenes of Christ's last days, grouped in alcoves above the main door and on either side of it. The scenes begin at the left with the **Last Supper**. The next scene to the right represents the night vigil in the **Garden of Gethsemane** and Peter awakening, followed by the kiss of Judas.

In front of the main door is Jesus, lashed to a post during his **flagellation**. To the right of the entryway is a rooster, and **Peter**, distraught over his third denial of Christ. Farther to the right Jesus, crowned with thorns, stands before **Pilate**, while just above, moving back to the left, is **Simon of Cyrene** coming to Christ's aid with the cross, after his first fall. Among this group, on the left, is the **sculpture of Gaudí** taking notes. Moving directly left from this is the mounted **centurion** lancing the side of the church, symbol of the body of Christ, with his spear. Above are the **soldiers rolling dice**

Detail of Subirachs's Passion Façade, showing a helmeted warrior, borrowed from the roof of La Pedrera, and a representation of Gaudí himself, taking notes in a pocket-book.

for Christ's clothing, and at the top, in the very center of the façade, is the **crucifixion** at Golgotha. The moon to the right of the cross refers both to the sudden eclipse-like darkness at the moment of Christ's death and to the full moon of Easter. To the right are **Peter and Mary at the sepulcher**, Mary under an egg symbolizing the resurrection of Christ. At Christ's feet is a figure with a furrowed brow thought to be a **self-portrait of Subirachs**, the agnostic searching for belief: will this body really rise from the dead? The letter 'S' on the figure's right arm and his giant hand, his attribute as sculptor, seem to support this interpretation.

The culminating element in the Passion Façade, not yet in place, will be an eight-and-a-half meter gilded representation of the risen Christ, dazzling proof of resurrection for all who still lack faith.

The Future of the Project

Architect Jordi Bonet, son of one of Gaudí's assistants, remembers playing on the construction site as a child. Now director of this colossus-in-progress, he claims that the end is truly in sight. The Sagrada Família project receives no official funding; it relies wholly on voluntary donations, making budgeting erratic and timetables difficult to predict. But recently there have been a couple of windfall years. Tourist entry tickets cover 95% of the construction costs. Since the year-long celebration of the 150th anniversary of Gaudí's birth in 2002, visitor numbers have skyrocketed, and well over half the

Stained glass glimmers through rounded stone tracery.

Scaffolding fills the interior.

building is now complete. New technology is also playing its part, Bonet says. A computerized diamond-tipped circle saw, for example, can carve perfect Gaudí shapes, working around the clock. And having plenty of funds available allows progress on various fronts at once. Soon, the immense central dome, supported by four columns made of Iranian porphyry, the hardest of all stones, will soar to its final height of 170 meters, making the Sagrada Família Barcelona's tallest building. By about 2023, the poet Joan Maragall's premonitory verse may well have become a reality: 'Like a great flower, a church blooms...awaiting the faithful...' (*New Ode to Barcelona*, 1909). Unless, of course, unexpected delays push the opening ceremonies back to 2026, the 100th anniversary of Gaudí's death.

ADDITIONAL INFORMATION AND VISITS
*English-language tours of the Sagrada Família
can be arranged through Guiart.
Tel: 669/482404. www.sagradafamilia.org
A 50% discount at this and other Modernist venues comes with a
Ruta del Modernisme ticket, available at Casa Amatller (see p. 99).*

THE BASILICA CHURCH OF SANTA MARIA DEL MAR

Plaça de Santa Maria, La Ribera
Open Mon-Fri 9am-1.30pm; 4.30pm-8pm.
For a walking tour that includes the church, see p. 177.

Barcelona's cathedral may be the seat of the bishopric, and Gaudí's Sagrada Família the city's most emblematic sacred structure, but the church closest to Barcelona's heart and soul is, beyond a doubt, Santa Maria del Mar. 'St Mary of the Sea', known in earlier times as Santa Maria de la Ribera, the waterfront church, was built to protect Catalan sailors, fishermen, ship's chandlers, stevedores and stowaways in fulfillment of a vow made by Jaume I el Conqueridor, upon capturing Majorca from the Moors in 1229 (*see p. 15*). When Jaume's great-grandson, Alfons III, completed Catalonia's conquest of the Mediterranean by taking Sardinia a century later in 1329, he immediately began construction of this exemplary Catalan Gothic basilica. Constructed near the

The bulky exterior of Santa Maria del Mar, showing its polygonal Catalan Gothic belltowers and enormous rose window.

site of an earlier 10th-century church, Santa Maria de les Arenes ('St Mary of the Sands', so called because, at that time, the beach began just beyond it), Santa Maria del Mar was the spiritual sanctuary for Catalonia's medieval maritime empire and the nerve center of this important medieval district of merchants and master craftsmen. The discovery, 500 years later, of the remains of Barcelona's early patron, Santa Eulàlia, hidden from the Moors in 717 in an early Christian cemetery on the site of Santa Maria del Mar, further consolidated the popularity of the seafarers' church. In 1714, when Barcelona surrendered to the forces of the Bourbon pretender to the Spanish throne, fallen resistance fighters were buried in the Fossar de les Moreres, the church graveyard, where Catalan nationalists still rally every 11th September to honor their heroic defeat.

The most gracefully classical of all Barcelona's churches, Santa Maria del Mar provides a lovely contrast to the ornate architecture of later Gothic, Baroque and - especially - Modernist Barcelona. Built in a record 54 years (1329-1383), it is the best existing example of early Mediterranean Gothic architecture, a shimmering continuum of symmetry and balance, its soaring verticality and delicacy especially surprising considering the bulky jumble of the exterior.

Criticized for seeming to be the work of engineers rather than of architects, Santa Maria del Mar was built by a mere *magister operis* (contractor), stonemason and sculptor named Berenguer de Montagut. He carefully selected and shaped each stone brought down from the Montjuïc quarry. The roof is supported by slender, unarticulated octagonal pillars, which spread out into simple rib vaulting. The symmetry is relentless: 16 eight-sided pillars, 2 meters in diameter, up to 16 meters from the floor, and another 16 meters to the keystones. The keystones in turn are 32 meters from the floor. Adding to the lightness is the height of the aisles, just 8 meters lower than the nave. All of these numbers are multiples of or divisible by 8, medieval mystic numerology's symbol for the Virgin. Meanwhile, the nave is exactly twice the width of the aisles; the combined height of the aisles matches the basilica's total width; and the width of the aisles is equal to the difference between their height and that of the nave. Berenguer's quasi-Pythagorean labyrinth of mathematical balance and proportion is suggestive of the Golden Section or Divine Proportion (A is to B as B is to the sum of A and B); the eurhythmy of Santa Maria del Mar is as seductive to the eye as that of Leonardo Da Vinci's drawing of the Vitruvian Man.

It has frequently been noted that Santa Maria del Mar owes much of its present grace and spirituality to the anti-clerical violence of the anarchists who torched it on July 18th, 1936, upon learning of the military uprising that started the Spanish Civil War (*see pp. 23-24*). Filled with Baroque side-chapels, heavy pews and choir stalls, and with royal boxes fixed to the south wall, the church burned for 11 days, until nothing but the bare bones remained. Restoration work began in 1939, when a new generation of post-Bauhaus architects, influenced by the functionalist teachings of Walter Gropius and Mies van der Rohe, recognized the mathematical purity of the basilica and endeavored to return to Berenguer de Montagut's original architectural vision.

INSIDE SANTA MARIA DEL MAR

THE CEILING BOSSES: These painted bosses represent, from the altar end downwards, the Coronation of the Virgin, the Nativity, the Annunciation, the equestrian figure of King Alfons, who laid the first stone, and the Barcelona coat of arms.

THE HIGH ALTAR: Against a backdrop of eight pillars, slender and tall as ships' masts, sits a simple statue of the Virgin and Child, with a model of a Barcelona galleon at her feet.

THE ST IGNATIUS STEP: An engraved stone riser to the left of the north door commemorates the spot where St Ignatius Loyola, founder of the Jesuit Order, begged for alms in 1524 and 1525.

TOMBS OF THE GUILDS: Let into the floor are a number of slabs marking the burial vaults of various guilds, stamped with their emblem: a hat for the hatters; a tankard and scales for retailers; a ship in full sail for mariners.

MUSIC IN SANTA MARIA DEL MAR

The church is frequently used for choral events and early music, much of which was written precisely for this kind of space. The six-second acoustic delay, which can create mayhem in modern compositions, was planned into medieval musical scores designed to be sung or played in large spaces.

At the sixth centennial of the church's completion in December of 1983, the trebles, countertenors, tenors, baritones, and basso profundos of St John's College Cambridge performed a program of Christmas music by Byrd, Tallis,

Guerrero and Tomás Luís de Victoria, the music, church, and the choir itself all written, built, and founded nearly simultaneously. Choirmaster George Guest, terrified by the acoustic delay as overtones echoed back from Santa Maria del Mar's nearly unbroken spaces, rehearsed his choristers ferociously, holding closing chords until the eight-to-twelve part polyphony going out finally matched what was coming back. The concert, performed before a packed basilica, was exquisite, the purity of the boys' voices musically mirroring Santa Maria del Mar's elegant sandstone simplicity, and confirming Saint Augustine's description of music and architecture as 'twin arts'.

The interior of Santa Maria del Mar, peaceful and uplifting, and in stark contrast to the prosaic strength of its massy exterior.

In April 2002, Harry Christophers directed The Sixteen here in a similar program of early music, possibly the most extraordinary musical experience the church has ever known. For those who had heard the St John's College concert 20 years earlier, it was an aural *déjà vu*, but for one tenor it was even more. Once an 11-year-old treble under George Guest's baton at St John's, he was now back at Santa Maria del Mar as a first tenor in The Sixteen. 'I could scarcely sing,' he confessed after the concert, 'the waves of sound just kept washing over me, floating back from the spaces as if…from my childhood…or from the ages…and I was choked up the whole time.'

Jordi Savall's Hespèrion XXI early music ensemble is always hauntingly powerful in this space; if a concert is scheduled during your stay in Barcelona, you should try and make time for it. If you are in town over the Christmas season, don't miss the Christmas Eve Midnight Mass: it is one of Santa Maria del Mar's most magical moments. At half an hour before midnight the ancient *Cant de la Sibil.la* (Song of the Sibyl) is sung. Derived from the pagan tradition, this chant became incorporated into the Christian ritual. A single countertenor backed by a choir of acolytes sing the prophetic words of the twelve sybils of the Mediterranean and Asia Minor, foretelling the birth of Christ, the coming of a messiah and the salvation of mankind.

Santa Maria del Mar is also a popular wedding venue (it once turned down the Spanish royal family, for historical and political reasons, when Princess Cristina asked to be married here in 1994). Other young hopefuls, less stigmatized by history, are often found exchanging vows here on weekends.

For information about concerts in Santa Maria del Mar, check the weekly Guía del Ocio, available at all newsstands.

ARCHITECTURE

Barcelona is one of the world's most comprehensive galleries of architecture. Formulas from the classical Roman to the post-Modern all cohabit here, making this a city of sharp architectural contrasts, often of extremes. The Modernist Palau de la Música Catalana and the Minimalist Mies van der Rohe Pavilion, for example, represent polar opposites of taste and style; both amply illustrate Barcelona's love of the avant garde. The city has never been suspicious of novelty or unwilling to embrace the future. Nor has it clung to the past. It has repeatedly and willingly re-designed itself, whether the century was the 1st, 4th, 14th, or 21st. Its most emblematic style is *Modernisme* (Modernism), the Catalan version of Art Nouveau, a flamboyant example of how one of Iberia's most ancient cities has perennially been its newest and most original. Art, architecture and design often overlap in Barcelona. It is a phenomenon summed up by Frank Gehry, architect of the Guggenheim Museum in Bilbao, and whose gilt-scaled goldfish presides over

Barcelona's famous twin skyscrapers with Frank Gehry's goldfish at their base.

Barcelona's Olympic Port: 'I don't know where you cross the line between architecture and sculpture,' he once said, 'For me, it's the same.' Antoni Gaudí would certainly have approved.

HISTORICAL OVERVIEW OF STYLES

ROMAN BARCINO

The remains of Roman Barcelona are concentrated around the cathedral (Catedral de la Seu), which stands on an area of high ground, the Roman Mons Taber, which formed the core of the early colony. Two cylindrical watch towers in **Plaça Nova** (on the far right as you stand facing the cathedral) are preserved along with a short section of the 2nd-century aqueduct that carried water into Barcelona from the Pyrenees. The entire Gothic Quarter is full of miniature vestiges, but most interesting of all is the **AEEF (Associació Expedicionari, Etnografic i Folklòric)** at Carrer Avinyó 19, where, upstairs on the main floor, you can walk between a 1st-century ritual enclosure and a hurriedly-assembled 4th-century rampart. The emotions of the Roman colonists are almost palpable:

using second-hand stones from earlier structures, some carved some plain, they threw these fortifications together in flurried panic before the next phalanx of barbarians marched over the horizon. AEEF is open weekday evenings except Thursday, 7pm-9pm. Downstairs in the back dining room of the El Gallo Kiriko restaurant, you can dine (on Pakistani food) between the lower parts of two watchtowers belonging to the same fortifications. The Pakistani fare here

Roman columns from the 2nd-century Temple of Augustus, in a courtyard in the Barri Gòtic.

is better than acceptable at bargain rates, while the 2,000 year old-walls add a powerful taste of eternity. For further Barcino sightings, have a look at **No. 1 Carrer del Call**, just off Carrer dels Banys Nous, where a Roman tomb can be spotted at the foot of the wall to the right at the back of the store. Roman tombs and a roadway are visible in **Plaça de la Vila de Madrid** (*see p. 35*); and for the pièce de resistance, the fluted columns at Carrer Paradis 4 are all that remain of the 2nd-century **Roman Temple of Augustus** (*see p. 157*). More can be seen in the Museu d'Història de la Ciutat in Plaça del Rei (*see p. 137*).

ROMANESQUE

SANT PAU DEL CAMP
Carrer de Sant Pau 101. Cloister open weekdays 4.30pm-7.30pm.
Sunday mass at 10.30am, 12.30 and 8pm.

Originally beyond the city walls (Sant Pau del Camp means St Paul's in the fields), Barcelona's oldest church occupies the site of a 2nd-century Roman cemetery later used by the Visigoths. The Moors sacked Barcelona in 985 and 1115, destroying Christian sites; the present church was built in 1127, its hunched, cowering shape reflecting the defensive spirit of the besieged early medieval Christians. The main entrance has 6th or 7th-century Visigothic marble capitals atop recycled Roman columns. The tympanum shows Christ in Majesty between SS. Peter and Paul. The symbols and images above seem to date from an earlier epoch in which human images were avoided, possibly the work of Mudéjar (Moorish-Spanish) artisans.

The ancient church of Sant Pau del Camp,
standing silent and alone amid
the raucous Raval.

The Divine hand, two fingers extended, centers the façade, surrounded by the symbols of the Evangelists. Inside the church is a sepulchral slab from the tomb of Sovereign Count Guifré II, dated 912, evidence that a 10th-century chapel existed on this site. The diminutive cloister is Sant Pau del Camp's best secret, a miniature gem and one of Barcelona's finest hideaways. The tri-lobed arches, clearly of Moorish descent, are unique Romanesque surprises, while the carved Corinthian capitals portray Adam and Eve, an archer shooting at a gazelle, and a woman tormented by toads, among other themes. Surrounded by the popular tumult of the Raval, this cloister is an oasis of sanctity and peace.

OTHER ROMANESQUE BUILDINGS

Església de Santa Anna - A secluded 12th-century church in its own little square, with a pretty cloister attached. The church once served a convent, now demolished (*see also p. 35*). *Santa Anna 29 (Barri Gòtic).*

Capella d'en Marcús - The tiny pre-Romanesque chapel was built in the 12th century by Bernardí Marcús, a wealthy banker and businessman who, according to legend, made frequent trips to France and became a benefactor of the guild of the *troters*, as Barcelona's early pony express was called. The chapel, which stands on what was once the main road out of town, is dedicated to La Virgen de la Guía, protector of wayfarers. *Carders 2 (Sant Pere - above La Ribera).*

Capella de Sant Llàtzer - Barely discernible on Plaça del Pedró, a square named for its stone pillar (*pedró*, large stone), marking a fork in the road. It is also the site of the crucifixion of Santa Eulàlia, co-patron of Barcelona (*see p. 50*). The present-day statue of Eulàlia is by Barcelona artist Frederic Marès (*see p. 139*) and was erected in 1952 to replace one destroyed in the Civil War. The dilapidated belltower at the end of the square belongs to the Sant Llàtzer chapel, built in the mid-12th century in what was then an area of open fields beyond the city walls. After the 15th century, when St Lazarus was officially named patron saint of lepers, the enclave was used as a leper hospital. The chapel is best viewed from the short Carrer de Sant Llàtzer, which cuts behind the church between Carrer del Carme and Carrer de l'Hospital. *Carrer de Sant Llàtzer (Raval).*

Three styles of Gothic tower on the Catedral de la Seu. Stubby Catalan Gothic, cut off abruptly at the top; Catalan Gothic topped with a metal lacework belfry; and neo-Gothic, complete with elaborately crocketed spire.

GOTHIC

Barcelona's Catalan Gothic architecture developed between the 14th and the 16th centuries, at a time when the city was a prosperous merchant town. Except for late 19th-century and early 20th-century Catalan Modernism, it is Barcelona's most archetypal style. The best place to see Gothic architecture is, logically enough, the **Barri Gòtic**, the area around the cathedral. Alongside this are the Gothic and Renaissance palaces on **Carrer Montcada**, and the church of **Santa Maria del Mar** in La Ribera. Other Mediterranean (or Catalan) Gothic churches include **Santa Maria del Pi**, the **Monestir de Pedralbes**, and the **Església de Sants Just i Pastor** just behind Plaça Sant Jaume. All are notable for their fortress-like walls, massive with buttressing, and pierced with windows only on the upper levels. The towers do not taper into spires: they are cut off unceremoniously, like the barrel of a musket.

SECULAR GOTHIC ARCHITECTURE

Casa de la Ciutat - The lateral façade of Barcelona's Town Hall remains Gothic despite the 18th-century Neoclassical main frontage. Inside is the splendid 14th-century Saló de Cent, where the medieval town council congregated. *Plaça Sant Jaume 1. Open Sun 10am-2pm, and for occasional concerts, lectures, and events held in the Saló de Cent.*

Palau de la Generalitat - The Gothic former main façade is on Carrer del Bisbe. Inside is a lovely courtyard built by Marc Safont, Barcelona's best-known Gothic architect. It is open to the public on the day of Sant Jordi

Sacred and secular Gothic: the Monestir de Pedralbes (above) and a full-bodiced gargoyle on the Casa de la Ciutat (left).

(April 23rd), and sometimes for concerts on Sundays. *Plaça Sant Jaume.*

La Llotja - Barcelona's maritime exchange (*see p. 180*). The façade was remodeled to conform to Neoclassical tastes between 1794 and 1802, but the Sala Gòtica, the Gothic trading hall inside, remains true to the original 14th-century style. *Pla del Palau, La Ribera.*

Saló del Tinell - In the Palau Reial Major (*see p. 155*). It is the palace's original banqueting and ceremonial hall, now often used for concerts and exhibits. *Plaça del Rei.*

Les Drassanes Reials - The medieval shipyards, built between the 14th and 17th centuries, are a Gothic tour de force at the end of the Rambla overlooking the port (*see p. 46*).

RENAISSANCE & BAROQUE

As happened with many cities whose wealth and development had come early, the Renaissance caught Barcelona in a period of political and economic decline. There is little really good Renaissance building; the best is along **Carrer Montcada**. The **Palau del Lloctinent** (1557) behind the cathedral on the Plaça del Rei, and the Italian Renaissance-style main façade of the **Generalitat** on Plaça Sant Jaume, built in 1596, are other examples. Baroque convents and churches began to appear in the early 18th century. The **Betlem church** on the Rambla, originally a Gothic structure, was reformed in 1729 in the Baroque style beloved by the Jesuits: massive and impregnable, with entranceways flanked by twisted Solomonic columns evoking the Biblical temple, and sculpted saints rolling their eyes heavenwards to immortal bliss. While the Baroque flourished in post-Inquisition Spain as a whole, however, Barcelona has few really good examples of it. The churches of **La Mercè** (1775) on Plaça de la Mercè, **Sant Felip Neri** (1752) on Plaça Sant Felip Neri in the Barri Gòtic (*see p. 159*), and **Sant Miquel del Port** (1755) in Barceloneta (*see p. 200*) are the best examples.

Twisted Solomonic columns flank a prominent saint of the Jesuit order on the Betlem church on the Rambla.

SGRAFFITO

The Baroque period left an enduring decorative mark on the city's façades: sgraffito, possibly Barcelona's third most characteristic feature after Catalan Gothic and Modernist architecture. The word sgraffito derives from *ex-graffito*: these are not engravings but 'ex-gravings'; the images are not carved into the surface, in other words, but are raised above it in low relief. Sgraffito attained the apex of its popularity in the mid-to-late 18th century, as Barcelona recovered from the ravages of the 1714 siege and defeat at the hands of Felipe V (*see p. 19*).

The technique itself consists, much as in etching or woodcutting, of creating a raised negative figure by cutting away the field around it. The backgrounds are generally dark and the figures lighter in color, although there are exceptions. Putti and cherubim engaged in allegorical activities provide the most frequent themes. Catalan sgraffito design, though it came a century earlier than Modernism, suggests the same playful approach to ornamentation that would explode into the color and form of late 19th-century Art Nouveau. Barcelona has hundreds of examples of sgraffito, most of them in the old town. Some of the best are listed below:

The Gremi dels Velers (Silkweavers' Guild) on the corner of Via Laietana and Carrer Sant Pere Més Alt (near the Palau de la Música). The sgraffiti on the façade over Via Laietena, composed of putti, atlantes, caryatids and a simulated entablature are originals, whereas those over Plaça Lluís Millet are a 1930 imitation.

Casa de les Quatre Estacions (House of the Four Seasons), on the other side of the Palau de la Música on the corner of Sant Pere Més Alt and Mare de Déu del Pilar is an example of a badly deteriorated sgraffito that, nevertheless, has a definite aesthetic appeal in its barely identifiable tracery.

Over Carrer de Sant Pere Més Alt, you can make out groups of cherubim weaving garlands, harvesting wheat, cutting grapes, and roasting chestnuts. The sgraffito around the corner on Mare de Déu del Pilar, when the light is right, clearly show the extruding edges of the figures.

The Gremi dels Revenedores (Retailers' Guild) at the corner of Plaça del Pi and Carrer Petritxol. These, over the Josep Roca knife store, are the earliest sgrafitti in Barcelona, dating from 1685. Around the archangel Michael are allegories for his attributes: angel of peace, serenity and health; herald of victory; messenger of God.

NEOCLASSICISM

In the late 18th century the Rambla was converted into a mid-city promenade, following the demolition of the medieval walls that flanked it. It became a fashionable place of resort, and a number of noble palaces went up in the new Neoclassical style. The **Palau Moja** (*see p. 37*) and the **Palau de la Virreina** (*see p. 39*) were both completed in the late 1770s. In the early 19th century the numerous convents which had lined the Rambla were dissolved, and their demise yielded space for Neoclassical construction, notably the **Hotel Oriente**, which is centered on an old monastery cloister, and **Plaça Reial** (1848) by Francesc Daniel Molina.

Graceful fluted Ionic pilasters on a late Neoclassical façade.

Molina also created the Plaça de Sant Josep, originally a gracious Neoclassical space, and now filled by the Boqueria market. The Ionic columns around the edges of the market give an idea of what this square was originally intended to be: formal, serene and elegant, not home to hurly-burly stallholders.

MODERNISM

Neoclassicism is all about symmetry and restraint. Ildefons Cerdà's post-1860 grid plan for Barcelona's expansion (Eixample, *see p. 55*) was all about order and uniformity. Suddenly, something in Barcelona's psyche snapped. Emotion was set loose. Straight lines began to writhe. Modernism - Catalonia's interpretation of Art Nouveau - was born. The movement's early flame was fanned into a blaze by new-found wealth and confidence. By the mid-19th century Barcelona had developed into a formidable industrial power, and its prosperity led to a resurgence of Catalanist feeling, the *Renaixença*; a search for

Modern buildings in the Eixample, a geometric grid of mainly 19th-century apartment blocks. Originally all had central courtyards.

a national identity that sought to express itself through literature, art and architecture. Modernism was the ideal vehicle. In a period of only three years (1890-93), known as the *febre d'or* ('gold fever') for the hurtling frenzy that characterized it, most of the Eixample's early Modernist architecture went up.

THE MODERNIST ETHOS

Known as *Style Moderne* in France, *Art Nouveau* in Britain and North America, *Sezessionstil* in Austria, *Jugendstil* in Germany, and *Stile Liberty* in Italy, what the Spanish-speaking world calls *Modernismo* was an attempt to break with the past in favor of new forms and ideas. For decades western art and architecture had contented itself with period imitation - Neoclassical, neo-Gothic and neo-Renaissance. Art Nouveau was something genuinely new and original. Characterized by a preference for the curved (organic or natural) line over the straight (man-made) line, asymmetrical shapes, elaborate and usually colorful decorative detail, Modernism made frequent use of natural, floral and vegetable forms as well as that of the human - particularly female - figure. Partly a reaction to early 19th-century optimism about the roles of science and technology in resolving humanity's social, economic, moral and spiritual problems - an optimism which had proved misplaced - Modernism reflected a trend away from the rational toward emotion, instinct, intuition and nature. Disillusionment with technology's failure to satisfy man's material and spiritual needs triggered a rejection of order and discipline in favor of spontaneity and passion. Irrationalism triumphed over logic and reason, nature over artificiality, the aesthetic over the practical, craftsmanship over mass production, and the simple life over the headlong pursuit of material wealth. In its intellectual inspiration Art Nouveau opposes the neo-Gothic in the way that the Baroque opposes the Gothic. Purity of line and the ideals of intellectual contemplation are out. Sumptuousness and theatricality are in. The aim is to seduce and bemuse the senses by the wealth of detail and ornament; to attack the soul via the body, not via the mind.What is interesting about Catalan Modernism is the way it fuses the Roman Catholic with the sinuous and the sensual. Elsewhere Art Nouveau is an expressly secular movement: the Catalan version finds space for devotion.

Modernism in Barcelona

NB: *Individual Modernist buildings and architects are dealt with in more detail on pp. 91-111.*

Barcelona's Modernist architecture exploded throughout the Eixample and spread to most middle-class neighborhoods. And as with all brash and exuberant styles, after the first flushes of enthusiasm, peoples' taste for it began to wane. Originally embraced as a national architecture and enthusiastically adopted by the Catalan bourgeoisie, the Modernism fervor began to abate after the First World War. Europe was in the clutches of depression; Catalonia's markets had collapsed, her wealth-creators were no longer so self-confident, her workers were half starved and politically volatile. Artistic tastes changed, becoming more modest. By the time of the 1929 International Exhibition, Modernism was regarded as a youthful indiscretion best forgotten. Senyora de Milà lost little time after the death of Gaudí in 1926 in ridding La Pedrera (*see p. 60*) of its Gaudí-designed furnishings and substituting them with Louis Seize. There were even moves afoot to have the Palau de la Música pulled down. Though now it is proudly trumpeted as Modernism's star exhibit, it was then execrated as 'a monument to the ostentatious vanity of an era of hopes and illusions'. Catalonia certainly had fewer illusions in the strife-torn 1930s. And as her nationalist fortunes waned, so did the fortunes of Modernism. When the Spanish Civil War ended in 1939 and Catalonia's 40 years of 'internal exile' began, Modernism was almost erased from the slate altogether. Scores of buildings were demolished, including works by such luminaries as Domènech i Montaner and Puig i Cadafalch. And as soon as Catalonia's once-proud national style was threatened with utter obliteration, people began to stand up for it again, and to recognize its merits. Architects, artists, journalists and historians began to stir up popular resistance in a bid to halt the destruction and save other condemned Modernist buildings. This is not to suggest that Barcelona underwent a Modernist revival. Throughout the middle part of the 20th century Catalan Modernism was regarded by the rest of Spain (and by many Catalans as well) as a manifestation of a frivolous, faintly unhinged tendency in the national psyche. It was only

Modernism, an ebullient style for an ebullient era, was used on store fronts all over town, with a particular fondness for pharmacies.

mad dogs and Englishmen like Graham Greene and Evelyn Waugh (perhaps no coincidence that both were Roman Catholics) who showed genuine enthusiasm for the style. Since the re-emergence of Catalan national pride over the past three decades, however, Modernism has been resuscitated as the epitome of all that is most creative in the Catalan genius.

NOUCENTISME

After Art Nouveau came Noucentisme ('nine-hundredism', a reference to the word *nou*, which means both 'new' and 'nine'). It was conceived as the new style for the nineteen hundreds, the beginning of the new century, although there was little about it that was truly innovative. In essence it was an attempt to return to a more classical canon, and not much of note resulted. It was even accused of destruction. When the ground floor of Domènech i Montaner's Casa Lleó Morera was remodeled, the pairs of female sculptures that had adorned it were hacked out and decapitated, some said by the Noucentistes, who loathed everything to do with Modernism. Noucentisme was more successful as a fine art movement (*see p. 118*). Its architecture consists largely of the **monumental structures on Montjuïc and around Plaça Espanya**, constructed for the 1929 International Exhibition. None is architecturally significant. The 1929 Exhibition did bring one of the century's most important buildings to Barcelona, but it was not a Noucentista one: **Mies van der Rohe's Barcelona Pavilion**, on Av. Marquès de Comillas, part of the German exhibition stand, embodies what at the time was a radically new approach to the use of space. Depending on your point of view, as a counterpoise to the burgeoning lushness of Modernist Barcelona, 'less is more' must have seemed, at the time, either next to nothing or an enormous relief.

RATIONALISM: JOSEP LLUÍS SERT

Josep Lluís Sert (1902-1983), a colleague and follower of Le Corbusier, was Barcelona's most important architect of the 1930s. His **Casa Bloc** (1932) in the north-eastern suburb of San Andreu (Passeig Torras i Bages) was the first workers' housing project south of the Pyrenees. Other major Sert buildings include the **Dispensari Antituberculós** (1935, Carrer Torres i Amat), and the

Exuberant - not to say overwhelming - interior of Domènech i Montaner's Casa Lleó Morera. It was precisely this sort of excess that the Rationalists wanted to flee from, bringing unadorned surfaces and purity of line into a cluttered, over-ornamented world.

Joieria Roca jewelry store at Passeig de Gràcia 18 (corner of Gran Via de les Corts Catalanes). During most of the Franco regime - which had no use for his style of architecture - Sert lived in the United States, where he worked as an urban planner (the layout of a number of Latin American cities is his) and designed many of the buildings of Harvard University. He was appointed Dean of Harvard's Graduate School of Design in 1953, and was instrumental in setting up its urban planning degree course. He returned to Spain at the end of the 60s. Sert's last and most important contribution to the Barcelona cityscape was the **Fundació Joan Miró** (1975) on Montjuïc (*see p. 123*), built in honor of his close friend Joan Miró, another artist purged by Franco, who had also lived much of his life in exile. The building is a bright and luminous series of geometric shapes, tacked together to form a unit, made of monolithic concrete, and painted plain white. Whatever may be said in its favor or disfavor, one thing is certain: it acts as an excellent foil for the multicolored, swirling madness of the paintings within.

CONTEMPORARY BARCELONA: RENEWAL

When the Franco regime ended in 1975, Barcelona embarked on a long-overdue project of urban renewal. Initially this concentrated on filling empty space with parks or the controversial *places dures* ('hard squares'), paved, vegetation-free lots such as the **Parc Joan Miró**, or Gràcia's **Plaça del Diamant**.

The 1992 Olympic Games provided further impetus for urban renewal. The Vila Olímpica extended Cerdà's Eixample grid plan north-east down the Diagonal as far as the Mediterranean shore. On Montjuïc the old 1920 Olympic stadium was completely refurbished, and Arata Isozaki's colossal **Palau Sant Jordi** went up. Isozaki is not the only contemporary international architect to be represented in the city. American architect Richard Meier's **MACBA** (Museu d'Art Contemporani de Barcelona, *see p. 130*) brings light and space into a traditionally dark and tortuous neighborhood (the Raval, *see p. 187*); Sir Norman Foster's **Torre de Collserola** radio mast pierces the sky from the heights of Tibidabo; Jean Nouvel's **Torre Agbar** rears above the rooflines of the lower Diagonal like a giant, 33-story lipstick case. Spanish architects are represented too. Piñón and Vilaplana's **CCCB** (Centre de Cultura Contemporània de Barcelona, Carrer Montalegre, Raval) adds a glass reflecting wall to a medieval convent. The angled upper section seems to conjure Montjuïc and the Mediterranean from thin air into the patio. Then there is Rafael Moneo's wood-paneled **Auditori** (Carrer Lepant 150, *see p. 146*) and Ricardo Bofill's Parthenon-in-aspic, the post-Neoclassical **Teatre Nacional** (Plaça de les Arts, near the eastern end of the Diagonal). In the middle of the Olympic Ring on Montjuïc stands Santiago Calatrava's **Torre Calatrava**, not only a telecommunications tower but also a sundial. The angle of its

Contemporary sheet glass at the CCCB throws back reflections of the former convent.

The distinctive roofscape of Domènech i Montaner's Hospital de Sant Pau. If a hospital is beautiful, the architect maintained, patients need not go there to die; they will go there to recover health and vigor.

pointer and the angle of the sun are in perfect alignment on the day of the summer solstice. Good examples of contemporary architecture breathing new life into redundant historic structures are Puig i Cadafalch's Casaramona (Av. Marquès de Comillas 6-8), once a factory now the **CaixaForum** art center, and Josep Fontseré's **Dipòsit de les Aigües** (Carrer Ramon Trias Fargas 25-27), once a water cistern and now the Universitat Pompeu Fabra library.

It seems certain that Barcelona will always find ways to delight and alarm the eye with new and surprising architecture. Meanwhile the Sagrada Família moves inexorably toward a conclusion that will nearly double its height and require the demolition of who knows how many apartment buildings to open up an approach to its main façade. Then, as now, Gaudí's masterpiece will continue to fascinate as the most original element in Barcelona's shifting architectural landscape.

MODERNISM IN DETAIL

NB: The Manzana de la Discordia, and Gaudí's La Pedrera and Sagrada Família are included in Major Sights on pp. 55-69.

MAJOR MODERNIST ARCHITECTS

LLUÍS DOMÈNECH I MONTANER (1850-1924) - Barcelona's first Modernist architect, and university professor of both Gaudí and Puig i Cadafalch. In 1878, at the age of 28, he published a manifesto exhorting Catalan architects to 'search for a national architecture'. His Editorial Montaner i Simó (1886, now the Fundació Tàpies) was the first Modernist building in the Eixample. It was Domènech i Montaner who brought

Domènech i Montaner, as seen through the eyes of Modernist artist Ramon Casas.

the *obra total* (total work of art, *Gesamtkunstwerk*) concept to Barcelona, bringing masters in fine and applied arts together in the Arts and Crafts tradition established by William Morris in Britain. Domènech i Montaner built in a distinctive, personal style, using brick, wrought iron and glazed ceramic, with an abundance of floral themes. His great-grandson, Lluís Domènech Girbau, remembers his 'passion for nature, for hikes in the mountains, and his devising of an architecture school course entitled *Flora i Fauna*, which emphasized the former'. His best-known surviving works in Barcelona are the Palau de la Música Catalana (1908, *see p. 143*), the Casa Lleó Morera on Passeig de Gràcia (1905, *see p. 58*), and the Hospital de Sant Pau (1902-1930, *pictured opposite*) at Carrer Sant Antoni Maria Claret 167 (one stop on the blue metro line - L1 - from the Sagrada Família).

Domènech i Montaner believed in the therapeutic properties of form and color. He also believed that patients were more likely to recover surrounded by trees and flowers, and thus set his hospital among gardens. (*Visits between 9am & 2pm and 4pm & 7pm every day.*) Active in journalism and politics, Domènech i Montaner was socially conservative and politically Catalanist, becoming president of the Catalanist Union in 1892, and a member of the Lliga, the Regionalist League, in 1901. During King Alfonso XIII's visit to Barcelona (1904) an anonymous newspaper article appeared criticizing aspects of the monarchy. Domènech i Montaner, widely suspected to have written it, never admitted authorship. Deeply shaken by the Great War of 1914-1918, Domènech retired from political activism and devoted the rest of his life to archeology and history.

JOSEP PUIG I CADAFALCH (1867-1956) - The most politically powerful of the Modernist architects, a true Renaissance man of the Catalan *Renaixença*, architect, scholar, writer, politician and statesman. Puig i Cadafalch's early style combined an affinity for Nordic Gothic forms with the lines and tradition of the Catalan

Bench by Puig i Cadafalch, part of the original furnishings for Casa Amatller.

mas or manor house. His most famous work in Barcelona is the Casa Amatller (1900, *see p. 57*) in the so-called Manzana de la Discordia, influenced by Flemish architecture because of Puig's admiration for cosmopolitan Brussels as a model for Barcelona. He also built the Casa Martí/Els Quatre Gats (1897, *see p. 240*), the Palau Quadras (1904, *see p. 97*), and Casa Serra (1908, *see p. 97*). In the Casa de les Punxes (1905, *see also p. 97*) Puig i Cadafalch realized his most extravagant Nordic Gothic fantasy. An expert on medieval Catalan art and architecture, Puig i Cadafalch authored important studies on these subjects throughout his life. Professor at the Barcelona School of Architecture (1901-02), he also taught at the Sorbonne (1925), Harvard and Cornell (1926) and at the University of Paris. Another prominent Catalanist politician, he was co-founder of the Regionalist League (1901), serving as a member of its Political Action Committee. It was Puig i Cadafalch who, much aided by the research of his teacher Lluís Domènech i Montaner, masterminded the transfer of Romanesque friezes from Pyrenean churches to what is now the MNAC (*see p.123*). He served as president of the Mancomunitat (*see p. 22*) in 1919, 1921 and 1923, and in this capacity

Josep Puig i Cadafalch, also by Casas.

worked to improve Barcelona's telephone network and public libraries. General Primo de Rivera's coup d'état (*see p. 23*) meant that popularly elected provincial deputies in the Mancomunitat were substituted with functionaries more to the dictator's liking. The president from 1924, Alfons Sala, initiated a defamation campaign against Puig i Cadafalch, and Barcelona's municipal government dismissed him from his post of architect to the 1929 International Exhibition. Franco's military rebellion of 1936 forced him into exile. He settled in Paris, and later in Roussillon, where he continued his Romanesque studies. Under Franco he was forbidden to work as an architect in Spain.

JOSEP MARIA JUJOL I GIBERT (1879-1949) - Jujol worked closely with Gaudí from 1906, collaborating on Casa Milà (*see p. 60*), whose wrought-iron balconies he designed, and Parc Güell (*see p. 107*), where his most famous creation is the undulating bench on the esplanade. Undulating forms recur on his Casa Planells (1924, Diagonal 332), a fusion of Modernism with Functionalism. The 20 years from 1906 until the death of Gaudí were the most creative of his career. His second period (from 1927 until his death) was less distinguished. His monumental fountain in the center of Plaça Espanya (1929) is remarkable for its size, but artistically uninteresting. While he failed fully to live up to this early promise, Jujol was technically brilliant, and was one of the finest draughtsmen Catalonia has ever produced. Though during his initial period, under Gaudí's influence, he created Surrealist works of striking originality, his later return to Classicism and Historicism suggests that his artistic inspiration failed to function without the external stimulus of a great master - or perhaps the aesthetic of the new Rationalist generation was simply alien to his instincts.

Undulating bench in the Parc Güell, the most famous creation of Josep Maria Jujol.

Berenguer's Gràcia Town Hall. The district contains many more of his buildings.

FRANCESC BERENGUER I MESTRES (1866-1914) - A close friend and key assistant of Antoni Gaudí (Gaudí had studied under Berenguer's father in Reus), Berenguer's role in Gaudí's work has been long debated. Berenguer went to work young, before receiving his architecture degree, and died young at the age of 48, before receiving full recognition for his contributions to the Modernist movement. When Berenguer married at the age of 21, Gaudí offered him a job as his assistant. Berenguer gave up his studies and became Gaudí's draftsman, organizer, construction foreman, and artistic alter ego.

Berenguer's practical skills and Gaudí's dreamy visions complemented each other well. Because never took his degree, however, Berenguer was not officially allowed to sign his blue-prints. The extent of the debt that the Barcelona cityscape owes him is still uncertain as a result. He is most associated with the district of Gràcia (*see p. 221*), and is generally credited with at least seven major buildings on Carrer Gran de Gràcia (Nos. 13, 15, 50, 61, 77, 196 and 237), although the official register attributes only half of those houses to him. The Gràcia Town Hall in Plaça Rius i Taulet is definitely his. A regular collaborator with Gaudí on the Sagrada Família (*see p. 63*), Berenguer identified with the style of the master to such an extent that his best known work, the Celler Güell in El Garraf (1888-90), just down the coast from Barcelona, is often taken for a Gaudí creation. His best known work is Barcelona is the house in which Gaudí lived in the

Parc Güell (1905). When Berenguer died on February 8th, 1914, leaving seven children and a widow behind him, Gaudí was deeply affected and said that he had 'lost his right hand'. Though Gaudí lived another 12 years, he became a virtual recluse, and dedicated himself solely to the Sagrada Família.

EXPLORING THE MODERNIST EIXAMPLE

A tour of six of the most visually impressive of the Eixample's buildings, by Barcelona's three greatest Modernist architects. Buildings are marked on the map below.

EIXAMPLE BUILDINGS BY JOSEP PUIG I CADAFALCH

CASA SERRA - Completed in 1908. The majolica-tiled turret bears witness to Puig i Cadafalch's love of northern European forms; the overall Gothic feel of the building is testimony to his interest in medieval architecture. The entrance is a copy of an old Renaissance doorway from the Barri Gòtic, demolished in the mid 19th century. The top floor windows imitate a low Gothic arcade. The sculptural decoration is by Eusebi Arnau. Look for the coat of arms created for the owner, Pere Serra, featuring a saw. *Serra* means 'saw' in Catalan. Its proportions are today dwarfed by the 1980s monolith-in-glass behind it. *Rambla de Catalunya 126.*

PALAU BARÓ DE QUADRAS - The neo-Gothic atmosphere of this building is unmistakable, from the impregnable iron door to the top-floor windows, which again imitate the kind of low arcade so typical of medieval Catalan architecture (as seen, for example, on the Casa de la Pia Almoina, *see p. 54*). It was built for Baron Quadras in 1904, and its main feature is the immense plateresque oriel. The plateresque is a notable feature of Spanish Renaissance architecture: clusters of intensely sculpted decoration erupt from an area of bare

The neo-Bavarian Casa de les Punxes.

stonework. Note the symbiotically writhing St George and the dragon, locked in inextricable combat, on the oriel's outer corner. The interior has been restored and remodeled to house the Casa Asia, a showpiece dedicated to the culture of an entire continent. *Av. Diagonal 373 (Casa Asia). Open Mon-Sat 10am-8pm; Sun 10am-2pm.*

CASA DE LES PUNXES (House of the Spikes) - This brick-and-stone extravaganza is from Puig i Cadafalch's so-called 'pink period'. It was commissioned in 1903 (completed in 1905) for the three Terrades sisters. Though it looks like a single entity, it is in fact three dwellings in one. Once again the oriel windows are covered in plateresque decoration. The six turrets could not be less Iberian: they seem to belong more to the Black Forest, and clearly demonstrate the architect's interest in Northern European forms. The building consists of private apartments and is closed to the public. *Av. Diagonal 416-420.*

EIXAMPLE BUILDINGS BY LLUÍS DOMÈNECH I MONTANER

PALAU MONTANER - Built between 1889 and 1896, for the architect's first cousin, the printer Ramon Montaner, who established the Montaner i Simó publishing and printing house (now the Fundació Tàpies, *see p. 128*), also by Domènech i Montaner. The exterior of the Palau Montaner is elegant and symmetrical, reminiscent of a Renaissance villa. It was begun by another architect, Josep Domènech i Estapà, who famously disliked Modernism and favored Historicist models. The point at which Domènech i Montaner took over must have been round about the second floor, hence the decorative explosion there. *Mallorca 101.*

CASA THOMAS - Built in 1898 for another printer, Josep Thomas. The ground floor and basement originally housed printing workshops; offices occupied the mezzanine; and the family's private apartments were on the upper floors. To the right of the wide ground floor arcade was the owner's and guest entrance: the door is carved with fierce greyhounds. The tradesmen's entrance was to the left, through a door carved with bibliophile owls. The façade presents an eclectic combination of straight and curved lines. Note the trademark Domènech i Montaner opera-box balconies. *Mallorca 291-293.*

Colorful ceramic decoration on the façade of Palau Montaner.

EIXAMPLE BUILDINGS BY ANTONI GAUDÍ I CORNET

CASA CALVET - (*NB: Walk down Roger de Llúria to Carrer Casp. Casa Calvet is marked on the map on p. 287.*)
The exterior of this building seems conventional for Gaudí. It was built in 1900 for the textile baron Andreu Calvet, and the sober sandstone façade gives every impression that Gaudí was treading with caution - it was his first commission in the Eixample. He gave his imagination free rein on his second and third commissions (Casa Batlló and La Pedrera (*see pp. 56 & 60*), with the result that he was never given another. Casa Calvet does reflect Gaudí's love of symbolism, however. A stylized letter 'C' for 'Calvet' appears over the door. The wild mushrooms above the central oriel window reflect Andreu Calvet's enthusiasm for fungi. The columns flanking the doorway look like bobbins from a weaver's loom (textiles being the source of Calvet's fortune). The door knockers are shaped in the form of massy iron crosses (symbols of good) that beat down on cast-iron bed bugs (symbols

Door knockers in the shape of crosses crash down upon cast-iron bedbugs.

of evil). The interior contains more of the Gaudí we have come to expect. For a truly synaesthetic Gaudí experience, dine in the same building's next-door Casa Calvet restaurant (*see p. 244 for details*). *Carrer Casp 48. For visits, consult the Ruta del Modernisme (see box below).*

RUTA DEL MODERNISME
For information on this tour of nine major Modernist sites, inquire at the Casa Amatller (Passeig de Gràcia 41), Tel: 93/488-0139 (*Mon-Sat 10am-7pm, Sun 10am-2pm*). The ticket gives you 50% discounts at each location.

ANTONI GAUDÍ

No architect has ever left his imprint on a major city as spectacularly as Antoni Gaudí (1852-1926) did on Barcelona. His still unfinished Temple Expiatori de la Sagrada Família (*see p. 63*) has become emblematic, while another dozen works in and around the city continue to draw curious and admiring crowds. Strange to think that for decades after his death he remained a virtual unknown, unlauded and unrecognized.

Strictly speaking, and considering his love of decorative detail and his interest in organic forms, Gaudí belongs to the Modernists. In truth his creations have little to do with Art Nouveau, and it is revealing that two of the early 20th century's greatest Functionalists, Le Corbusier and Walter Gropius, saw and appreciated in Gaudí what the rest of the world did not: his architecture was revolutionary. He approached construction like no one else before him had ever done. He was a true original - and he defined originality literally: as a 'return to origins'. Throughout history, he maintained, architects had become prisoners of the forms they were able to create with the tools of their trade. Buildings were composed only of circles, triangles and rectangles. But in nature, Gaudí pointed out, such shapes do not exist. Bones are not cylindrical; leaves are not triangular; the sides of an apple never curve in a perfect arc - and yet they all have strength and structural integrity. What Gaudí discovered was that all organic forms take their strength from an inner support system composed of fibers. Gaudí translated this into architecture, and the shapes he ended up with were conoids, helicoids, hyerboloids and paraboloids. The terms sound outlandish, but they all describe everyday shapes. The arches between fingers are neither pointed nor rounded, for example. They are hyperbolic paraboloids. In this lies the secret of Gaudí's genius. He was doing much more than just experimenting with aesthetics; he was putting function before form, and devising an alternative system of construction.

EARLY CAREER

Gaudí's life and personality have always been surrounded by mystery and controversy. While a movement to have him canonized progresses inexorably, other voices claim that he was a Freemason and not even a Christian, much less a saint. Even his 1852 birthplace is disputed between the towns of Reus and

Riudoms, both just inland from Tarragona. His father was a coppersmith, and the molding and casting of copper pots has been cited as important in Gaudí's ability to visualize three-dimensional form. After graduating from Barcelona's Escola Superior d'Arquitectura de la Llotja de Mar in 1878, Gaudí's first major project was the house of the ceramics mogul Manuel Vicens, on Carrer de les Carolines in Gràcia (*see p. 220*). Not long afterwards, Gaudí met the wealthy industrialist and patron of the arts Eusebi Güell (*see p. 104*) - and the young architect was never idle again. Parc Güell (*see p. 107*), Palau Güell just off the Rambla (*see p. 103*), Colònia Güell just outside of Barcelona, and the gate and gatehouse at the Güell estate (Finca Güell), now the Càtedra Gaudí, in Pedralbes (*see p. 215*) all attest to this symbiotic relationship between patron and architect.

ARCHITECTURAL DEVELOPMENT

Gaudí's architectural evolution is easy to trace. His first project, Casa Vicens (1883-85, *see also p. 220*), is much the most conventional, despite its bravura polychrome façade. In essence it is still a house built of right-angled planes. In Palau Güell (1885-89, *see p. 103*) the parabolic arch makes its triumphal entrance, though overall Gaudí is still in thrall to the neo-Gothic. With La Pedrera (Casa Milà, 1905, *see p. 60*), Gaudí abandons convention more entirely. There are no supporting walls; the structure rests on an inner fretwork of beams. Casa Batlló (1907, *see p. 56*), in outward appearance as well as structural concept, is still way ahead of its time. And finally, there is the project that consumed the last 40 years of Gaudí's life, the Sagrada Família (*see p. 63*), more a geological formation than a building, the ultimate experiment in monumental

Gaudí's first Barcelona project: Casa Vicens in the district of Gràcia. It was Barcelona's first polychromatic façade.

organic architecture, which Gaudí himself once compared to Montserrat, the famous serrated mountain and holy shrine just west of Barcelona.

GAUDÍ'S FINAL YEARS

Throughout his major works, Gaudí continued to develop his own personal architectural language, largely oblivious of the Modernist movement raging around him. Gaudí stories abound: said to have been an extravagant and epicurean dandy as a young man, he became more ascetic as he grew older and nearly starved himself to death fasting for Lent in 1894. A devout Catholic, religious mystic, and eccentric genius, Gaudí's affairs of the heart led to sentimental crises that finally convinced him that he 'lacked the aptitude for family life'. A staunch Catalanist on a purely emotional level (he was as devoutly apolitical as he was asexual), Gaudí was briefly imprisoned at the age of 72 for refusing to speak anything but Catalan to a policeman. His famous encounter with Basque philosopher Miguel de Unamuno turned into a fiasco for the same reason: Gaudí reasoned that Unamuno, as an erudite scholar of the Classics, should surely be able to understand Catalan. Unamuno did not, and the meeting devolved into an autistic standoff with the Catalan building origami paper sculptures and the Basque, 12 years Gaudí's junior, tapping his pencil and staring out of the window. Increasingly reclusive and ethereal as the years went on, Gaudí lived with his niece in Parc Güell for nearly twenty years before moving into his studio in the Sagrada Família, his only active project after completing Casa Milà. Perennially penniless, near

Trencadís, pottery broken into fragments and haphazardly pieced together again: one of Antoni Gaudí's many decorative innovations.

the end of his life Gaudí was known to do without underwear and dressed in the same suit for months at a time. When he was struck by a trolley car on June 7th, 1926, three weeks before his 74th birthday, he was taken for a pauper and remained unidentified for some time, until his absence at the Sagrada Família building site came to someone's notice and inquiries were made. Gaudí, hospitalized in the medieval Hospital de la Santa Creu (*see p. 191*), never regained consciousness. 150 years after his birth, his magnum opus continues, and his vision continues to shape the city that became his personal sand box.

PALAU GÜELL AND PARC GÜELL

Of all of the schemes put together by Antoni Gaudí and Eusebi Güell (*see overleaf*), it is these two that seem to speak to each other much as the architect and the patron did, as kindred but opposing spirits. One is light, the other dark; one at the edge of the port, the other high up behind the city; one is an urban private palace, the other a leafy public park; both were much criticized when unveiled; and while the downtown palace was their first mutual venture in 1885, the garden city, finished in 1914, was their last.

PALAU GÜELL
Carrer Nou de la Rambla 3-5. Open Mon-Sat 10am-6.15pm; Sun 10am-1pm.
Tickets are sold for guided tours at set times only. No advance tickets;
same-day-only bookings. Tel: 93/317-3974.

With its parabolic arches and Gothic upsweep, its Mudéjar jalousies and ceramic collage chimneys, Palau Güell was a bold beginning for a young architect's first commission from the man destined to become his main patron. Though work continued until 1890, the palace was officially opened in 1888, to coincide with the World Exhibition of the same year. Princesses Paz and Isabel de Borbón, daughters of King Alfonso XII, were guests of honor at the inaugural gala.

Initial reactions were mixed. Epithets ranged from 'Babylonian' to 'dungeon-like'. Gaudí patiently insisted that 'Count Güell and I like it', but we also know that the Countess, Isabel López, hated it, and was frightened of going from one floor to another at night. It is certainly austere. The somber façade, which looks like a medieval baronial hall, provides little more than a foretaste of what is in store inside.

GAUDÍ'S PATRON - EUSEBI GÜELL

If Eusebi Güell i Bacigalupi (1846-1918) had not been struck by Gaudí's work at the Paris World Exhibition in 1878, Barcelona and the world might have seen little or nothing of the great Modernist's unique vision. The piece on show was a display window that Gaudí had designed for a Barcelona glove boutique: a six-faced glass prism containing a two-way shelf. The prism rested on a decorative wooden frame holding a circular metal railing protecting the glass from spectators. The originality of the piece so dazzled Güell that he immediately sought out the young architect in Barcelona. So began a close and complementary relationship that would endure until Güell's death. Güell's great-great-granddaughter, Carmen Güell, has described the friendship as an alliance of opposites based on profound mutual admiration. The two men would argue endlessly about artistic and aesthetic matters, though they fervently agreed on the importance of a powerful Catalonia within a plural Spain, and spoke to each other only in Catalan.

Eusebi Güell was the son of a self-made man, Joan Güell, who had gone to seek his fortune in Cuba, and returned to found one of Barcelona's largest textile factories, the Vapor Vell. Eusebi was born to opportunities his father had only dreamed about. Brought up in a world of art and culture, the young Güell studied in Barcelona, England and France. Italy, his mother's ancestral country, was of great interest to him; he learned Italian, to add to his fluent English, French, Spanish and Catalan. Though profoundly Catalanist and a staunch believer in protectionism for Catalan industry, he enjoyed cordial relations with the Spanish king, Alfonso XII, who granted him the honor of visiting the palace without booking a prior audience. Alfonso XIII was later to create him Conde de Güell (Count Güell). He married the daughter of Antonio López y López, first Marqués de Comillas and the most opulent magnate of his time (*see pp. 37-8*). All in all, he couldn't have been better positioned to catapult the young Gaudí into the thick of Barcelona's most powerful and influential circles, allowing him to work out his architectural vision independent of prevailing tastes. 'Don Eusebi,' affirmed Gaudí after the financier's death, 'was a gentleman in the full sense of the word...a person of excellent sensibilities, education, and position. Being pre-eminent in all areas, he envied no one...and liked seeing those around him demonstrate their talents.'

INSIDE PALAU GÜELL

ENTRANCE & STABLES: Tours begin downstairs in the stables, a nether region of fungiform columns forming a system of parabolic arches that support the entire building. The yard where the horses were groomed receives light through a skylight, one of several devices Gaudí used to illuminate this tenebrous edifice, tightly hemmed in on all sides. Other tricks include mirrors and even frosted-glass panels placed over artificial light sources, giving the impression of light coming in from outside. The chutes on the roadward side of the basement were for delivering feed straight in from street level overhead, while the spiral ramp was the servants' access to the main entrance hall. The stones underfoot are worn to smoothness now: it is difficult to walk up the ramp in leather-soled shoes. Note the pine-block flooring in the ground-floor entranceway, used instead of cobbles to deaden the sound of horses' hoofs. Spare a thought also for the political prisoners who were held in the

Palau Güell. Note the stylized 'G' for Güell, and the coat of arms incorporating the Catalan banner, crested by a phoenix symbolically rising from its ashes.

basement during the Civil War, when the stables were used as a Republican secret-police dungeon. One such prisoner was Andreu Nin, a purged Trotskyite. He was never seen again.

MAIN SALONS: Upstairs there is an enfilade of three reception rooms, the wooden ceilings progressing from merely splendid to Byzantine in the complexity of their molded floral and leaf motifs. The third reception room, which has the most elaborate ceiling ornamentation, has a latticed jalousie in the gallery above, a double screen through which Count Güell was able to inspect and - to put it baldly - eavesdrop on his visitors. The central salon has a three-story parabolic cupola, lined with alabaster, which reaches up above the roofline. This was the grand function room, used for parties, receptions and musical evenings (not dances - polite Barcelona society in those days frowned on dancing for young ladies. The Güell daughters were never allowed even so much as a staid minuet). Musicians played from the balcony, and the overhead balcony window was for the main vocalist. A

Cavernous interior of Palau Güell. The walls are of gray marble, polished to a dull sheen, and the overall effect is one of strangely medieval discomfort.

chapel of beaten copper with retractable kneeling pads and a small two-seater bench built into the right side of the altar is enclosed behind a double door. Around the corner is a small organ, the pipes in rectangular tubes climbing the mansion's central gallery.

The dining room has a Modernist fireplace in the shape of a deeply curving horseshoe arch at one end, beside which stands a large mahogany dining table, with space to seat ten. The long bench and sitting area under the window in front of the table to the right boasts upholstery and carpeting that looks forward to the fashions of the 1970s. The louvered window blinds and

mechanism for adjusting their angle are the originals. From the outside rear terrace, the polished gray marble of the main part of the house is visible. The marble came from Count Güell's own quarry in El Garraf, just south of Barcelona. The servants' quarters, made of brick, rise up on the left. A passageway built out toward the Rambla linked Palau Güell with the Count's father's house, which overlooked the Rambla dels Caputxins.

Upstairs are the bedrooms of Count Güell and his wife, Isabel López. The countess has built-in closets padded in lilac plush, and the initial letters of her and her husband's names intertwined in wrought-iron fancywork. The couple's bathroom is also preserved, appointed with all the modern conveniences of the age.

ROOF: It is here that we encounter Gaudí as the world popularly knows him, in his 20 zany, polychrome *trencadís* chimneys, which make you feel you must be looking through a kaleidoscope. The main chimney features a weather-vane in the form of a bat, the emblem of Jaume I el Conqueridor, the sovereign count who conquered Majorca and paved the way for Catalonia's Mediterranean empire-building. Jaume is said to have chosen the bat as his emblem in gratitude after his Majorca campaign. One night, as the opposing forces lay sleeping in their camps, a bat became trapped in Jaume's tent. Woken by its flutterings, the count-king found that the Moors were planning to attack under cover of darkness. He was able to rouse his men to arms and beat the attackers back.

PARC GÜELL

Carrer d'Olot s/n. Metro to Lesseps; then walk 10 minutes uphill or catch Bus 24 to the park entrance. Open Oct-Mar 10am-6pm every day; Apr-June 10am-7pm every day; July-Sept 10am-9pm every day.

While Palau Güell partly satisfied Eusebi Güell's ambition to reinvigorate Barcelona's urban landscape and to position himself prominently within it, he missed the peace and pleasures of a country estate. More importantly, perhaps, his wife Isabel, daughter of the Marqués de Comillas (*see pp. 37-8*), always longed for the lush and leafy Cantabrian village where she had spent childhood summers. Following a visit to England, during which he had admired the garden city movement, Eusebi Güell returned to Barcelona with a new project in mind.

Gaudí accompanied Güell to the 15-hectare area of high ground in upper Barcelona known as *muntanya pelada* (Bald Mountain) for its scarce vegetation. Güell planned to develop it as a private residential compound, in which individual lots would be sold off for house construction. He let his imagination carry him away, envisaging the bald hill as a Mount Parnassus. He instructed Gaudí to build him his very own Delphi, complete with tripod from which the Sybil conjured her oracles. There were to be three fountains, a Doric temple and a wide esplanade, to be known as the Greek Theater.

Gaudí set to work on the steep and rocky hillside, respecting the orography, leaving the vegetation as untouched as possible, and planting thyme, rosemary, ivy, broom, agave, palms and wisteria. Using the rock excavated on the site as his main construction material, he built two gatehouses and viaducts made with rough-hewn, rocky pillars leaning into the hillside and supporting roadways overhead. The mosaic inscription at the entrance announces 'Park Güell', spelled deliberately in the English way, to emphasize the Anglo-Saxon garden city concept.

The final result is a Modernist anthology with gingerbread gatehouses topped with, on the right, the hallucinogenic red-and-white fly ammanite wild mushroom (of which Gaudí is clandestinely rumored to have been a user), and, on the left, the *phallus impudicus*. Both are reproductions of sketches drawn by Gaudí to illustrate a publication of *Hansel and Gretel*: the house crowned by the fly ammanite represents the witch's house, while the one under the phallus (and Gaudí's beloved double-armed cross) is the children's. The interiors of both gatehouses make interesting exploring: the left-hand house is a bookstore with twisting stairways leading to upper landings. Gaudí's curious mingling of innovative brilliance with naïve infantilism is at its most marked here. It is said that when the mother of one of his childhood friends first came to Barcelona and saw his work, she exclaimed that he was 'doing the same things he always did as a boy'.

Leaving the gatehouses behind you, go up the steps straight ahead. Here you will see the most famous motif of the whole park, the patchwork lizard, lolling on the central balustrade. At the top of the steps you come to the so-called Hall of a Hundred Columns (there are only 86) - conceived as a covered

View of Parc Güell. The Hansel and Gretel-style cottages beside the entrance can clearly be seen, as can the house, designed by Berenguer, where Gaudí lived in his latter years.

market for the community. The roof is supported by Doric-style columns, the outermost ones inclined at an angle to better bear the weight. The ceiling is decorated with a collage of *objets trouvés*: fragments of bottles, plates, cups, and even china dolls recovered from dumps and trashcans around Barcelona; and *trencadís*, broken pieces of tile, are assembled seemingly haphazardly as Modernist ceiling bosses. Carmen Güell recounts that workers, smashing tiles at the entrance to the park, were regarded with utter bewilderment by passers-by unfamiliar with this decorative approach.

Above this hall of pillars is the 'Greek Theater', the esplanade and *mirador*, hemmed around the edge with an undulating polychrome bench. This bench is

the work of Gaudí's assistant Josep Maria Jujol, and is probably the most celebrated example of the *trencadís* technique.

And yet despite all the romantic planning that went into it, Güell's garden city scheme never caught on. Barcelona's bourgeoisie seemed happier living closer to the middle of

Left: Doric pillars in the famous Hall of 100 Columns, originally intended as the market place for the community.

Above: An early example of low-impact architecture: man-made buttresses support an overhang, but are fashioned as if by nature herself.

town; no one wanted a plot of land on Bald Mountain. The Güell family eventually turned the area over to the city as a public park, a perfect place to be on a sunny afternoon when the blue of the Mediterranean is illuminated from the west.

Only two houses were ever built in the park. One of them, designed by Francesc Berenguer (*see p. 95*) in 1905, was home to Gaudí for twenty years: he lived here with his niece. Today it houses the Gaudí Casa-Museu (*Open Jan-Mar & Oct-Dec 10am-6pm; April-Sept 10am-8pm*). It contains furniture from Palau Güell, Casa Calvet and Casa Batlló, along with personal objects and paraphernalia that help bring the eccentric genius into focus. In the garden are pieces of wrought iron in the shape of the palmetto leaves used by Berenguer in Gaudí's first major commission, Gràcia's Casa Vicens.

ART GALLERIES & MUSEUMS

The Gothic and the Modernist styles, for both aesthetic and economic reasons, proved the most fruitful inspirations for Barcelona's genius. In art this is manifest from the tenderly lovely altarpieces of 15th-century master Jaume Huguet and the Modernist creations of Ramon Casas. And just as Barcelona is certainly not a city to sit on the laurels of its past, but a town that grasps the future with both hands, modern art is also well represented. Picasso spent many years in Barcelona; Dalí was a Catalan; Joan Miró tried to fill the city with as many public works as he could; Antoní Tàpies continues the tradition of tortured shapes, twisted religious imagery, and a sinisterly playful approach.

MAIN ART GALLERIES

THE MUSEU D'ART MODERN
Plaça d'Armes, La Ciutadella
Open Tues-Sat 10am-7pm; Sun 10am-2pm. Tel: 93/319-5728.

This collection is a superb compendium of late 19th and early 20th-century Catalan paintings and sculptures, a must for all those who want to understand the hearts that used to beat behind Barcelona's Modernist façades. The collection is also an ideal size: neither too large to be tiring nor too slight to make a trek to the Ciutadella disappointing. It is housed in what was formerly the arsenal for the Ciutadella fortress. The building's walls are suitably thick; it is the only surviving remnant of the citadel built by Felipe V, after his victory in the War of the Spanish Succession in 1714. The museum currently shares the premises with the Catalan Parliament.

NB: plans are in motion to move this collection to Montjuïc. No date has been set, but check carefully to confirm before you visit.

Detail of a 12th-century altar from the church of la Seu d'Urgell, now in the MNAC.

PHOTO: MUSEU NACIONAL D'ART DE CATALUNYA

A Handful of Artists on Display in the Museu d'Art Modern

Realism

Marià Fortuny i Marsal (1838-1874) - Painter, draughtsman and engraver, Fortuny, in his brief 38-year life, became one of Catalonia's first internationally recognized painters. In his day he was known for his accuracy at recording scenes and events and was sent to Morocco in 1859 as a sort of pictorial war correspondent. The result is the enormous canvas *Battle of Tetuan* (1863, *pictured on p. 21*), showing the battlefield on which Spain defeated Morocco in 1860. His keen sense of the sensuality of the exotic is also reflected in *Odalisque*. A meticulous and highly skilled painter, Fortuny's talents were well used in canvases such as *La Vicaria* or *The Stamp Collector*, where the detail of the (deliberately period) interiors is extraordinary, as well as the skilfully hinted physiognomy of the characters, and the lavish atmosphere of silk

'La Vicaria' by Fortuny (1870), one of his meticulously detailed genre scenes.

PHOTOS: MUSEU NACIONAL D'ART DE CATALUNYA

A brooding sky and bowed figures lend a mournful atmosphere to 'Sorrow' (1876) by Joaquim Vayreda, Catalonia's most celebrated 19th-century landscape artist.

and brocade. His international reputation rested mainly on his Moorish subjects, which were then fashionable in Western art. In Catalonia, a country just beginning to forge a sense of its own nationhood, he was considered one of the greatest painters of all time.

JOAQUIM VAYREDA I VILA (1843-1894) - Born in Girona province, Vayreda's philosophy studies took him to Barcelona in 1860. In 1865 he exhibited his first work, *Arri Moreu*, at the Society of Artists, and the following year at the Sala Parés he exhibited a number of landscapes, the genre that was to make him famous. In his early period browns, greens, ochres and dark earth hues predominate. After a visit to Paris he changed direction, deciding that he needed to develop in accordance with modern European trends. The result revolutionized Catalan landscape painting. Vayreda's best-known canvas is the ominous *Recança (Sorrow)*, with its melancholy atmosphere of gathering dusk, black rooks flocking like vultures, and a family on the move, with all their meager possessions heaped into ox carts.

MODERNISM

RAMON CASAS I CARBÓ (1866-1932) - Modernism's leading painter. Casas studied in Paris, where he established himself in 1890 with Santiago Rusiñol (*see below*) and Miquel Utrillo at the Moulin de la Galette in Montmartre. The paintings produced at that time, such as *Plein Air* (1891), with its wonderful drizzly atmosphere, clearly show the influence of Symbolism and of Whistler. From 1889, Casas exhibited annually at Barcelona's Sala Parés (*see p. 166*). The Barcelona public, brought up on the narrative canvases of the time, was initially unenthusiastic, considering his subject-matter flimsy and his palette

PHOTOS: MUSEU NACIONAL D'ART DE CATALUNYA

too restricted. Casas' most famous work is in fact a narrative one: *Garrote vil* (Museum of Modern Art, Madrid, though a sketch for it is housed here), reflecting the social upheaval of contemporary Barcelona. In 1897, with Rusiñol, Utrillo and Pere Romeu, Casas opened the famous tavern Els Quatre Gats (*see p. 241*), a key meeting point for young artists. Other works by Casas include the mermaid murals in the Fonda Espanya (*see p. 43*), and the paintings he produced for the Cercle del Liceu, still hanging in the opera house clubroom (*see p. 142*). In the popular imagination Casas will always be known for his poster art, especially for his advertisement for a syphilis clinic and for the cartoon of himself and Pere Romeu riding on a tandem bicycle.

SANTIAGO RUSIÑOL I PRATS (1861-1931) - Playwright, short story-writer, painter and collector, Santiago Rusiñol came from a well-to-do family whose money came from textiles. Uninterested in the family business, however, he broke ranks and went to Paris, emerging later as a leading

Tousled hair and rumpled bedlinen - bohemianism arrived in Catalonia with the painting of Casas and Rusiñol.

'Figura femenina' by Rusiñol, a typical example of the focus he gives to human subjects - and to himself in the mirror.

exponent of Catalan Modernism, and an advocate of the 'art for art's sake' philosophy of the British Decadents. Rusiñol was a key member of the Els Quatre Gats group, and from 1892 to 1899, between sojourns in Paris, held the Festes Modernistes de Sitges, in the coastal artists' colony south of Barcelona, where he owned a house. In both his painting and his short story writing he criticized the social disparities between bourgeois and working-class Barcelona, pointing out the intransigence and narrow vision of both sides. He ignored family pleas to give up his bohemian existence, and was a frequent exhibitor at the Sala Parés. His best paintings take human subjects as their focus, for example the study of a woman sitting beside a fireplace, *Figura femenina*.

MODERNISM & EXPRESSIONISM

ISIDRE NONELL I MONTURIOL (1872-1911) - Son of a Barcelona noodle manufacturer, Isidre Nonell was the most charismatic of the post-Modernist generation of painters and - as a result of his early death at the age of 39 - the most mythologized and famous. As early as 1891 he showed paintings at Sala Parés, works described as Impressionist by the critics. The following year, as part of the Acadèmia Lliure group, he participated in a group exhibition headed by Rusiñol. In the summer of 1896, Nonell went to the Boí valley in north-western Catalonia, where he produced oil paintings and made drawings of cretinism, then endemic in that area. From then on he continued to be interested in society's outcasts, producing a number of paintings of gypsies. His work, which

'Reclining Figure' (1908) by Isidre Nonell.

slowly became darker and more Expressionist, shocked and disturbed Barcelona sensibilities, much as the work of Kokoschka did in Vienna. Although he was on good terms with Picasso, Nonell had few friends in artistic circles, and he alienated critics by his abrasive response to their articles. His premature death contributed enormously to his recognition and appreciation: posthumously he became a role-model for young artists.

NOUCENTISME

Derived from a play on *nou* ('new') and *nou cents* ('nine hundred'), as in the year 1900 and the turn of the century, Noucentisme was a reaction to the unruly excesses (as the Noucentistes regarded them) of Modernism and a confirmation of Flaubert's *'Le mauvais goût c'est le goût de la génération antérieure'*.

Allergic to the spontaneity and chaos of Modernism, Eugeni d'Ors, Josep Carner, and Ismael Smith, among many others, attempted to revive organization over inspiration and Classicism over anarchism in a movement that ranged from the poetic 'Parnassianism' of Carner and d'Ors, to the anti-floralism and formal dandyism of Smith, or the Cézanne-inspired landscapes of Joaquim Sunyer. Eugeni d'Ors elaborated the aesthetic doctrine he called Noucentisme in his *Almanach dels Noucentistes*; in its first publication, Isidre Nonell (*see above*), Pablo Picasso, Pau Gargallo (sculptor and disciple of Eusebi Arnau, who worked with many Modernist architects), Ismael Smith, and indeed nearly anyone coming of age around the turn of the century, were among the artists and poets included in the movement.

Enric Prat de la Riba, first President of the Mancomunitat, Catalonia's early 20th-century semi-autonomous government (*see p. 22*) provided a political rallying point for the Noucentistes, who believed that art should contribute to social reform in an orderly and practical manner. The architect Josep Puig i Cadafalch (*see p. 92*), a subsequent President of the Mancomunitat, helped Prat de la Riba with a number of social reform programs, and the Noucentista sculptor Gargallo collaborated with

Puig on several buildings. Eugeni d'Ors called Prat de la Riba the 'ordering wisdom of Catalonia', a turn of phrase that reflects the Noucentistes' concern to create order out of what they regarded as the mayhem of Modernism.

But while the Noucentistes were tidy-minded, they were not prudish. Many were ardent admirers of the work of the English writer and illustrator Aubrey Beardsley (1872-98), a member of the so-called Decadents, whose aestheticism espoused art for art's sake in reaction to art as a mechanical process, a response to commissions from a patron, a means of making a living.

Portrait of the artist's father, a Noucentista work by Salvador Dalí (1925).

Noucentisme, therefore, was in no way a reactionary movement. It embraced anti-materialism and idealism, which it saw as antidotes to Modernism's romantic - and pragmatic - consumerism. D'Ors defined the process of artistic creation as a flight from sentimentality toward ethical and ideal aesthetic truth. Artistically, this meant a return to structure over ornament. Noucentisme, a modern form of Classicism, seeking both novelty and tradition at once, often looks as paradoxical as it sounds: both disciplined and confused at the same time, a sort of Modernism on Prozac. By far the best Noucentista work in the Museu d'Art Modern is Salvador Dalí's portrait of his father (1925). It is interesting that Dalí the Noucentista, member of a generation who attempted to impose rational structure on basic instinct, should have gone on to become the father of that supreme expression of basic instinct unleashed and reason undermined: Surrealism.

THE GALLERIES OF MONTJUÏC

This jutting promontory overlooking the port has long been said to be named for a Jewish cemetery that once occupied its slopes. Another tradition claims a Roman origin for the name, citing a 3rd-century Roman document referring to the construction of a road between Mons Taber (around the cathedral) and Mons Jovis (Mount of Jupiter), present-day Montjuïc. Compared to the immediate attractions of central Barcelona, Montjuïc may seem distant and not worth the trek: if you enjoy art, though, you will find it amply rewarding. The Miró Foundation, the Museu Nacional d'Art de Catalunya's collection of Romanesque Pyrenean murals and frescoes in the Palau Nacional, and the minimalist Mies van der Rohe Pavilion are all among Barcelona's most important sights, not to mention a handful of other attractions along the way. It is well worth taking half a day out to explore. Other Montjuïc options include the Castell de Montjuïc military fortress, the Olympic stadium, Isozaki's Palau Sant Jordi, and the Poble Espanyol. Take your pick. All are of interest, though these are perhaps less important than other Barcelona sights to make time for, such as Parc Güell or the Monestir de Pedralbes.

All sights and museums mentioned in this section are marked on the map opposite.

Inside the Miró Foundation, which also has a restaurant, a good place for lunch. The work shown here is 'Figure in front of the Sun', 1968.

How To Get There

The most memorable way to get to Montjuïc is by cable car (Transbordador aeri) from Barceloneta or from the mid-way station in Port Vell. This drops you at the Jardins de Miramar, a good 15-minute walk from the Fundació Miró. If Miró is your primary object, your best option is to take the funicular from the Avinguda del Paral.lel (Paral.lel metro stop, Line 3). The funicular is under ground, and consequently unpicturesque, but it drops you right where you want to be. For the MNAC it is quickest to take Bus 61 (or walk) from Plaça Espanya. The Telefèric de Montjuïc takes you from the funicular terminus up to the Castell de Montjuïc.

Montjuïc is also an extended city park, and dallying in its groves and gardens is extremely pleasant. Unless you have the time and the disposition for hiking, though, walking from A to B can be long and wearisome, and you won't have the stamina for the museums themselves. If your main aim is to see the art, it is best simply to take a taxi door to door.

The Museums and Sights

Fundació Miró
Av. Miramar 71. Open Tues, Wed, Fri, Sat 10am-7pm; Thurs 10am-9.30pm; Sun 10am-2.30pm.

The permanent collection of the Miró Foundation is a gift from Joan Miró to his native Barcelona. During the Franco regime, which Miró strongly opposed, the artist lived in self-imposed exile, first in Paris and then on Majorca. After Franco's death he embarked on a campaign to fill Barcelona with as much of his art as possible. The Functionalist building that houses the collection was designed by Miró's personal friend, the architect and planner Josep Lluís Sert (*see p. 87*). The foundation opened in 1975 - almost but not quite before Franco was in his grave. Miró's unmistakable style, filled with Mediterranean sunshine and shadow, is a perfect counterweight to its surroundings. Miró himself rests in the cemetery on Montjuïc's southern slopes.

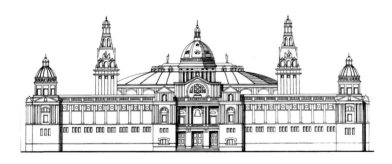

Museu Nacional d'Art de Catalunya
(MNAC; Catalan National Art Gallery)
Mirador del Palau 6. Open Tues-Sat 10am-7pm; Sun 10am-2.30pm.
www.mnac.es

The grandiose Palau Nacional, which houses the museum, was built as the main pavilion for the 1929 International Exhibition. It was renovated in 1995 by Gae Aulenti (architect of the Musée d'Orsay in Paris), and is currently in the process of becoming what its name implies: a repository for all Catalan art, from antiquity

Baldachin from the village of Tost (c.1200).

to the present day. As yet it has three main collections: Romanesque, Gothic, and the Cambó Collection (a diverse anthology, donated by lawyer, politician and financier Francesc Cambó). In the future Renaissance and Baroque art will also be represented, as well as the 19th and 20th-century works due to be relocated from the Ciutadella's Museu d'Art Modern (*see p. 113*). The Romanesque section is possibly the world's finest collection of early ecclesiastical art, most of it moved from chapels in the Pyrenees during the 1920s to preserve it from deterioration and theft. Reproductions of many of the finest friezes have been reproduced and replaced in their original settings. The Gothic collection contains treasures from Catalonia's medieval zenith.

A Major Artist on Display in the MNAC

JAUME HUGUET (c. 1415-1492) - After Bernat Martorell (d. 1452, *see p. 52*), Huguet is the best-known painter of the Catalan school. His work exercised a profound influence on contemporary painting in the Iberian peninsula. Although he was without doubt a medieval, with no knowledge of perspective, he went beyond the primitivism of Martorell to invest his

Detail from Huguet's 'Last Supper' (1470), part of the MNAC collection. Note Mary Magdalene on Christ's left.

PHOTOS: MUSEU NACIONAL D'ART DE CATALUNYA

work with a deep and touching humanity. These are more than just icons: the wealth of detail and everyday observation give his work warmth and intimate appeal, and are largely what contributed to the dubbing of his style as Hispano-Flemish. His best-known surviving work is his altarpiece of the Flagellation (now in the Louvre in Paris). The finest work housed in this museum is his St George altarpiece, and there are several other lesser works as well, notably the *Last Supper* (*pictured opposite*). Often Huguet achieves a 3D effect by the use of embossed metal plates, a technique also seen in his Epiphany altarpiece in the chapel of Santa Àgata in the Palau Reial Major (*see p. 156*).

OTHER SIGHTS ON MONTJUÏC

MUSEU D'ARQUEOLOGIA DE CATALUNYA - The collection includes important finds from the Greek ruins at Empúries on the Costa Brava, as well as artifacts and information about megalithic Spain. *Passeig Santa Madrona 39-41. Open Tues-Sat 9.30am-1pm & 4pm-7pm; Sun 9.30am-1pm.*

POBLE ESPANYOL - An outdoor museum of Spanish vernacular architecture, created as a showpiece for the 1929 International Exhibition; a magic-carpet ride round the country. Poble Espanyol (Spanish Village) takes you from the walled towns of Old Castile to the sherry bodegas of the Costa de la Luz. None

of it is real, but if you want a textbook lesson in Iberian architecture, this is the place to come. And if you think Spain can't be Spain without flamenco, it is worth knowing that a

The gardens of Montjuïc are perfect for a relaxed wander between museums.

ticket to the Tablao del Carmen flamenco club gives you free access to the rest of the complex. *Av. Marquès de Comillas s/n. Open Mon 9am-8pm; Tues-Thurs 9am-2pm; weekends 9am-4pm. www.poble-espanyol.com*

CASTELL DE MONTJUÏC - A fortress built in 1640 during the War of the Reapers (*Guerra dels Segadors*), a rebellion against Felipe IV, the poet-king much portrayed by Velázquez. It wasn't his poetry that was the problem so much as that his reign presided over Spain's decline, as gradually she lost her trading supremacy to England and Holland.

This castle has been repeatedly besieged, most famously in 1705 during the War of the Spanish Succession (*see p. 18*). In 1808, during the Peninsular War, it was seized by the French. During a flare-up of civil unrest in 1842, the city was shelled from its heights by Spanish artillery. The moat is now drained and grassed over, and one side has been turned into an archery range. The castle itself houses Barcelona's military museum. *Ctra. de Montjuïc 66. Open Tues-Sat 10am-2pm & 4pm-7pm; Sun 10am-2pm (Oct-Mar); Tues-Sat 10am-2pm & 4pm-7pm; Sun 10am-8pm (Apr-Sept).*

WHERE TO EAT ON MONTJUÏC

The best places to have lunch are either Poble Espanyol or the Fundació Miró, which has a good restaurant (Tel: 93/329-0768) and self-service cafeteria. Alternatively ride the cable car down to Barceloneta and dine on the Mediterranean shore. A selection of Barceloneta's best restaurants is given on p. 246.

IN AND AROUND PLAÇA ESPANYA

Descend to Plaça Espanya down the wide steps directly outside the main entrance to the MNAC (escalators are also available). The walk takes you down past monumental cascading fountains, past Barcelona's twin trade-fair exhibition pavilions, down to the giant mock-Venetian towers at the beginning of Av. Reina Maria Cristina. The whole of this ensemble was created for the 1929 International Exhibition.

The Mies van der Rohe pavilion: cool calmness and balance after the opulence of MNAC and the hyper-activity of Miró.

THE MIES VAN DER ROHE PAVILION
Av. Marquès de Comillas s/n. Open 10am-8pm every day.

This Minimalist structure was created by Ludwig Mies van der Rohe (1886-1969) as the German pavilion for the International Exhibition of 1929. Though dismantled when the exhibition ended, the building was reassembled between 1983 and 1986, and now stands as a cool and classy exercise in interlocking planes of marble, onyx and glass, a superb architectural template of the Bauhaus School. There is little else like it in Barcelona, a city which has traditionally had difficulty believing that less could ever really be more - witness the hyper-Art Nouveau Palau de la Música and the florescent Gaudí spectaculars. Here serenity rules. The veins in the green onyx panels are carefully matched, and the black carpet inside the pavilion is deliberately made to mirror itself in the dark water of the pool outside. The interior is minimally furnished with the famous Barcelona chair (also designed by Mies van der Rohe), reproductions of which still grace design-conscious interiors all over the world.

The CaixaForum, former factory turned police station turned exhibition space.

THE CAIXAFORUM (CASARAMONA)
Av. Marquès de Comillas 6-8.
Open Tues-Sun 10am-8pm.
Free entry. Tel: 93/476-8600.

This neo-Mudéjar former factory (1911) is the work of Modernist architect Josep Puig i Cadafalch (*see p. 92*). It was reopened in 2002 as a center for exhibitions, concerts and other cultural events. The restoration makes full use of ultra-modern design, while respecting the original industrious ethos of the place. Still buzzing, Casaramona, now CiaxaForum, is a superb arts venue. Check the daily listings to see if there is anything on that catches your eye.

OTHER MAJOR ART GALLERIES

FUNDACIÓ TÀPIES
(Casa Montaner i Simó)
Carrer d'Aragó 255. Open Tues-Sun 10am-8pm.

This former publishing house was built in 1880 by Lluís Domènech i Montaner (*see p. 91*). Made of red brick, it looks like a cross between a Moorish palace and a 19th-century railroad station. It was the city's first building to incorporate iron supports. To reinforce the publishing theme, sculptures of Europe's three greatest men of letters, Shakespeare, Dante and Cervantes, were incorporated in the façade. The interior has been converted to house a permanent collection of works by contemporary Catalan painter and conceptual artist Antoni Tàpies. The building also hosts temporary exhibitions.

ANTONI TÀPIES

Catalonia and Spain's most famous living artist, Abstract Expressionist painter (and sometimes conceptual artist) Antoni Tàpies is known for his use of mixed media (sand, cloth, straw) and *objets trouvés*. His intensified collages demonstrate a passion for materials and a fascination with texture. Oddly, since the Catalan word *tàpies* means 'walls', many of Tàpies's works have an informal, spontaneous, graffiti-like quality, as if in the process of materializing semi-autonomously on some abandoned city wall.

Born in 1923, Tàpies studied law, though a long illness prior to his studies helped him understand that he was not destined to be a lawyer: instead he discovered a passion for drawing and painting. Largely self-taught, Tàpies owes much to Surrealism, particularly in his early works. Max Ernst, Joan Miró, and Paul Klee were important formative influences, along with elements of magic and dreams. Mysterious spaces populated with boxes, and often with blocked doors and windows, appear frequently in a sort of post-Freudian vision.

After 1952 Tàpies veered more towards the abstract, and began to work with sand, marble dust and clay, making graffiti-like incisions in his materials and working on creased or uneven surfaces. His *'pintures matèriques'* (material paintings) are his hallmark: what matters is neither the texture nor the color, but the form the material takes and the semiotic symbols, taking the works beyond the merely pictorial. An example of such a work is his 1959 *Pintura Ocre*, in the MACBA, where the lack of form is expressed through movement and constant change, a portrait of the transitory existence of an object in the process of acquiring or losing form. His most accessible (in the physical sense) work is the billowing tangle of metal entitled *Núvol i cadira* (Cloud and Chair) atop the Fundació Tàpies (*pictured right*).

MUSEU D'ART CONTEMPORANI DE BARCELONA (MACBA)

Plaça dels Àngels s/n. Open Mon & Wed-Fri 11am-7.30pm; Sat 10am-8pm; Sun 10am-3pm. Free guided tours Wed & Sat at 6pm, Sun at noon. Tel: 93/412-0810. www.macba.es

Barcelona's museum of contemporary art, known simply by its acronym MACBA, was designed by American architect Richard Meier in 1992. It is a sudden apparition of shimmering light and space in what was until recently the cramped and noisome Raval. Behind the glass and concrete is a permanent collection of international contemporary art, with temporary shows hosted as well. Meier's exercise in Minimalism did not meet with universal acceptance in Barcelona; in fact it was much debated. One social group has granted it unanimous approval, however: the skateboard surfers. The wide open, traffic-free space that is the museum's forecourt doubles as a perfect rink for perfecting post-contemporary maneuvers. The art collection inside, which includes works by Calder, Rauschenberg, Oteiza, Chillida and Tàpies, is excellent, as is the guided tour, which gives explanations of the philosophical and aesthetic bases of contemporary art.

MAJOR MUSEUMS

CARRER MONTCADA - THE PICASSO MUSEUM & TEXTILE MUSEUM

Carrer Montcada, for centuries Barcelona's most aristocratic street, is also one of its straightest and most historically coherent. After Guillem Ramon de Montcada organized and financed Ramon Berenguer IV's victorious campaign against the Moors in Tortosa in 1148, the sovereign count ceded the land to the Montcada family in gratitude. Along with nine other prosperous Barcelona merchants, Montcada set up an unusually rectilinear trace through what had up to then been known as Vilanova del Mar, translatable as New-Town-on-Sea, one of the earliest neighborhoods to appear outside the Roman walls. Originally waterfront, before landfill and construction pushed the edge of the Mediterranean farther east, the sandy soil permitted an orderly layout of streets unlike the curved and

The narrow thread of Carrer Montcada, filled with former noble palaces, plain on the outside because of the cramped space, but with lovely inner courtyards and stairways. Most now house museums and art galleries.

foreshortened alleys and byways of the Barri Gòtic. Carrer Montcada became an enclave for Barcelona's most honored and wealthy families, and the *cases nobles* these eminent burghers built between the 13th and the 18th centuries are some of the city's finest examples of medieval and Renaissance architecture.

Museu Picasso
Carrer Montcada 15-19. Open Tues-Sat 10am-8pm; Sun 10am-3pm.
Tel: 93/319-6310. Free entry on 1st Sun of the month.
www.museupicasso.bcn.es

The museum occupies three adjoining palaces, the finest being the old Palau Aguilar, with its lovely inner courtyard by the acknowledged master of the Catalan Gothic, Marc Safont (*see p. 80*). The collection of the Picasso Museum, while by no means a monopoly of the artist's best paintings, is nevertheless the world's most comprehensive chronicle of his development and evolution. The exhibit is particularly strong on his early works: the sketches, oils and caricatures from Picasso's childhood years in La Coruña are perhaps the most fascinating part of the museum, showing the artist's early talent for drawing. His *La Primera Comunión* ('First Communion'), painted at the age of 16, gives a clear idea of his youthful mastery of classical painting techniques, as does *Ciencia y Caridad* ('Science and Charity'), where a doctor and a nun hover around the sickbed of a young mother, pondering whether either of their ministrations will be sufficient to stave off the final hour. There are also works from Picasso's blue and rose periods, and the famous 1950s Cubist variations, all 58 of them, on Velázquez's *Las Meninas*, as well as ceramics and engravings.

© HUNGART

'Picasso and Junyer arriving in Paris' (1904), one of a series of early drawings on show in the Picasso Museum. It was in 1904 that Picasso moved to Paris for good, leaving his formative Barcelona years behind him, and embarking on a career that was to make his name.

The drawing *Traginer* ('Carter') demonstrates Picasso's break with the classical tradition, introducing a more Modernist line, and betraying the influence of Isidre Nonell (*see p. 117*).The museum originated in 1962 on the suggestion of Picasso's friend Jaume Sabartés, who donated the first collection of works. Later Picasso himself donated some early works and in 1981 his widow, Jacqueline Roque, added many more. Barcelona friends and art gallery owners were of major importance in convincing the Franco-era mayor, Josep Maria Porcioles, to permit the museum to open at all, as Picasso was openly hostile to the Generalísimo's regime.

PICASSO AND BARCELONA

Pablo Ruiz Picasso (1881-1973) lived in Barcelona between 1895 and 1904. His father was art professor at the academy in La Llotja and the Ruiz family lived nearby. Picasso, a precocious draftsman, began advanced classes in the academy at the age of 15, and at 19 had his first exhibition at Els Quatre Gats (see p. 241). Much intrigued by the life of Barcelona's popular neighborhoods, Picasso's early Cubist work *Les Demoiselles d'Avignon* was inspired not by the demure virgins of the French town but by the ladies of the night on Barcelona's Carrer d'Avinyó, then known for its brothel. In 1904 Picasso moved definitively to Paris, where the artistic soil was more fertile. After his move he returned occasionally to Barcelona until his last visit in the summer of 1934.

Barcelona's claim to Picasso has been contested by Málaga, the painter's birthplace; by Madrid, where *Guernica* graces the Reina Sofia Contemporary Art Center; and by the town of Guernica itself, victim of the 1937 Luftwaffe saturation bombing that inspired the famous canvas. A staunch Franco opponent after the war, Picasso refused to return to Spain. In turn, the Franco regime allowed no Picasso work to go on public display until 1961, when the artist's sardana frieze on the façade of the Barcelona Guild of Architects building (on Plaça Nova) was unveiled. Picasso did not set foot on Spanish soil for the last 39 years of his life, dying two years before Franco himself.

Picasso and Barcelona, in fact, may not seem to have much to do with each other. But the years that span the ages of 14 and 19 are arguably the most dramatic and indelible in the life of a young man, and in Picasso's case, because he was an artist and a passionate young blood (judging from subsequent escapades), and because he was coming to this steamy Mediterranean fleshpot straight from Atlantic Galicia, those years perhaps had more influence than ever. It was in Barcelona that Picasso first saw the work of Isidre Nonell (see p. 117), which was to influence him greatly and help him break with the orthodoxy of his training up to that time. A year later, it was a Ramon Casas (see p. 116) show at the Sala Parés that caught the 18 year-old artist's eye. His series of charcoal drawings in the Casas style show just how much he was influenced by Catalan art of the day. Casas was one of the founders of Els Quatre Gats; Picasso began to exhibit there too, and he continued to experiment with different styles. By the time of his second Quatre Gats show in 1900, he had turned himself into a violent Colorist. The suicide of a close friend after that turned him suddenly in the direction of Primitivism. It has also been suggested that a somber-hued Nonell exhibition of paintings of gypsies propelled him towards the mournful cobalt of his blue period.

1903 and early 1904 were dark times for Picasso in Barcelona. The early euphoria centered around Els Quatre Gats vanished. His *Terrats de Barcelona* ('Rooftops of Barcelona', 1903) portrays a forlorn roofscape of condemned buildings soon to be torn down to push Via Laietana through the Barri de la Ribera. Many of these houses were available to impecunious artists, and he and a number of his artist friends lived and had their studios there. On April 12th, 1904 Picasso returned to Paris, never to live in Barcelona again. His rose period began a new and more optimistic cycle; by 1907, when he came to paint *Les Demoiselles d'Avignon*, his Cubism was fully developed, leaving the artistic styles of old Barcelona, Modernism and Noucentisme, little more than a distant memory.

Museu Tèxtil i de l'Indumentària
(Palau de los Marqueses de Lló)
Carrer Montcada 12-14. Open Tues-Sat 10am-8pm; Sun 10am-3pm.
Free entry 1st Sat of month 3pm-8pm.

The textile museum's collection includes clothing worn from prehistoric times through the late 19th century. It also charts the history of what was to become Barcelona's most important industry: textiles. The medieval guilds of carders, weavers and drapers bred the dyed-in-the-wool manufacturing expertise which was to be the engine of the city's 19th-century boomtime. The textiles industry created a wealthy bourgeoisie that became, in a kingless province, the capital city's answer to an aristocracy. The factories that made the fortunes of these families (many of whom - the Batllós, the Güells and the Calvets - became patrons of the arts) also created an urban underclass. Working conditions were appalling and the workers themselves underfed and badly housed. Eventually social upheaval caused by the misery of the urban poor led to anarchy and terrorism, as in the 1893 bombing of the Liceu Opera House, a direct attack on the

Interior courtyard of the Museu Tèxtil, a popular place for coffee or a light lunch.

Barcelona bourgeoisie and the inequities of the Industrial Revolution. The chaos was exacerbated by the fact that Barcelona mill-owners, though they might have wanted to use force to crush their workers' riots themselves, lacked the political means to do so: those were in the hands of Madrid, whose agenda was often different. Most of Spain in the 19th century was agricultural and pro free trade. Catalonia was industrialized and fiercely protectionist, because of the perceived threat of imports from France and Britain, whose industry was better developed and more competitive. Some textile barons tried to solve the problem by going abroad, as Joan Güell, father of Eusebi Güell, did when the manager of his factory, Vapor Vell, was murdered by rioting workers. Others sought a solution in a return to nature, and to the splendor of the medieval decorative arts. English poet, artist, craftsman, designer and social reformer William Morris (1834-1896), in conjunction with the Arts and Crafts movement and the Pre-Raphaelites, linked aesthetic reform with social and political reform, and saw design and craftsmanship as the salvation of industrialized society. Eusebi Güell met Morris, and was won over to the cause. But handicrafts were never seriously going to solve the problems of the masses, and Barcelona's calico barons were eventually wrecked between the Scylla and Charybdis of opposing social forces in the Spanish Civil War.

The courtyard of El Cafè Tèxtil is an ideal spot for a drink or a snack, as you sit and muse on these matters. In the winter the sun still manages to visit this sequestered space at certain times of day. In summer it casts long shadows that offer welcome shelter from the glare. The museum store has good books and cards, beautiful scarves, and fun, textile-related artifacts.

OTHER MONTCADA LANDMARKS

PALAU NADAL (No. 14) - home to the Barbier-Mueller pre-Columbian art collection. The façade is notable for its 14th-century window and top-floor solar.

CASA DE LA GELOSIA (House of the Latticed Blind, No. 21) - Here an 18th-century *mashrabiya* jalousie designed to allow discreet (often jealousy-inspired) observation from the shadows within, peeks from the middle level of a plain 17th-century Baroque façade. (**Galeria Surrealista**, at No. 19, specializes in Dalí, Miró, and Picasso drawings.)

CASA DE LA TORRE TRIFORADA (House of the Three-Light Tower, No. 23) - One of the best preserved palaces on the street, with a square tower perforated by a triple window and an open loggia overlooking the street.

L'ASIL BRESSOL DEL NEN JESÚS (No. 18) - An early day-care center, now a kindergarten. The 16th-century architecture fuses Gothic and Classical elements with great simplicity.

PALAU DALMASES (No. 20) - The nine gargoyles on the façade, alternating griffins and lions, appear to be identical to those on the Hospital de la Santa Creu over Carrer Hospital in the Raval, no doubt from the same gargoyle artist,

or at least the same molds. Once through the doors (note the knocker up at horseback level) you find yourself in Barcelona's best late Renaissance patio, built in the 17th century during alterations to a 15th-century palace. A carved relief of the Rape of Europa adorns the stairway at the far end. Neptune's chariot, cherubic putti, naiads, dancers, tritons and musicians all bear witness to Europa's abduction by Zeus, who, in the form of a bull, carries her off to Crete where she bears him three sons, one of them Minos, who continues the bull theme with his Minotaur. On either side of the door leading up the stairs, look for the minuscule representations of either putti or maidens covering their nakedness with their arms. These, along with the Gothic chapel and the vaulting in the reception area and in the main salon, are the only remnants of the original 15th-century palace. Now seat of the Òmnium Cultural, a center for the diffusion of Catalan culture, the building hosts lectures, book presentations and other public events. On the ground floor you will find the Espai Barroc, a Baroque-theme café with period furnishing. *Open 9am-2pm & 4.30pm-7pm every day. Café Tues-Sun 7pm-1am.*

Late Renaissance stone stairway in the courtyard of the Palau Dalmases.

CASA CERVELLÓ-GIUDICE (No. 25) - A handsome combination of Catalan Gothic, flamboyant Gothic, and Renaissance. Originally built in the 15th century by the Cervelló family (whose chapel to Santa Maria de Cervelló overlooks Carrer de la Cirera out behind), the house became the property of the Giudice family, merchants from Genoa, in the 18th century. Home of the Galeria Maeght since 1974, this is a restful spot to browse through whatever is on display in the midst of some of Barcelona's finest architecture. Look for the early well to the right under the staircase, the sculpted ornamentation around the windows leading up the stairs, the small flamboyant Gothic window at knee level on the way out, and the empty flamboyant Gothic niche higher up on the right. Next door in what was once the stables of the Cervelló house is the 0.925 designer jewelry store, so-named for the traditional stamp embossed on sterling silver.

EL XAMPANYET (No. 22) - This has been Carrer Montcada's tavern of choice since 1929 (*see p. 235*).

OTHER MUSEUMS

MUSEU D'HISTÒRIA DE CATALUNYA (Catalonia History Museum) - Housed in what used to be a freight depot, this museum traces 3,000 years of Catalan history, from prehistoric times right up to the present day. Captions to the exhibits appear in Catalan, Castilian, and English, and many of the displays are interactive as well. Guided tours are available on Sundays at noon and 1pm. The rooftop cafeteria has excellent views over the sea and the harborfront. *Plaça Pau Vila 1. Open Tues-Sat 10am-7pm; Sun 10am-2.30pm. Tel: 93/225-4700. Free entry 1st Sun of month.*

MUSEU D'HISTÒRIA DE LA CIUTAT (City History Museum) - Situated under and around Plaça del Rei, this museum's display follows the development of Barcelona from the first Iberian settlement to Roman and Visigothic times and beyond. The Roman remains are the most fascinating. The vestiges of an entire civilization lie beneath your feet: mosaic floors, wine cellars, dyers' workshops: you wander above it all on metal and transparent glass walkways. *Carrer del Veguer 2 (corner of Plaça del Rei). Open Tues-Sat 10am-2pm & 4pm-8pm; Sun 10am-3pm. Tel: 93/315-1111.*

MUSEU MARÍTIM (Maritime Museum) - A superb museum housed in the 13th-century Drassanes Reials (Royal Shipyards), on the harborfront at the foot of the Rambla (*see p. 46*). This vast 14th-century complex is the world's largest and best-preserved medieval arsenal, a grand testimonial to Barcelona's former maritime might. King Jaume I conquered Majorca in 1229. His *Consolat de Mar*, drawn up in 1259, was the first code of maritime law in Europe. After Majorca, Jaume and his successors went on to conquer other strategic points in the Mediterranean, giving Catalonia footholds all the way to Athens, and creating a maritime power to be reckoned with - until the 15th century, when Ferdinand and Isabella limited Catalan trade to the Mediterranean, effectively turning Barcelona into a backwater. The museum is filled with vessels, including an excellent collection of models, best of all the life-size reconstruction of the galley of John of Austria, commander of the Spanish fleet at the Battle of Lepanto. There is also a chart that once belonged to Amerigo Vespucci. Figureheads and other nautical trappings make this a wonderful experience for all would-be seadogs. The headphones and

Museu d'Història de Catalunya, situated beside the marina and old port.

infrared pointers make navigation easy. The cafeteria is strong on medieval atmosphere. *Plaça Portal de la Pau 1. Open 10am-7pm every day. Tel: 93/342-9920. Free entry on 1st Sat of month after 3pm.*

MUSEU DE L'ACADÈMIA DE BELLES ARTS DE SANT JORDI (Museum of the St George Academy of Fine Art) - The Escola de Belles Arts (Fine Arts School) occupied the south-western corner of the Llotja from 1849 until 1960. Its alumni include many famous Barcelona artists, including Gaudí, Miró and Picasso, whose father was a professor there. The Reial Acadèmia de Belles Arts de Sant Jordi still has its seat here, and its museum is one of Barcelona's secret sites. 19th-century sculptor Damià Campeny's Neoclassical sculpture of Lucretia, swooning from her self-inflicted stabwound, is on the main floor upstairs to the right, and is one of the building's prized possessions, as are the Marià Fortuny (*see p. 114*) drawings from his student days in Rome. *Passeig d'Isabel II 7. Open Mon-Fri 10am-2pm. Admission free. Tel: 93/319-2432.*

MUSEU FREDERIC MARÈS - The theme here is early 20th-century sculptor-collector Frederic Marès himself and the delightful jumble of art and curios he collected throughout his life. The 1537 polychrome wood Pietà, by Juan de Juní, is the star attraction. The courtyard café is a cozy and quiet place for a break. Public sculpture by Marès is scattered across Barcelona, from the 1940 Ciutadella Park statue of General Prim, the Catalan soldier who helped topple the Bourbon monarchy in 1868, to the 1952 Santa Eulàlia at Plaça del Pedró in the Raval. The 1982 reclining bronze *L'esperit del Mediterrani* at the bottom of the left-hand stairway descending from the Saló de Cent in the Casa de la Ciutat is one of Barcelona's most erotic sculptures. *Plaça Sant Iu 5. Open Tues-Wed & Fri-Sat 10am-7pm; Thurs 10am-5pm; Sun 10am-3pm. www.museumares.bcn.es*

ARTICKET BCN

A combined ticket giving entry to seven major galleries and museums: MNAC, Fundació Miró, MACBA, CCCB, Fundació Tàpies, Museu d'Art Modern and the Espai Gaudí in La Pedrera. Tickets are sold at all these venues.

CASTELLERS

As if Barcelona's vast architectural patrimony weren't enough, Catalonia also builds castles - *castells* - out of human beings. Different squads or clubs, known as *colles*, practice and compete to establish records and build ever higher and more complex structures. The custom reportedly originated as a siege tactic for elevating sappers over ramparts: another tradition asserts that *castells* developed peacefully in south-western Catalonia, in imitation of a dance from neighboring Valencia with a human tower in its choreography. Popular in the 1880s as part of the 19th-century resurgence of Catalan nationalism, *castellers* are now back in force, with nearly 100 *colles* currently active.

A typical Monday morning newspaper *casteller* review might bear the headline '*Els Xiquets de Valls cargan un quatre de nou amb folre*' (The Valls Boys load a nine-story tower of four with lining), which means that the historic team from Valls built a nine-story human tower with four people at each level and a 'lining', or supporting layer, atop the *pinya* (literally 'pineapple'), the mob at the bottom, who press together in a scrum to create a foundation for this human skyscraper.

Castells are studiously planned feats of engineering using building blocks of both sexes and of all ages. At the bottom level are the barrel-chested forty and fifty year-old men, wrapped in weight-lifters' sashes to support backs and bellies. The next level is composed of lighter, more athletic - but still powerful - twenty year-olds, while the succeeding levels are built of descending ages and weights, all the way up to the very top element, the *enxaneta*, a tiny but intrepid eight-to-ten year old boy or girl who, using carefully practiced toe holds in tightly wound sashes, scrambles up the outside of the *castell* and, when he or she reaches the top, raises a hand in a hurried wave of triumph before quickly slithering down.

When a *castell* crumbles apart before completion, which they do with some regularity, the smallest children from the uppermost levels, trained to relax in the air, seem to float leaf-like down onto the older generations below. It is a frightening moment: mothers rush in to comfort sobbing *enxanetes*, and sometimes there are injuries. Even when *castells* are successful, tears are common. The level of excitement created is highly charged, and the *enxaneta*'s tense little wave always unleashes a surprising emotional catharsis. This is a multi-generational event, with fathers and even grandfathers in the tightly-packed base, building through sons and daughters to the youngest and most exposed top story, the youngest generation. There is a beauty, watching this family raising its child; a sense of genetic memory in action; of a culture doing, for no good reason, what it has always done.

MUSIC

MUSIC VENUES

GRAN TEATRE DEL LICEU
La Rambla 51-59. Tel: 93/485-9900.
Guided tours daily at 10am. www.liceubarcelona.com

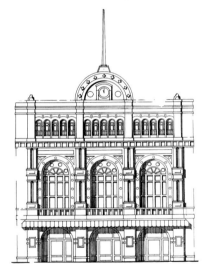

Barcelona's opera house, the Liceu, looks somewhat plain from the outside. The glittering salons within have established its reputation as one of the most beautiful opera venues in the world. Its auditorium has a seating capacity second only to Milan's La Scala, and the acoustics are superb. As well as being Barcelona's most cherished cultural institution, it was also, in the 19th century, the city's prime social playroom.

The site on which it stands was once occupied by a monastery of Discalced Trinitarians. This was demolished in 1844, and construction work on the opera house began. But the history of the Liceu has been one long saga of natural and unnatural disasters. The first building was badly damaged by fire, so much so that it had to be completely rebuilt. The man entrusted with the task was Josep Oriol Mestres, who created the neo-Gothic façade of the cathedral (*see p. 49*). The new Liceu promised to be a runaway success. Season tickets to all the boxes were sold out well before the building was completed - and then disaster struck again. It was gutted in a blaze in 1861. Pious members of Barcelona society said that this was surely divine retribution, for pulling down a house of God and building a pleasure dome in its stead.

When the Liceu was finally completed, it quickly became the focal point of social contact for Barcelona's elite. Bourgeois Barcelona lacked a royal court. There were no king's levées for ambitious young men to attend, no palace balls for debutantes to make their society entrances. Instead they came to the Liceu: to see and be seen, to further their careers, to flirt and find husbands, to hatch plots and intrigues. It was here that Isabel López met her future husband Eusebi Güell, patron of Gaudí. Gaudí built the couple a town residence just around the corner (*see pp. 103-7*). The Liceu was sumptuous and grand, and much as everyone loved it, they loved to complain about it too. The candles in the chandeliers dropped wax onto the taffeta ballgowns. When electric lighting was installed that was no good either: it was so garish that it made the women ghoulish to look at, and took the luster out of their complexions.

In 1893 the building was bombed by anarchists, in one of the rumblings of civil unrest that were part of Barcelona life until after the Civil War. Call it the curse of the barefoot friars if you will, but even today the jinx has not been completely exorcised. In 1994 the Liceu was once again gutted by a blaze of mysterious origins. Five years later, restored as far as possible to its former glory, supremely equipped for modern productions, the Liceu opened anew. Even if you don't see an opera, don't miss a tour of the building; some of the Liceu's most spectacular rooms (including the glittering foyer known as the Saló dels Miralls, or Hall of Mirrors) were untouched by the 1994 fire, as were those of Spain's oldest social club, El Cercle del Liceu. If they admit you at all, remember that a necktie is *de rigueur*. The Cercle's dozen Ramon Casas (*see p. 116*) paintings, all brilliantly illuminated in the club's penumbral smoking room, comprise Barcelona's best Casas stash. The Espai Liceu downstairs, with entrances on both Carrer Sant Pau and the Rambla, puts the city and the opera house in cultural and commercial contact. If you love opera, this is the place to be. Alongside the inevitable café and shop, there is also a small, 50-seat concert hall, and a mediatheque featuring recordings and filmings of past productions.

PALAU DE LA MÚSICA CATALANA
Sant Francesc de Paula 2. Tel: 93/295-7200.
Tours daily 10am-3.30pm, except when
there is a concert or event in the hall.
www.palaumusica.org

This is very possibly the most unconventional auditorium in the world. Most music halls cater first and foremost to the ear. The Palau de la Música won't set your eyes free either. The polychrome ceramic ticket windows on the Carrer de Sant Pere Més Alt give only the merest hint of what is to come inside. This Modernist tour de force was designed by Lluís Domènech i Montaner (*see p. 91*) in 1908. Today it is considered the *ne plus ultra* of Barcelona's Modernist movement, an anthology of the Arts and Crafts-inspired, comprehensive deployment of the best decorative artists and artisans of the day. Modernist sculptors Eusebi Arnau, Miquel Blay and Pau Gargallo all worked with Domènech i Montaner here, as did stained glass worker Antoni Rigalt i Blanch and ceramicist Lluís Bru. The venue was originally conceived by the Orfeó Català,

an avowedly Catalanist musical society that wanted a forum to propagate their theories about the importance of music at a popular level. This was in direct opposition to the Liceu opera house, where music was rarefied, and which was frequented by an haute bourgeoisie who, in defense of their own position and interests, were often Castilian-speaking and monarchist in their political allegiances. The Palau and the Liceu were for many decades opposing forces in Barcelona's musical, social, political and ideological debate.

Palau de la Música ticket office. Note the inscription: Orfeó Català.

THE EXTERIOR

Over the corner of Carrers Amadeu Vives and Sant Pere Més Alt is a sculptural group by Miquel Blay: an allegory of Catalonia's popular music. National patron St George the dragon-slayer heads the procession; after him come the people, from every walk of popular life; women, children, fishermen; all swelling the chorus. Not all of it is totemized, though. For a lifelike detail, look for the little boy peeking fearfully over the balcony rail, or the rolled up *barretina*, the traditional Catalan peasant cap, to the right of the flowing maiden. At the top of the main façade is a ceramic mosaic portrayal of a choral scene, the Orfeó Català in full concert. Over and above everything, barely visible, is a ceramic egg, a symbol of fertility and rebirth much used by the Modernists, adorned with floral motifs, the Catalan colors, and the red and white cross of St George.

THE INTERIOR

The Palau's auditorium is all clamor and commotion before the first note of music is even struck. In a tribute to European classical music, Wagnerian cavalry leads the charge from the right side of the stage over a bust of Beethoven framed by classical columns. On the left is Catalonia's own music, represented by Josep Anselm Clavé, whose workers' choruses connected classical music and the proletariat; and by the supple maidens of the song *Flors de Maig* ('May Flowers'). In the center of the ceiling a stained-glass cupola-chandelier seems to drop the divine gift of music onto the audience below. The hallowed theme continues on stage, which is shaped like an apse, turning the Palau into an Orphean temple. Daylight concerts are particularly spectacular as both the north and south façades are nearly all glass, with brightly colored garlands and crosses of St George alternating with the yellow and red Catalan colors. In the upper reaches of the hall, winged Pegasus-like horses, sculpted by Eusebi Arnau's disciple Pau Gargallo, and fitted with real leather reins, sail out of the wall.

   As the clubhouse of the Catalan nationalist Orfeó Català and epicenter of Catalan Modernism, the Palau was bound to run into trouble with Franco's centralizers. The truth is that it barely escaped the regime intact. It was even

Even if your ears don't like the music, your eyes will certainly never be bored.

rumored, when a church was erected over the Palau's south façade, that this was a Potemkin village-like effort to ensure that the Generalísimo would never have to contemplate the lurid fact of its existence during motorcades up Via Laietana. In 1960 the Orfeó Català at last obtained permission from the censors to sing their traditional song, *El Cant de la Senyera* ('Song of the Flag'), at a memorial tribute to the *Renaixença* poet Joan Maragall. When, at the last minute, permission was withdrawn, Catalan nationalists, rallied by a physician named Jordi Pujol, leapt to their feet to sing the forbidden verses, and all hell broke loose. Dozens of secret agents, strategically placed among the audience, drew pistols; the riot police charged in; skulls were cracked; arrests were made; 25 young nationalists were dragged off to prison. One of them, Dr Pujol, court-martialed and sentenced to seven years in jail, was elected President of the Generalitat de Catalunya in 1980. Today when the Coral Sant Jordi, Catalonia's national chorus, sings *El Cant de la Senyera* here, the entire audience rises to join them, and dry eyes are few and far between.

L'AUDITORI DE BARCELONA
Carrer Lepant 150. Tel: 93/247-9300.

Near Plaça de les Glòries, the Rafael Moneo-designed Auditori opened in 1999, and is the perfect counterpoint to the Palau de la Música. The classical and minimalist interior, often compared to the inside of a guitar, is an immense (42,000 sq.m) and resonant maple-paneled sound chamber, soothing to the eye and spirit. Even the poet and playwright Ramón de la Valle Inclán, supreme exponent of the School of the Grotesque, found that the Palau de la Música's 'mixture of brick, ceramics, glass, stone and steel do not help me in the least to relax and listen to concerts': he would have loved L'Auditori. With a capacity for 2,340 spectators, complete visibility from every seat in the house, and universally praised acoustic excellence, the Auditori, with its Music School, Music Museum, 700-capacity chamber music hall, and polyvalent hall with a capacity of 500, is a virtual musical city. The austerity of its exterior belies the harmonious interior, beginning with the cubic glass atrium modeled after the Roman impluvium or water cistern in an interior patio. Painter Pablo de Palazuelo's blue stripes are the sole decorative element in the linterna or skylight. For all its relaxing lines and tones, the Auditori seems chilly compared to other Barcelona music venues, which are either intimate and warm or, in the case of the Palau de la Música, ablaze with color and ornamentation. Perhaps this is a result of its sheer size, or perhaps it is the price one pays for perfect visibility and acoustics. The Auditori schedules a full program of classical music with occasional jazz or pop concerts, and is home to the Orquestra Simfònica de Barcelona i Nacional de Catalunya.

CONCERT INFORMATION

For details on concerts throughout the year, check the agenda page in either *La Vanguardia* or *El País*, or ask at the tourist offices listed on p. 269. The weekly entertainment bulletin, *La Guía del Ocio*, is sold at all newsstands. The easiest place to buy tickets is from the box offices at the venues themselves. To get good seats at the Liceu you need to book well in advance.

MUSIC FESTIVALS

El Grec: Held annually from late June until the end of July. A series of concerts, theater and dance performances are on offer, many of them outdoors in venues such as Plaça del Rei in the Barri Gòtic, the Teatre Grec on Montjuïc, and the Mercat de les Flors (Carrer de Lleida 59).

Festival de Música Antiga (Early Music Festival): Some of the best early music groups from all over Europe congregate in Barcelona from late April to mid-May. Concerts are held at venues all over town, though

Street musicians provide impromptu entertainment.

most are at the CaixaForum, a converted 19th-century factory building (Av. Marquès de Comillas 6-8. *See p. 128*).

International Music Festival: Held in late September, this festival forms part of the feast of Nostra Senyora de la Mercè (Our Lady of Mercy), Barcelona's *Festa Major* (*see p. 252*). The main venues are Palau de la Música (*see p. 143*), Mercat de les Flors in Carrer de Lleida, and Plaça del Rei in the Barri Gòtic.

MUSICAL CATALANS

ANTONI SOLER (1729-1783) - Priest and monk, born in the province of Girona. Soler began his career as a choirboy at the monastery of Monsterrat. After his ordination, he accepted a post as organist at the Escorial, where he later became a monk. He was raised to the post of Maestro de Capilla, and was tutor to the musically gifted Infante Don Gabriél de Borbón, son of King Carlos III. Soler went on to become the greatest composer of the Spanish Enlightenment, the age of transition from the Baroque to the Classical. He is best known today for his harpsichord sonatas, beautifully crafted pieces which mingle a serene monastic chastity with twinges of adventurous mischief. They are full of a playfulness and joy that almost seems to foreshadow Mozart.

Old poster advertising the Ballets Russes at the Gran Teatre del Liceu.

PAU CASALS (1876-1973) - Pau (Pablo in Castilian) Casals was one of the finest cellists of the 20th century. He was born in El Vendrell, 75 kilometers south of Barcelona, as the son of an organist. Casals showed great talent as a young boy. When the composer Isaac Albéniz heard him

play in a café in Barcelona's Gràcia, he recommended him to Queen María Cristina, under whose patronage he went to study in Barcelona, Madrid, Brussels and Paris. When the Civil War ended in 1939 Casals went into voluntary exile in Prades, in the Pyrenees just north of the Spanish border, where he helped Spanish refugees in concentration camps and silenced his cello in protest against war and against the Franco regime. This silence was only broken with the summer music festivals of Prades, founded to commemorate the bicentennial of the death of J. S. Bach. Casals had first discovered Bach's Cello Suites in a pile of old sheet music in a shop on Barcelona's Carrer Ample. His recordings of them remain unmatched.

ENRIC GRANADOS (1867-1916) - Composer and pianist known principally for his Andalusian themes. Granados was born in Lleida (Lérida), and came to Barcelona as a child. Together with Albéniz, he was the creator of the modern Catalan school of piano, producing romantic harmonies that betray the influence of Schumann and Liszt. In 1901 he founded the Granados Academy, where he taught piano technique. His masterpiece, *Goyescas*, was first performed in Barcelona in 1911. He died returning from a trip to New York, where he had gone with his wife to the opening of the stage version at the Metropolitan Opera. The ship in which he was traveling was torpedoed by a German submarine in the English Channel. Though unable to swim, Granados panicked and leapt into the sea. His wife dived in to save him, and both drowned. The ship made it safely to port: Enric Granados and his wife were the only casualties.

ISAAC ALBÉNIZ (1860-1909) - Pianist and composer. Born in northern Catalonia, Albéniz came to Barcelona as a baby. A child prodigy, he was giving concerts by the age of eight. In 1869, the Albéniz family moved to Madrid, where Isaac studied at the Conservatorio. He traveled to various Spanish cities, and soon began a nomadic musical life that took him through Europe and America. On returning to Catalonia in 1883, Albéniz established himself in the village of Tiana, just outside of Barcelona. He gave a series of concerts at the Barcelona World Exhibition in 1888. In 1893 he settled in Paris, where he became the friend of Fauré and Debussy. Albéniz's best-known compositions are those that were inspired by the Iberian Peninsula and its landscapes. The most famous of all are *Sevilla* and *Granada*.

MONTSERRAT CABALLÉ (1933 -) - One of the greatest operatic sopranos of this century. She shot to fame in 1965, when she replaced Marilyn Horne at short notice at the New York opera, in a performance of Donizetti's *Lucrezia Borgia*. After that Donizetti became her specialty - and her 1977 La Scala performance of Bellini's *Norma* was so breathtakingly brilliant that Milan has never staged a Bellini opera since. Her recording of *Barcelona*, with Freddie Mercury, in 1992 propelled her into the pop charts.

JOSEP CARRERAS (1946 -) - One of the world's greatest living tenors. Carreras's teacher father found his career ruined because he had fought on the Republican side during the Civil War. He eventually found work as a traffic policeman, while his mother opened a small hair-dressing shop, where the young Josep would sing to customers. One of his great formative experiences was seeing Mario Lanza in *The Great Caruso*: *La Donna è Mobile* became his favorite aria. He sang it so relentlessly that eventually his mother arranged for him to take singing lessons. It was Montserrat Caballé who first noticed

Carreras's talent, and asked him to sing alongside her in *Lucrezia Borgia*. It was the role that launched his career. In 1987, at the height of his success, he was diagnosed with leukemia. He recovered, and set up the José Carreras International Leukemia Foundation. The Three Tenors concerts, which he organised with Plácido Domingo and Luciano Pavarotti, were aimed at raising money for the foundation.

JORDI SAVALL (1941 -) - Viola da gamba master Jordi Savall was born in a small industrial town west of Barcelona. After studying at the Barcelona Conservatory, his interest in early music took to Belgium, where he studied under Wieland Kuijken, and to Basel, where he succeeded August Wenzinger as director of the Schola Cantorum Basiliensis in 1974. That same year he founded the group Hespèrion XX, especially dedicated to the study and performance of early Hispanic pieces. In 1987 he formed the Capella Reial de Catalunya, an instrumental and vocal group specializing in church music. Acknowledged as one of the world's finest early musicians, Savall is often accompanied by his wife (soprano Montserrat Figueras), his daughter Arianna (medieval harpist and vocalist) and son Ferran (guitarist and vocalist).

THE SARDANA

It is said that Catalans are so penny-wise they count even while they dance. Maybe so, but the real reason for the counting is the numerical intricacy of a dance that comes in four sets of nineteen steps, each of which needs to be accounted for. Dainty, subdued and mathematical, the sardana is everything the athletic Aragonese jota is not. An allegorical reference to the passing of time, a metaphor for the revolutions of the moon and stars, the sardana is a circular dance chronicled by Greek historian Strabo (63 BC-AD 21), who recorded Iberian peoples of northern Spain paying homage to the full moon with dances in the round. The

Llibre Vermell, Catalonia's medieval songbook, records 14th-century pilgrims performing 'the round dance' on the way to Montserrat. Popularized by the oboe master and composer Pep Ventura after his debut in 1837, the sardana is danced in small or large circles of dancers young and old. The *cobla* (band) is composed of five wind instruments, five brass, and a director, who, with one hand, plays a three-holed flute (*flabiol*) and, with the other, taps on a small drum (*tabal*).

Whether in local fiestas, village squares, or in Barcelona in front of the cathedral Sunday midday or in Plaça Sant Jaume Sunday evenings, the sardana is always moving for spectators, the dancers rapt in concentration and counting, deep in two thousand years of culture and ritual.

PART III

WALKS & NEIGHBORHOODS

Each of the four city-center walks is designed to take about an hour.
Tours of farther-flung neighborhoods can occupy a whole morning or
afternoon.

GUIDED WALKS

NEIGHBORHOOD TOURS

Narrow street in the Barri Gòtic, beside the cathedral.

WALK ONE

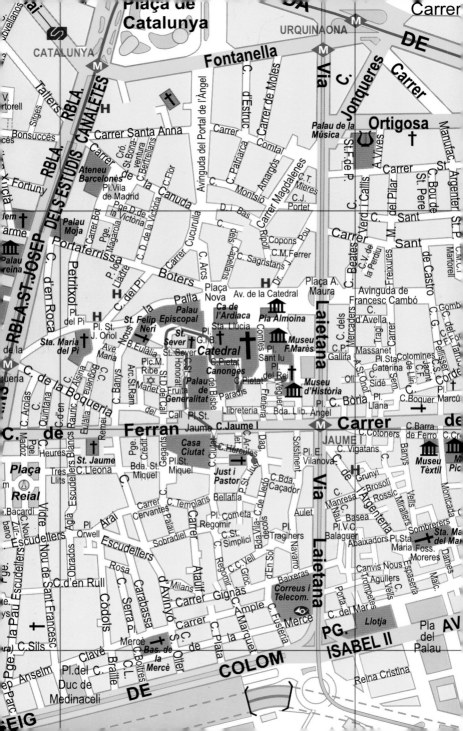

THE BARRI GÒTIC: AROUND THE CATHEDRAL

The Gothic Quarter is a warren of medieval streets clustered around the cathedral. This is the oldest part of Barcelona, with half-hidden vestiges of the ancient Roman colony, and proud reminders of medieval prosperity. But it is more than just a monument to the past. In these reverberating spaces, life still goes on.

This walk begins in **Plaça del Rei**, a purely medieval square once thought to have been the scene of Columbus's return from his voyage to the New World. Ferdinand and Isabella have been portrayed receiving 'the Discoverer' and his entourage on the circular steps at the top of the square. Later evidence has indicated that the Catholic monarchs were in fact at a summer residence near Badalona: but the **Palau Reial Major** (royal palace) in Plaça del Rei was the official royal residence in Barcelona at

The flags of Spain and Catalonia flying from the Palau de la Generalitat on Plaça Sant Jaume.

Entrance to the Palau Reial Major, where
Ferdinand and Isabella once resided.

the time. The entrance to the palace is up the circular stairway. On your left as you enter is the old ceremonial chamber, the **Saló del Tinell**, a magnificently barrel-vaulted banquet hall built in 1362 and nicknamed for the *tinells* (vats) containing the royal grain supply. The windows that originally gave out onto the square are walled up now, lending the hall an even more tenebrous, medieval atmosphere. To the right of the main entrance is the 14th-century **Capella Reial de Santa Àgata** (Royal Chapel of St Agatha), a typically slender-naved Catalan Gothic chapel with a handsome, coffered ceiling. Its altarpiece, almost 3D in the effect of its gilding, is an Adoration of the

Magi, painted by medieval master Jaume Huguet (*see p. 124*) in 1465, and is the chapel's main treasure. To the left, don't miss the portrait of Santa Àgata, with the attributes of her martyrdom (her severed breasts) on a plate in her right hand.

Coming back out into the square again you have, on your right, the 16th-century **Palau del Lloctinent** (Governor's Palace, 1557). The window hoods are decorated with dozens of tiny sculptures, testimony to late Barcelona's early Renaissance creative and ornamental energy. This palace was inhabited by the governor-general of Catalonia during the 16th and 17th centuries, after the houses of Aragon and Castile joined, and royal power had been transferred to Madrid. Above it looms the dark 15th-century Torre Mirador del Rei Martí (King Martin's Watchtower). At the bottom of the square, on the left, is the **Palau Clariana Padellàs**, moved to this spot stone by stone from Carrer Mercaders in the early 20th century and now the Museu d'Història de la Ciutat (*see p. 137*). The hulking bronze sculpture *Topo* ('space' in Greek), by Basque sculptor Eduardo Chillida (1924-2002) stands outside it, while a tiny **shrine to La**

Mercè, Our Lady of Mercy, Barcelona's protector, is embedded in the wall to the left.

Leave Plaça del Rei by turning right up the short Baixada de Santa Clara. Overhead on the corner as you leave, and at the next corner as well, look for the teams of angels bearing coats of arms emblazoned with the Cross of St George, patron saint of Catalonia. Note the overhanging gargoyles too, in particular the enormous locust. The apse of the cathedral abuts the intersection of Carrer dels Comtes and Carrer de la Freneria. Look up to see its protruding gargoyles portraying an assortment of fauna - a dog, a cow, a ram, a pig, a unicorn - while along the lower sections of the wall inscriptions marking the tombs of members of medieval artisans' guilds can just be made out. At this corner are two very disparate dining establishments: Buenas Migas, a good place for a coffee and a focaccia, and La Cuineta, a gorgeous location over the cathedral apse filled with priceless furniture, heirloom tapestries - and undistinguished cuisine.

Leaving the apse on your right, go up Carrer de la Pietat now. The first turning on your left, Carrer Paradís, leads up to a corner where a millstone is embedded in the pavement. This is old Barcino's highest point at 16.9 meters. Inside you will find the hiking club Centre Excursionista de Catalunya (CEC). Turn into the courtyard (*open Mon-Sat 10am-2pm & 5pm-8pm; Sun 11am-2pm*) and then right at the rear of the patio, where you will see four tall pillars bathed in a sort of green light. These are the 2,000 year-old columns of one corner of the Roman **Temple of Augustus**: massive, fluted pillars with Corinthian capitals. They remain here only because Barcelona's early Christians elected, atypically, not to build their cathedral over the site of the previous temple. Dedicated to the Roman emperor Caesar Augustus, the temple

Rear entrance to the cathedral cloister.

occupied the northwest corner of the Roman forum, which coincided approximately with today's Plaça Sant Jaume (*see below*). Carrer Paradís, in fact, is named for the Roman garden or 'paradise', once part of the temple, which overlooked the forum.

Backtrack now, back into Carrer de la Pietat, and turn left. On your left you will pass the 14th-century **Cases de les Canonges** (Canonries), somewhat over-restored in 1929, but reasonably representative of the medieval structures that originally stood there. The entrance to the **cathedral cloister** (*see p. 52*) is straight ahead. If it's open, it is a tempting shortcut, cool and leafy, through to Plaça de Garriga i Bachs. If

not, continue down Carrer de la Pietat into Carrer del Bisbe. Looking to your left you will see the much-mocked '**Bridge of Sighs**', built in neo-Gothic style by the Modernist architect Joan Rubió y Bellver in 1928. It was built to link two buildings used by the Generalitat, the regional government of Catalonia. Beyond the bridge on the right is the original Gothic façade of the main **Generalitat building**, with its Sant Jordi medallion in bold relief, six gargoyles, and two dozen smaller sculpted heads. Turn right up Carrer del Bisbe and into Plaça de Garriga i Bachs. On your right is another entrance to the cloister, with Santa Eulàlia (*see p. 50*) carved on the tympanum, complete with her X-shaped cross and palm of martyrdom. On your left is a **bronze statue by Josep Llimona**, foremost sculptor of his day, depicting handcuffed captives, whose story is also told in the sepia-and-white ceramic plaques that decorate the benches: the men in question were heroes of the Catalan resistance to the invasion of Napoleonic troops in 1809. The first three scenes (moving from left to right) show the five resistance leaders

Cathedral cloister with its famous geese, said to be descended from those that guarded the Capitoline Hill in Rome.

Statue of handcuffed Catalan resistance heroes in Plaça Garriga i Bachs.

for early music concerts; Jordi Savall's (*see p. 150*) viola da gamba is very haunting here. His daughter Arianna's medieval harp is even better. The Museu del Calçat, the tiny Shoe Museum on the left, includes a pair of clown's shoes and a pair worn by Pablo Casals (*see p. 148*). The building that houses the museum is, appropriately, the old shoemakers' guildhall, moved from its original location during urban redevelopment in the 1940s, and rebuilt here, stone by stone. Note the shoe motifs all over the façade, and even around the door handle (*Plaça Sant Felip Neri. Open Tues-Sun 11am-2pm*). The main building on the square is the **church of Sant Felip Neri**, dedicated to the Florentine priest and founder of the Oratorians, Filippo Neri (1515-1595). It is appropriate that this square should be such a popular music venue: the Oratorians were great lovers of music. The oratorio is named after them, and they used music frequently in their services. In his latter years Antoni Gaudí would walk to this church every afternoon, to relieve his rheumatism. It was on his way here that he was run over by a trolley car in 1926. The large pock marks on the walls of the church were

waiting their turns to be garroted or hanged (the *garrote vil*, or vile garotte, was reserved for the clergymen, as hanging was considered a meaner form of execution). The fourth scene depicts the surrender of three agitators who attempted to rally a general Barcelona uprising by ringing the cathedral bells. Though promised amnesty by the French, all three were subsequently executed.

The narrow alley to the right of the tiles as you face them leads into the intimate **Plaça de Sant Felip Neri**, once a cemetery for Barcelona's executed felons. In the centre of the square stands a small fountain, whose solitary trickling fills the space with soothing sound. This is a favorite spot

caused by shelling during the Spanish Civil War. In 1938 the bombardment of Barcelona by the Italian air force killed over a thousand civilians, some of them schoolchildren, in this tiny square.

With the church behind you, leave Plaça Sant Felip Neri and go into Carrer Sant Sever. Go left past the handsome new designer-medieval Hotel Neri and up to the tiny **Sant Sever church**, a diminutive structure built in 1705, and one of Barcelona's best Baroque secrets. It is only open on Thursdays from 5pm to 7.30pm, but its Churrigueresque (named for the exuberant Baroque style of José Churriguera, 1650-1725) altar is a rarely-seen treasure. Backtrack now

and go left down Carrer de Sant Honorat, which brings you out onto **Plaça Sant Jaume**.

As you emerge into this great open space, try to imagine the Roman Forum, three times the size of the present square, that stood here a mere two millennia ago. The square is still a city hub, housing both of Barcelona's government buildings, the **Palau de la Generalitat** to your left, and the **Casa de la Ciutat** or Ajuntament de Barcelona (Town Hall) opposite. A quick glance around the square already tells much. The flags atop the town hall are three, the Catalan *senyera* with its four horizontal red stripes on a gold field, the Spanish *bandera* with the same colors arranged in blocks, and the city flag, Catalan colors around the red on white cross of St George. The Generalitat flies just two flags, the Catalan and the Spanish. The Generalitat building is mainly 15th-century. Look through the front windows and you will see the ornate ceiling of the grand Saló de Sant Jordi (Hall of St George). The Generalitat is closed to the public except on certain holidays, notably St George's Day (April 23rd) and the Festa de la

Mercè (begins 24th September). There are sometimes concerts here on Sundays at noon.

The Casa de la Ciutat's mid-18th-century Neoclassical façade stares coolly across at the Generalitat. Barcelona's administration is reasonably open to things Spanish; the Catalan regional government is militantly Catalan nationalist. On the façade of the Casa de la Ciutat are two large statues: on the left is Jaume el Conqueridor, the Catalan sovereign count who conquered the Balearic Islands from the Moors and wrested much of the Mediterranean from pirates, thus launching Catalonia's 15th-century commercial empire (*see p. 15*). On the right is Joan Fivaller, *conseller* or chief representative in the city parliament known as the Consell de Cent (Council of 100, *see p. 15-16*), founded by King Jaume in 1265. Fivaller (sometimes spelled Fiveller) was five times head councillor between 1406 and 1427, and was a relentless champion of municipal liberties over royal prerogative. He is most famous for his 1416 protest to King Ferdinand I over the payment of a tax on meat purchased in Barcelona. The king died that same year: people said that Fivaller's constant harassment had given him an apoplexy, and Fivaller became a hero overnight.

From Plaça Sant Jaume walk into Carrer de la Ciutat to the left of the Town Hall. You will find a surprise in store: the original early 15th-century flamboyant Gothic façade lost part of an arch when the Neoclassical frontage was added. Instead of removing it entirely, the masons stuck it back on, at right angles, providing a strange, *trompe l'oeil* effect. Inside is the Gothic **Saló de Cent** (Hall of the 100, *see p. 80*, open Sundays 10am-2pm), from which the Council of 100 ruled Barcelona from 1373 (though the Council was founded in 1265) until 1714, when central authority was transferred once and for all to Madrid.

Go left down Carrer d'en Hércules, named for the mythical founder of Barcelona. At the corner, stop in for a lungful of the fragrant Anormis herb and medicinal plant shop before continuing down to **Plaça Sant Just**. The Església de Sants Just i Pastor is one of the oldest churches in Barcelona, dating from the 4th century, and dedicated to the boy martyrs Justus and Pastor. The church is also one of the few in Spain in which, even now, legally binding verbal wills can be sworn and witnessed in front of the Capella de Sant Feliu (Chapel of Saint Felix) near the apse on the left. Largely a Baroque jumble inside, the best work of art is the altarpiece in this same chapel painted by the Flemish master John of Brussels.

The **Gothic fountain** across from the church was Barcelona's first. The spring that feeds it was discovered by Jaume Fivaller, older brother of Joan the famous agitator, while he was out hunting in the Collserola Hills above the city. He subsequently had the water piped into this square. The fountain bears an image of Sant Just and the Barcelona coat of arms. The Cafè de l'Acadèmia, which puts tables and parasols out by the fountain in summer, is a good choice for light Mediterranean cuisine (NB: reservations advised). If you don't feel like a full meal, the following detour might be of interest: leave Plaça Sant Just by Carrer de la Dagueria, named for the medieval knife-makers who once worked here. Across from the feminist bookstore Pròleg is Scotswoman Katherine McLaughlin's artisanal cheese shop, La Seu, a

Preparing for Festa Major in Plaça Sant Just.

brilliant little spot with ingenious painter's palette-like cheese and wine-tasting plates available with samplings of sheep, goat and cow's cheese. The ancient butter churn in the back room is a unique treasure.

St Dominic stands guard over the street that bears his name, site of a former Dominican monastery.

Plaça de Catalunya

URQUINAONA

CATALUNYA

Fontanella

M

Via

Jonqueres

Carrer

Ortigos

Palau de la Música

DE

C. Jovellanos

C. Ranelleres

Tallers

RBLA.

H

Pl. V. Martorell

Sitges

còrdia

Bonsuccés

Pl. B.Succés

C. Bertrellans

Cró. St. Bona-ventura

C. de la C.

Carrer Santa Anna

Avinguda del Portal de l'Àngel

Carrer d'Estruc

Carrer de Moles

Comtal

C. Patriarca

Amargós

St.F.de P.

A.Vives

C.T. Mieres

Montsio

C.J. Portet

Pintor Fortuny

Carme

Carrer C.C.Flor

La Canuda

Pge.D.de la Victòria

D. Bas

Magalenes

Sant

Carrer

Betlem

Carme

Palau de la Virreina

Palau Moja

Portaferrissa

Carrer Bot

Pge. Magarola

C.D. de la Victòria

Carrer Cucurulla

dels Capellans

C.C. Sagristans

Ripoll

Copons

C.M.Ferrer

Carrer

Beates

C.V. de la Perdiu

Freixures

Pge. Virreina

Pl.Vila de Madrid

C. Arcs

Boters

Palla

Plaça Nova

Av. de la Catedral

Plaça A. Maura

Avinguda de Francesc Cambó

Mercat Boqueria

Pla de la

Petxina

Cabres

Pl. del Pi

St. Felip Neri

H

Palau Episcopal

Ca de l'Ardiaca

Pia Almoina

H

Laietana

C.d'Avella

C. dels Mercaders

Tragi

Sta. Maria del Pi

St. J. Oriol

Ave Maria

St. Sever

St. Sever

Sta. Llúcia

Catedral

Comtes

Museu F.Marès

Pl.Sta Caterina

C.Sidé

Massanet

C.P. Gallifa

LICEU

M

Boqueria

C. de la Boqueria

C.C. Banys

Arc St.Ram.

St. Honorat

C.St.

Pietat

Canonges

C. Pietat

Sant Iu

Pl. del Rei

Museu d'Història

C. Bòria

Colom de Lliri

Oli

A.St.Onof.

Pau

C. d'en

C. Arolas

Quintana

C.C.

Rauric

C.d'en

Madoz

C. Arai

Boqueria

Bobca

Marlet

Fruita

Palau de la Generalitat

Paradís

C. del Bisbe

Llibreteria

Bda. Llib. Àngel

Frenería

C. Llana

C.Boc.

atre ceu

C. de la Boqueria

Alsina

Remei

Eufalla

Call

Pl.St. Jaume

Ferran

C.Jaume I

M

Carrer

JAUME I

C.Cotoners

CAPUTXINS

St. Jaume

C. Lleona

Tres Llits

Escudellers Blancs

Bda. St. Miquel

Pl.St. Miquel

Casa Ciutat

Gegants

C.Hércules

Dag.

Sotstinent

Pl. E. Vilanova

C. Vigatans

Via

Laietana

H

Grunyi

Brosoli

Manresa

C. d'Argenteria

Rossic

Plaça Reial

Colom

Pge.Bacardi

Vidre

Nou de Sant Francesc

Aglà

Pl. Orwell

Carrer Cervantes

C. Templaris

Palau

Pl. Cometa

Regomir

C.St. Simplici

Just i Pastor

Bellafila

C.Bda. Caçador

Aulet

Pl. Traginers

Navarro

C.Nou.

Basea

Pl.V.C.

Balaguer

Abaixadors

Pl. Sta. Maria

Canvis Nous

Agullers

Espaseria

Pge. Ginjol

C. Escudellers

Pge. Escudellers

C.d'en Rull

Escudellers

Rosa

Còdols

Carabassa

Serra

Milans

Carrer d'Avinyó

Ataülf

Regomir

C.C. Vell

Gignàs

C. del Sol

decols

Baixeras

Correus i Telecom.

Porta

Trompetes

Canvis Vells

Carrer del Mar

au March (seu de Cera)

C. Sils

Pge. Banys

Clavé

Braille

Pl. del C.

C. Boltres

Merce

Bas. de la Mercè

C. de Oller

C. Plata

C. Marquet

Fusteria

Merce

Llotja

Banca

de Josep Anselm

Parc

Duc de Medinaceli

Pl. del C.

DE

COLOM

Reina Cristina

PG.

ISABEL II

ASSEIG

THE BARRI GÒTIC: FROM PLAÇA DEL PI THROUGH EL CALL

The Gothic Quarter is built over the ancient Roman town, on high ground which the Romans knew as Mons Taber. The walls that protected this settlement can still be traced in the curve of the streets. The pretty Plaça del Pi, occupying former marshland just outside the old Roman walls; the medieval Jewish Quarter or Call; and any number of treasure-trove shops and cafés complete this tour.

From the fountain with the ceramic representation of the Rambla at its intersection with Carrer Portaferrissa, continue down Portaferrissa for a few paces before turning right into **Carrer Petritxol**, one of the Gothic Quarter's favorite little streets, a slender succession of *xocolaterias* (hot chocolate

Fresh cheese and honey market in the Plaça del Pi.

emporiums) and art galleries. At No. 11 on the right, mock curtains are carved into the door and colorful flowers decorate the entryway at the top of the walls. A plaque outside commemorates Montserrat Caballé, who worked here in 1950. Next door is the Granja la Pallaresa, a café with an emphasis on dairy goods. Next, at No. 9, is Xocoa, an artisanal chocolate store. Their candied oranges are excellent. Sala Parés, at No. 5, is the most famous of Barcelona's art galleries, and a hallowed city cultural center, where Picasso, Casas (*see p. 116*), Miró, and nearly all of Barcelona's most important artists have shown their work at one time or another. In the corner to the left of the gallery is an image and poem dedicated to Our Lady of Mercy, Barcelona's patron. The Galeria Trama across the street is another good place to look at paintings. Further down on the left is Llibreria Quera (No. 2), Barcelona's best hiking and mountain-climbing bookstore, with maps, magazines, and volumes of advice for trekkers, climbers, and anyone interested in mountaineering. Dulcinea, the hot chocolate and tea room next door, offers a cozy retreat for a wet winter afternoon. Above the fireplace is a photograph of the 19th-century poet and playwright Àngel Guimerà, who died in the house at No. 4 next door, and who returns a little later.

As you progress down Petritxol, a slender church tower has been looming ahead. Suddenly, at the end of the street, the immense rose window of the **Església del Pi** bursts into flower before you, impossibly huge in the small Plaça del Pi: it is said to be the largest rose window in the world. The Plaça del Pi is named for the pine tree (*pi*) that has always marked the spot, and still does, diagonally to your left. To the immediate left is the **Ganiveteria Josep Roca**, Barcelona's best knife store, with some of the city's oldest and best-restored sgraffito decorations (*see p. 82*) on the building's upper façade. The appropriately ominous-looking building on the right side of the square is the Casa de la Congregació de la Puríssima Sang, usually called the **Casa de la Sang** (House of Blood), headquarters of the Cofradia de la Sang, the Brotherhood of Blood, a religious order entrusted with the spiritual preparation and physical delivery, removal and burial of criminals condemned to death. In the Ramon Casas painting *Garrote Vil* (it hangs in Madrid, but a preliminary sketch for it is housed in the Museu d'Art Modern, *see p. 116*), the members of the Cofradia can be seen around the gallows dressed in the long robes and pointed conical headgear of penitents. Look carefully and over the right-hand door of Casa de la Sang, you will be able to make out the Latin inscription *'Erit sanguis in signum edibus vobis in quibus eritis'* ('Blood shall be a token upon the houses where ye are.' Exodus XII, official motto of the Cofradia de la Sang, referring to the Israelites' slaughter of a lamb, whose blood they daubed on their lintels to protect themselves from God's wrath.). The putti over the door are holding a shield bearing bleeding incisions, the brotherhood's insignia, while the numbers '13' and '42' on either side

make up the dates of the founding of the order. On the corner nearest the Església del Pi is another coat of arms held between another pair of cherubs, the wounds and blood even more clearly identifiable. The '1615' on either side is the year of the construction of the building, while a window up above to the left has yet more insignia of the Cofradia. Presently abandoned, this eerie house may have been overhauled and converted into an ice cream parlor by the time this book is out, so…beware. The Estamperia d'Art postcard shop (with another Cofradia de la Sang shield, this time in wood, over the

Lavish cutlery displays in the Josep Roca knife store on Plaça del Pi.

Putti bearing the emblazoned blood-wounds of the medieval Cofradia de la Sang.

door) offers excellent reproductions, in postcard size, of some of the greatest paintings in the world. Incidentally, the first chapel on the right inside the Església del Pi is the Capella de la Sang, the brotherhood's official chapel, home of the cross of El Crist de la Sang, which members of the order continue to carry during Easter processions.

Walk left round the church now, into **Plaça de Sant Josep Oriol**. These three adjoining squares, Plaça del Pi, Plaça de Sant Josep Oriol, and Placeta del Pi, are some of the most appealing spaces in the old quarter, filled with outdoor cafés and used as a venue for markets, as well as for street musicians, of varying levels of talent, who come to pester or to entertain, depending on your outlook. The seated bronze is Àngel Guimerà, 19th century poet and playwright known for his macabre sensuality and his play *Terra Baixa*, translated in 1914 as *Martha of the Lowlands*. The house at No. 4 Plaça de Sant Josep Oriol across from the lateral façade of the church is the Palau Fivaller, once home of Joan Fivaller, a famous medieval town councillor (*see p. 161*). It now houses the Agricultural Institute. The church wall bears a plaque commemorating the miraculous delivery of Josep Mestres, a stout priest who slipped and fell from the narrow walkway round the outside of the apse in 1806. He survived the fall unhurt.

Leaving Plaça Sant Josep Oriol now, with the Bar del Pi on your left, go straight ahead up Carrer de la Palla, named for the straw once collected and sold at this point outside the Roman walls. A series of art galleries and antiques stores takes you down to Carrer Banys Nous and the corner shop Caelum, which sells honeys, candies, candles and pastries made in convents and monasteries around Spain. **Philippus** across the way, named for the monastery of Sant Felip Neri, for which this vaulted space once served as wine cellar and stables, offers breakfasts and a selection of beers in medieval surroundings, while **Xaloc** just opposite serves a fine selection of cheeses, hams, and wines - either buy to take home or sit and taste. Make a jack-knife right turn now into Banys Nous. The street follows the curve described by the line of the 4th-century Roman walls, which, if you look carefully on a good map, you can detect circling the cathedral. This is the very heart of the ancient city. More antiques stores, the timeless **El Portalón** restaurant (it has been going as long as anyone can remember),

and, at No. 20 on the left, L'Arca de l'Àvia ('Grandmother's Trunk'), selling linens and lace. Go left into Baixada de Santa Eulàlia. Opposite L'Arca de l'Àvia, the ceramic tiles on the wall commemorate the public baths for which the street is named (*banys nous* means 'new baths'; the previous baths were in the Ribera district, covered in Walk 3). The co-ed composition of the ceramic representation is certainly historically incorrect, no doubt a product of the artist's fantasy life. Climbing up the Baixada (all *baixades* were caused by the crumbling of the early Roman walls and the elevation difference inside and outside them, just as all streets called *arcs* were alleys that hugged the walls along their outside edges) you will see, on your right at the first curve, a small **shrine dedicated to Santa Eulàlia** (*see p. 50*), a 4th-century martyr persecuted by the Romans, and co-patron of Barcelona. Eulàlia was rolled down this incline in a barrel filled with swords and double-edged knives - as the ceramic-tile verse on the wall tells you. The verse is by the priest-confessor and nationalist poet Jacint Verdaguer (*see p. 184*). When she emerged unrelenting from this ordeal, her Roman persecutors had no more tortures left to inflict. She was sentenced to death by crucifixion.

Continuing on, up Carrer Sant Sever, the first street on the right, Carrer de Sant Domènec del Call, in front of the very good little restaurant La Cassola, takes you into the **medieval Jewish quarter**, el Call. Its name derives from the Hebrew word *qahal* (kahal, council of elders). Barcelona's Call spanned the area between the Palau de la Generalitat (on Plaça Sant Jaume) and Carrer Banys Nous, with Carrer del Call, Carrer de Sant Domènec del Call, Carrer Marlet, and Arc de Sant Ramon del Call marking the heart of it. It flourished between the 9th and the 14th centuries, only to be brought to a bloody end in August 1391, when an outbreak of anti-Semitic violence, originating in Seville, reached Barcelona with tragic results: more than a thousand Jews were murdered. Ten years later, almost a century before the official Expulsion Decree of 1492, Barcelona's remaining Jews were expelled from the Call, only reprieved if they consented to convert to Christianity.

Carrer Sant Domènec del Call leads through a little square, past the Vinissim wine bar, to the corner of Carrer Marlet. Continuing for a few steps down Carrer Sant Domènec del Call will reveal the surprising Modernist entryway of the tiny Pensión Sant Domènec del Call, with its floral numerals 1892 carved over the door, and colorful ceramic tiles lining the stairs. Directly across the street is a restored Renaissance façade with, just overhead, ceramic tiles of Sant Dominic in prayer. It commemorates the Dominican monastery that used to stand here. Just beyond on the right, the Fernández antiques and furniture restoration shop is a magnificent jumble of everything from frames to sideboards to ancient books and paintings. The deep grooves cut into the walls at waist and knee level on either side of this narrow street, one of the Barri Gòtic's slenderest, were caused by the hubs of horse-drawn wagon wheels grinding through up to the middle of the 20th century.

Return to Carrer Marlet now, and go left down it. No. 5 on your right is the former **Sinagoga Major de Barcelona**. Now restored, it lays claim to being the oldest synagogue in Europe. Inside is a *menorah* in wrought iron, donated by the Majorcan sculptor Ferran Aguiló in honor of his ancestors. After the murder or expulsion of the Jews, the synagogue became home to the master mason Marc Safont (*see p. 80*), who was working on the nearby palaces on Plaça Sant Jaume. The vats under the plexiglass floor were used in the 15th century by Jaume

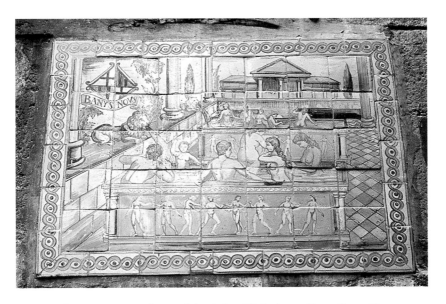

Ceramic tiles commemorate the site of the city's public baths, on Carrer Banys Nous.

d'Arguens, a dyer who occupied the building before the Inquisition accused him of 'crypto-Judaism' and he was forced to flee to France. The synagogue's eccentric orientation within the surrounding grid, facing southeast to Jerusalem, is one of its identifying characteristics. Tours of the synagogue are given in English, Hebrew, and Spanish, and a booklet available in English explains the history of the city's Jewish community (*Carrer Marlet 5. Open Tues-Sat 11am-2pm & 4pm-7pm; Sun 11am-2pm. www.calldebarcelona.org*).

Continue down Marlet to the corner with Arc de Sant Ramon del Call. Fixed to the wall is a facsimile (the original is in the City History Museum) of a **stone tablet with Hebrew inscriptions**. The lettering is translated twice, both times erroneously. Chiseled into the stone are the Spanish words '*El santo Rabino Samuel Hasareri nunca se acabe su vida*' (The holy Rabbi Samuel Hasareri may his life never end). The glass plaque reads, in Catalan, '*Fundació pia de Samuel Ha-sardí. El seu llum crema permanentment*' (Pious foundation of Samuel Ha-Sardí. His light burns everlastingly). A group of Hebrew scholars from Israel gathered at the site in summer 2003 agreed that both versions were incorrect; the plaque simply names and honors in permanent memory Rabbi Samuel Ha-Sardi or *el Sefardi*.

Turn left down Arc de Sant Ramon del Call, past the lovely Momo storefront with its six-meter windows and doors, and come out onto Carrer del Call. A few meters up to the left at No. 14 stands what was once the legendary **Cormellas printing press**, which functioned from 1591 to 1670. The elaborate sgraffito decoration on the façade overhead to the right shows an image of bookshelves amid other more pastoral scenes. The MAE THA MOR FOSEOS at the bottom refers to the printing of Ovid's *Metamorphoses*. The Cormellas press was made famous by *Don Quijote*. In Part II, Chapter LXII, when the doddery knight-errant arrives in Barcelona, he *'looked up and saw written over a door in very large letters BOOKS PRINTED HERE…which made him very happy, because he had never seen a printer's shop and was curious to see how one worked'*. During his tour of the process, Don Quijote discourses on the vagaries of translation and how certain translators are so skillful that they

Hebrew tablet in Carrer Marlet, one of the few reminders of the former Jewish inhabitants of El Call.

'cast doubt on which is the translation and which is the original' (an idea echoed by Jorge Luís Borges in his famous remark about having grown up reading *Quijote* in the English Palmer version, and how on first reading it in Spanish it had sounded to him 'like a bad translation'). Don Quijote then chats with an Italian author who says *'What? You expect me to give my work to a book seller, who will give me three cents for the privilege and pretend he's doing me a favor? I don't write books for fame, which I already have as a result of my deeds. What I want is profit, without which fame isn't worth a nickel'*. And finally, in a perfect example of Cervantine fictional craft, Don Quijote finds workers correcting another book, which turns out to be the Second Part of *Don Quijote de la Mancha*, composed by 'a certain resident of Tordesillas'. This is, of course, the notorious Avellaneda, author of the 'false Quijote' (probably,

Pondering questions of style outside the Sombrereria Obach.

Castell Nou, the tower where the besieged victims of the 1391 pogrom made their final stand. The jewelry store is filled with Roman stones, while the next store, Tantra, at No. 1, has a 4th-century Roman watchtower and section of wall in the back room. Look carefully for the Roman tomb tucked in at the foot of the wall at the far right end.

On the corner of Banys Nous, the **Sombrereria Obach**, a 100-year old hat emporium, rounds the corner with a classic wood and mirror storefront. Above the second 'E' of Sombrereria on Carrer del Call, is an unusual tiny medieval stone window frame. Opposite the shop's main entrance, the house with the handsome sgraffito on Carrer Banys Nous stands on the exact site of the medieval Jewish *mikveh* or ritual baths. After a few steps up Carrer de la Boqueria take a left turn into the Volta del Remei, a tunnel-like arch descending to Carrer Ferran and the Sant Jaume church, **site of the Sinagoga Menor**, the Call's second, lesser synagogue. Don't miss the blocked-up ancient archway, probably Roman, on the immediate right inside the Volta, or the stone ring near the top of the wall as you look back once through the arch. The stone ring is

in fact, written as a jealous prank by Cervantes's great rival Lope de Vega). '*I have heard of that book,*' said Don Quijote, '*and in truth thought it had been burned to dust for its impertinence…but his day will come… as every pig's does…because fake stories are only as good as they are true, and true ones are all the better for being real.*' Could Pirandello have done it better?

Retrace your steps down Carrer del Call now, past the Sant Jordi-slaying-the-dragon image over the corner to the right, opposite Cormellas, and past the jagged broken stone above the Fills M. Sala store at No. 5, a piece of the Roman wall and all that **remains of the**

St James 'Matamoros' in action on the tympanum of the church of Sant Jaume, on the site of a former medieval synagogue.

thought to have been part of the Roman circus that is said to have occupied this spot. Immediately in front of you as you come out into Carrer Ferran is a doorway on the site of the **former door to the synagogue**. The main façade of the church next

door, with its escutcheon of St James, slayer of the Moors, bears the Latin inscription *Diliges proximum tuum sicut te ipsum* (Love thy neighbor as thyself) - an ironic motto, perhaps, for the lynch-mob of 1391 who slaughtered their Jewish brethren.

Gleaming brass door-knocker on Passeig del Born.

WALK THREE

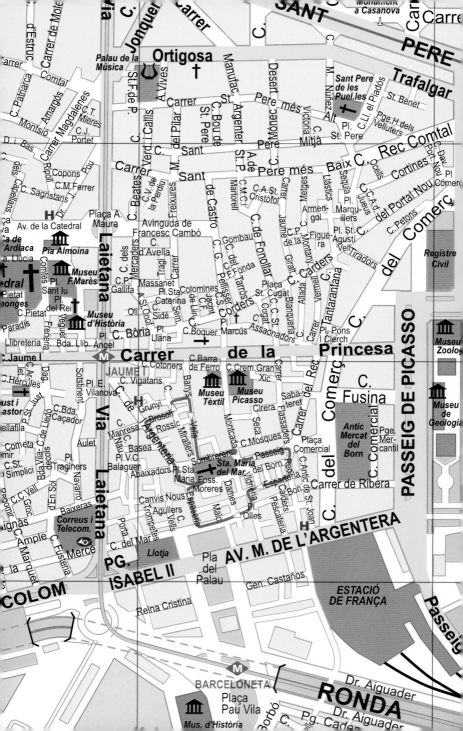

LA RIBERA

The old waterfront district of La Ribera is a jumble of narrow streets centered on the church of Santa Maria del Mar. Old craftsmen's workshops and stylish new boutiques, lively bars and quiet alleyways all happily exist side by side.

Passeig del Born, which runs from the apse of Santa Maria del Mar to the Born market on Carrer de Comerç, is more a rectangular square than a *passeig* or promenade. '*Roda el món i torn al Born*' (Go round the world and return to the Born) was Barcelona's 19th-century way of describing **El Born** as the center of the universe, and indeed until the city's main produce market moved out of town in 1971 and in-town foodstuffs were left to the Boqueria (*see p. 41*), it was El Born, not the Rambla, that generated most of the city's epicurean energy. This square was the site of medieval jousting

The church of Santa Maria del Mar, reflected in the windows of La Vinya del Senyor, an excellent wine-tasting bar.

tournaments: one explanation for the name '*born*' was the early Catalan word for lists or jousts. Inquisitional *autos da fé* were held here as late as the 18th century, and all processions, carnivals, and trade fairs - especially ceramics and glass displays - were invariably held in the Passeig del Born. Only one house has managed to retain its original Gothic physiognomy: No. 17, with its typical towers, gallery, and six Gothic windows. The numbered bronze **cannon balls and trunk** that adorn the center of the square outside it are a 1992 work by sculptor Jaume Plensa, commemorating the bombardment and subsequent destruction of the La Ribera neighborhood by the victorious Spanish and French armies under Philip of Anjou, the Bourbon claimant to the Spanish crown in the 1700-1714 War of the Spanish Succession (*see p. 18*).

The **Born market** itself, the great iron hangar at the opposite end from the church, was designed in 1874, modeled after the mother of all markets, Les Halles in Paris. A project to convert El Born into a public library has recently uncovered remains of that lost city of 1714, complete with kitchen fireplaces, tiled floors, wells, and the Rec Comtal (county canal) itself, which brought water into this part of town. The site is due to be turned into an archeological museum. Detailed municipal records compiled on the inhabitants of La Ribera specify who lived in each house, what they did for a living, what they possessed down to the last vat of wine - and even how good the wine was.

With the Born roof in front of you, turn right down **Carrer del Rec**, named for the canal, or *rec* (as in irrigation) that flowed through here. The right side of the street is lined by the arcades and porches that once backed onto the watercourse as it ran - no doubt pungently - through the neighborhood. Now lined with new boutiques opening daily, the most tenacious emporium here is the vegetable and fruit stand at the corner of Carrer Esparteria, marked simply 'Almacén', and the only survivor of the many that once operated as satellite produce vendors near the Born market. Carrer Esparteria is named for the wicker manufacturers who once worked there. It leads past two attractive sister taverns on the right, La Tinaja (wine vat or barrel), and the La Tinajilla (wine cask) next door. Further down, at the corner of Carrer Vidrieria, across to the right is the **Origens 99.9%** store and restaurant, selling purebred Catalan food products in what was once the workshop of a glassblower, source of

The soaring slender belltower of Santa Maria dominates the Ribera district almost everywhere you go.

the street name. Look for the carved wooden balconies and shelves and the overhead effigy of St Anthony of Padua, patron saint of artisans and of lost possessions.

Turn down Carrer Vidrieria in the other direction now, and you will come out into **Plaça de les Olles**. Named for the makers of *olles*, or earthenware pots, this little enclave is a popular spot; people are attracted by the square's secluded feel, by its two little bars and, more famously, by Cal Pep, where some of Barcelona's most celebrated delicacies are served (*see p. 231*). The balconies at No. 6 over the Café de la Ribera are decorated with colorful blue and yellow floral patterns in ceramic tile on the second and top floors. At No. 2 is a house with a castle-like turret, complete with gargoyles over the street. It was built in 1910 by Enric Sagnier i Villavecchia, the architect responsible for the meringue-like Temple Expiatori del Sagrat Cor (Barcelona's answer to the Sacré Coeur) that gushes over the city with saccharine importunity from the top of Tibidabo. This town house is a much nicer example of Sagnier's work. Look for the two vertical rows

of tiny tri-lobed windows on the side of the façade facing the square.

Go straight ahead now to an adjoining square, **Pla del Palau**, which means the plain (*pla*) of the palace (*palau*), and originally referred to an open space in front of the Palau Reial, a royal palace used by the military governors of Catalonia from the late 17th century, and destroyed by fire in 1875. The Prince of Darmstadt, the Habsburgs' proconsul in Barcelona during the War of the Spanish Succession, imitated the passageway which the Medici family had built in Florence between the Pitti Palace and the Uffizi, and had his palace connected by covered walkway with Santa Maria del Mar, so he and visiting royal personages could attend mass without walking through the street and thus risking their lives. Though the Catalans supported the Habsburg claimant during the War of the Spanish Succession, they still hated the Habsburg presence in Barcelona. The Prince of Darmstadt was in an impossible position - it is easy to see why he thought a walkway necessary. The narrow Carrer Malcuinat, to the right as you enter Pla del Palau from Plaça de les Olles, was filled with this overhead passage until 1987.

The old palace stood just about where the excellent tapas restaurant La Estrella de Plata now resides, on the north side of the square. On the far side of the square is **La Llotja**, the Maritime Exchange, once one of the best secular Gothic structures in Barcelona. Like the other *llotjas* (in Spanish, *lonjas*) in major port cities of the Crown of Aragon, Barcelona's was extremely fine. Originally little more than a tarpaulin stretched across poles to protect merchants and their wares from the elements, Barcelona's present *llotja* was constructed between 1380 and 1392, a more fitting reflection of the city's mercantile importance. At the end of the 18th century the façades were remodeled in the fashionable Neoclassical style. The interior was

left untouched, however, and the great Saló Gòtic (Gothic Hall) was used as a grand venue for balls and functions throughout the 19th century. It functioned as the Barcelona stock exchange until 1975 and, until late 2001, as the grain exchange. The hall has now been restored, though a system for public visits has not yet been formally established.

A right turn from Pla del Palau into Carrer Espaseria provides a perfect view of **Santa Maria del Mar**'s belltower (*NB: The church is described in detail on pp. 70-74*). The street was named for the medieval swordmakers, as the Granja L'Espaseria sign at No. 12 on the right bears witness. A right turn at the end of the street takes you past the beautifully restored Candela clothing design store (drop in and have a look at the painted beams revealed when a false ceiling was removed) and into **Fossar de les Moreres**, the Graveyard of the Mulberry trees. The low red marble parapet running across this open space is in fact a monument to the anti-Bourbon resistance fighters who lost their lives in the 1714 siege that ended the War of the Spanish Succession and established Philip on the Spanish throne as Felipe V. The monument is carved with the inscription '*en el* *fossar de les moreres no s'hi enterra cap traïdor'* (no traitors are buried in the graveyard of the mulberry trees), lines written by the playwright Frederic Soler, whose statue adorns the Rambla (*see p. 46*). The lines refer to the story of the sexton who refused to bury those who had fought on the Bourbon side, even when one of them turned out to be his own son. This square has always been a favorite rallying place for Catalanist militants. During the Franco years many ugly confrontations took place here. Today it is the most vociferous elements of Catalonia's separatist movement, Terra Lliure ('Free Land') who make their feelings felt here. Blood always

runs high on September 11th, Catalan national day.

From the middle of the square, one of Santa Maria del Mar's external peculiarities is clearly visible: a rectangular, peaked patch of lighter-colored stone, covering two of the lancet windows, running from the ground to just above the second string course. This is all that remains to tell of the Prince of Darmstadt's covered bridge, which led directly into the royal box over the south side of the altar. The mulberry-colored steel arch holding an eternal flame over the street was erected in 2002.

From Fossar de les Moreres, go back to the square in front of the church, where **La Vinya del Senyor** (The Lord's Vineyard) is always a tempting spot for a taste of one of the fortnightly changing, by-the-glass selections. Walking ahead with La Vinya to your right, you will pass under a sailing vessel suspended from the façade of the restaurant Vascelum, both the ship and the name of the restaurant in honor of Santa Maria del Mar's role as protector of the Catalan

An eternal flame burns in Fossar de les Moreres, commemorating those who fell in the siege of 1714. Note the lighter-colored patch of church wall, clearly marking where the Prince of Darmstadt's notorious passageway was attached.

fleet. About here begins the shortest street in Barcelona (about two and a half meters long), Carrer de l'Anisadeta, allegedly named for a woman who sold shots of anise at this corner during the 18th century. Swinging to the right behind La Vinya is one of early Barcelona's most ancient and archaic corners, **Carrer de les Caputxes** (named for medieval cowl or hood makers) where heavy wooden beams support tiny apartments overhead and octagonal Gothic stone pillars are wedged under overhanging porches and wooden arcades. Passing the restaurants Vox Populi and Caputxes, a right turn leads out to the **Gothic fountain** in front of the corner of Santa Maria del Mar. Atop this rectangular structure, with its stone escutcheons of Catalonia and Barcelona, is a tiny terrace garden with a minuscule alabaster image of Santa Maria in a little grotto. A look over at the corner of Santa Maria del Mar will reveal an elevated brazier, once used for the torches that lit the streets before the advent of gas or electricity.

Here, a left up Carrer Argenteria, named for the medieval silversmiths, takes you past La Pelu, a hot-as-a-pistol hairdresser; past Cafés El Magnífico, always a good place to

Colorful murals and an urban 'garden' decorate an empty lot on Carrer Banys Vells.

take a deep breath; and Sagardi, a popular Basque cider house and tapas bar on the corner. Two streets up from Sagardi, a right into Carrer Brosolí takes you down to the corner of Carrer Mirallers. Down to the left at No. 6 is a fragrant coffee-toasting shop, and further on, at the end of the street on the corner to your right, is *La Carassa*, a full-faced female countenance with flowers in her hair: she once marked a bordello. Return to Carrer Brosolí and turn left into Carrer Banys Vells, an almost uninterrupted succession of boutiques and galleries, nearly each of which has elegantly restored spaces within medieval buildings. Africa Negra at No. 7 to the left has vats below glass panes underfoot, which were once storage tanks (the central sumps were for collecting sediment) for olive oil sold in the Born. Both L'Ametller (also at No. 7) and Ull de Llebre (literally 'hare's eye', Catalan for the Tempranillo grape) at No. 6 are excellent wine, ham, cheese and honey shops. At the end of the street turn left down Carrer Sombrerers, past the Modernist Carpanta restaurant, to the **Gispert** store, Barcelona's best sensorial feast, especially for the nose and eyes, at No. 23. The ancient almond-toasting oven in the back of the store is the top prizewinner, but the baskets of nuts, the acid engravings on the office windows, and everything else up to and including the rickety glass back door opening into Carrer Sant Antoni dels Sombrerers are all irresistible (and a pocketful of lichi nuts can be a secret resource while tasting wine or just staying on your feet).

At the far end of Carrer Sombrerers is the **Taller Cuixart**, a foundation, museum, and gallery dedicated to Modest Cuixart, one of Catalonia's greatest 20th-century artists, influenced by Surrealism, by Joan Miró, and by Middle European trends in an obscure and enigmatic artistic vision. Over 50 of his paintings are on display upstairs.

JACINT VERDAGUER (1845-1902)

National poet of Catalonia and the most revered voice of the *Renaixença*, Verdaguer (or Mossèn Cinto, 'Mossèn' being Catalan for Monsignior) suffered repeated spiritual crises, while his physical health was ravaged by tuberculosis. Priest, poet and mystic, he wrote works of great religious, telluric and patriotic fervor, as exampled by his long masterpiece *Canigó* (1886). In *L'Atlàntida* (1877), eventually to become a Manuel de Falla opera-oratorio, he converted into epic poetry the prehistoric myths of the Iberian Peninsula and the Pyrenees.

Born near Vic, son of a poor quarry-worker and a deeply religious mother, the young Verdaguer was pushed toward the Church by poverty and maternal religious fervor. As a young seminarist he was ascetic and competitive, challenging peers to barefoot races through fields of corn stubble. His early poetic efforts were satirical until a fellow student convinced him to write serious epic and religious verse. He went on to become the leading voice in Catalan letters and father of modern Catalan.

Portrait of Verdaguer by Ramon Casas.

Verdaguer was handsome as a young man. His poetic talents gave him great appeal, and he made a dashing impression on the Barcelona bourgeoisie. He was appointed chaplain to the wealthy shipping magnate Antonio López, Marqués de Comillas (*see p. 37-8*), and went to Cuba as chaplain on López's Transatlantic Company steamers. His fame spread widely during his lifetime, and 100,000 copies of his *Oda a Barcelona* were distributed to the city's schoolchildren. He travelled extensively, and was received by Popes, monarchs and grandees around the world.

His death at age 57, weakened by tuberculosis, depression and disgrace, was a tragic contrast to his glamorous life. His travels to the Holy Land had inspired him to regard his life of ease with increasing suspicion. When he returned to Barcelona he began to give away large sums of his benefactor's money, espousing the cause of the poor and oppressed. Eventually his conduct became so eccentric that it gave rise to gossip and suspicion. He began to conduct exorcisms, believing it was a way to eradicate evil from society. He was excommunicated as a heretic, disowned by López and defrocked by Bishop Morgades of Vic (one of the propagators of the Sagrada Família project). A public scandal ensued, and Catalonia found itself divided into pro and anti-Verdaguer camps. Verdaguer's enemies attempted to have him dismissed as mentally ill. His series of essays *En defensa pròpia*, published in the anti-establishment press, attacked the bourgeoisie and Bishop Morgades. Though he was eventually pardoned, he died penniless and abandoned by all but a last few friends and admirers, in the house of the Miralles family in Vallvidrera on June 10th, 1902. His death provoked massive mourning. Verdaguer's funeral was one of the greatest and most multitudinous events in Barcelona history, comparable only to Antoni Gaudí's in spontaneity and emotion.

'Men flee with the wind; the truth of God endures forever'. Ceramic-tile homily adorning the courtyard of the CCCB, formerly a convent and now a cultural center.

WALK FOUR

ELS HOMES PASSEN COM EL VENT;
LA VERITAT DE DÉV ROMAN ETERNAMENT.

EL RAVAL

El Raval is the area to the west of the Rambla, on the right as you walk toward the port. Originally a rough outer edge of town, the Raval used to be notorious for its Barrio Chino red-light district, the lurid attractions of which are known to have fascinated, among many others, the young Pablo Picasso.

Starting from Plaça de Catalunya, take an immediate right after the Font de les Canaletes into Carrer Tallers, named for the butchers, tailors or small textile factories that used to exist here. **Boadas**, on the immediate left, has been Barcelona's most famous cocktail bar since 1933, when Miguel Boadas first opened this Havana-style saloon openly derivative of Hemingway's beloved Floridita in the Cuban capital. The compass on the wall outside indicating the four cardinal points more or less backwards is a tip-off that you're about to enter Barcelona's Bermuda

Old men congregate under the trees in one of the Raval's squares.

Old-fashioned barber shop, still managing to survive a few paces from the Rambla.

Triangle of ethylic disorientation. Everyone from Papa Hemingway to Joan Miró to Sophia Loren has knocked back a mojito, a frozen daiquiri, or a dry martini here, so why not?

Across the street at No. 2 is a Modernist *forn de pa*, literally, bread oven. Its carved wooden storefront is one of Barcelona's best. Farther down Carrer Tallers, at the corner with Carrer de les Sitges, an old-fashioned barbershop has somehow survived. No piercings, no rastas, no extensions, no tattoos, just a buzz cut in one of the three desolate looking barber chairs.

Turn left now down Carrer de les Sitges, past La Oveja Negra beer hall on the right, an interesting medieval tavern to have a look through or even breakfast in - by night teenage beer drinkers take over. The Caribbean Club next door is a Boadas branch office, known for superior frozen daiquiris. At the next corner, Bar Castells has a handy outdoor marble corner bar and a splendid carved wooden and mirrored 'altarpiece' behind the bar inside, flanked by Ramon Casas (*see p. 116*) prints.

Turn right into a small square, and right again through an opening into Plaça Vicenç Martorell, a leafy, grassy spot with two interesting cafés at the far end: Kasparo, with outside tables in the sun particularly useful in winter, and the Cafè d'Annunzio, named for the Italian poet, novelist, dramatist and soldier Gabriele d'Annunzio (1863-1938), early Fascist and inventor of the black shirt uniform. Going left across the square brings you to the **Casa de la Misericòrdia**, at No. 17 Carrer de les Ramelleres, a street said to derive its name from a Catalanized version of the Spanish *ramera*, 'whore', in reference to a famous nearby brothel. The Casa de la Misericòrdia was a home and school for girls from poor families, transforming into 'useful and productive women' many who 'might otherwise have perished in poverty or stumbled into the pitfalls of immorality', as one historian put it. The complex also included a foundling hospice. To the right of the main entrance of No. 17 is a wooden porthole set into the wall. This is an ancient *torno* or turntable, where, up until well into this century, unwanted babies were spun into the safe and supportive arms of the nuns of the House of Mercy. Now cemented in, this wooden circle once contained a partitioned revolving shelf. Answering the knock of a woman in distress, the nun on duty would answer 'Ave Maria', to which the new mother replied in kind as the turntable creaked her newborn out of one life and into another. The coin slot above to the left, fed by wealthy gentlemen, poor cleaning girls and wayward matrons alike, was used for contributions to the hospice. The handsome stone doorway into what is now the Barcelona Town Hall's Ciutat Vella branch came from the Casa d'Infants Òrfens (House of Infant Orphans), in what is now Plaça dels Àngels, founded in 1578, as the inscription reads, and torn down in 1995. Further down to the left, the

Carrer Elisabets is the leafiest street in the Raval, filled with former convent gardens.

slender six-story house at No. 9 is a classic Barcelona structure, cozy and intimate in its peculiar way, while the handsome vermilion Drogueria Gomara sign further up on the corner is an ancient vestige of a late 19th-century paint, soap, and liquid goods store.

Turn right down Carrer Elisabets, named for a convent torn down during the 19th century. On the right you come to **La Central del Raval** book and music store, built into the late Gothic (1693) former Casa de la Misericòrdia church. Over the door a brace of angels sustains the city coat of arms. Next on the right are the four immense, light-seeking, 25-meter palm trees in the lush green garden

of the Casa de la Misericòrdia, with the former Col.legi de Sant Guillem d'Aquitània on the left end of the patio, now a school of international relations. At the end of the street, again on the right, is another chapel, the chapel of the orphanage, at Elisabets No. 24. The wooden plaque on the door reads: 'Charity for the Poor of the Hospital of Our Lady of the Orphan Children - year 1785'. Look up to see the verdant jungle growing on the roof behind the belfry.

The harshly bright open space beyond the chapel is dominated by the white-tiled, glass and plastic Museu d'Art Contemporani de Barcelona (**MACBA**), designed by Richard Meier (*see p. 130*). Straight ahead to the left is the chapel of the Convent dels Àngels, usually open and showing contemporary art and design. To the right beyond the MACBA is the Centre de Cultura Contemporània de Barcelona (**CCCB**), housed in the partly-restored, partly-remodeled Casa de la Caritat, a former medieval convent and hospital. The CCCB's main courtyard offers a successful combination of traditional architecture and contemporary design. The right-hand

wall of the patio is made up entirely of panes of glass, which throw reflections of the world outside into what was once a gated nunnery. The CCCB hosts concerts, lectures, art shows and exhibitions of all kinds. (*Montalegre 5. Tues-Fri 11am-2pm & 4pm-8pm; Wed & Sat 11am-8pm; Sun 11am-7pm. www.cccb.org; entry to patio and bookstore free.*) Next door is the Centre d'Estudis i Recursos Culturals de la Diputació de Barcelona (Barcelona Study and Cultural Resource Center), in a restored 14th-century Carthusian convent with a pretty inner patio. (*Montalegre 5-9. Open weekdays 11am-7pm; Sat 10am-8pm; Sun 10am-3pm*).

Back in the Plaça dels Àngels, the Convent dels Àngels is the only

Skateboarders take a break from the action outside the MACBA.

Ceramic angel in the patio of a Carthusian convent turned study center.

the street, a brief probe to the right will take you past the monumental sculpture of St Paul (namesake of the hospital's founder Pau Ferran) leaning wearily on his sword in the overhead niche. Another 50 meters down the street is the Modernist **Bar Muy Buenas**. Inside is a handsome arrangement of curving wooden arches, acid-etched glass, and marble former codfish-salting basins, once used here to hold ice and chill drinks.

Return to the hospital entrance now. This is one of Europe's earliest medical complexes, founded in the 10th century, though most of the present buildings date from the 15th and 16th centuries. The first stone was laid by King Martí l'Humà (Martin the Humane) in 1401. As you come in from Carrer del Carme, the first door on the left is the Reial Acadèmia de Cirurgia i Medicina (Royal Academy of Surgery and Medicine). Open for visits until 1.30 pm on weekdays, it contains, under a large stained glass window, a lovely circular hall with an operating theater originally used for the observation of surgery and dissections. The plaque on the wall to the right outside is dedicated to Dr Santiago Ramón y Cajal (1852-1934), the eminent

escape from the aggressively sheer and dazzling MACBA across the way. It boasts the FAD (Foment dels Arts Decoratives) restaurant, a popular and appropriately design-happy space with post-modern 'newglobalcuisine' (*sic*) served on pre-graffiti-ized paper tablecloths under the vaulted roof inside or out in the courtyard beyond. As well as the restaurant and bar, this former 16th-century Augustinian convent also boasts an exhibition hall (El Fòrum dels Àngels), bookstore and 150-seat auditorium.

Go straight ahead down Carrer dels Àngels. Ahead of you is the hulking lateral façade of the medieval **Hospital de la Santa Creu**. Although the entrance is just to your left across

Spanish histologist who won the 1906 Nobel Prize for Physiology and Medicine. As the inscription attests, Ramón y Cajal taught histology in Barcelona from 1887 to 1892. The large crowned coat of arms overhead honors King Carlos III, during whose reign the Surgeons' College was originally built.

Across the way is the door into the patio of the 17th-century **Casa de la Convalescència**. The walls of the vestibule are decorated with ceramic scenes of the life of St Paul, beginning to the left of the door into the inner courtyard with a depiction of the moment of the saint's conversion. Created in 1680 by the Passolas brothers (though one of them, Llorenç, seems to get most of the credit), the tiles employ a 20th-century comic strip technique: ribbons of dialogue, to dramatize key moments. Using Paul's pre-conversion Hebrew name, Saul, the upside down script reads '*Savle, Savle, quid me persegueris?*' (Saul, Saul, why persecutest thou me?), to which Paul, blinded by the light, having come to Damascus to suppress Christianity around 33 AD, answers '*Dom quid me vis facer?*' (Lord, what would you have me do?). The next nine scenes around

the vestibule recount episodes from St Paul's life: preaching to the Jews; the flight from Damascus, when he was lowered over the walls in a basket; with St Barnabas curing the infirm in Listra; and embarking at Milet. On the other side of the door back out to the Surgeons' College, is the sixth scene, the saint taken before the magistrate for having exorcised a priestess, and, in the background, in jail; in an olive grove writing his Epistles, which are chronologically listed; Saints Peter and Paul in Rome flanked by large buildings; and, finally, the scene of Paul's martyrdom, his severed head bouncing several times and the blood turning to water on the third bounce (portraying the

The statue of St Paul stands guard over the ancient Hospital de la Santa Creu.

Scenes from the life of St Paul adorn the Casa de la Convalescència vestibule.

Rodoreda, is visible. Visitors are welcome to look around the patio, while tours of the chapel and other interior rooms are given on Thursdays (*Tel: 93/270-1620 to reserve*).

Turn right now, and you will reach the **hospital patio**, centered on a Baroque cross and filled with orange trees, blue jacaranda blossoms in season, and students from the Escola Massana art school at the far end on the right, mingling with the derelicts for whom this hospital is, was and ever shall be a refuge. The stairway under the arch on the right, which leads to the main entrance of the **Biblioteca de Catalunya**, was built in the 16th century. The statue at the base of the stairway is the hermit-saint St Roch, patron saint of invalids, who owed his own life to the kind offices of a dog. The stairway on the opposite side of the courtyard has a statue of La Verge de la Caritat (Our Lady of Charity) near the bottom, a woman with several little children clinging to her.

Inside the library you can admire the wide 15th-century vaulting of what was once the hospital's main ward, designed by the architect of Santa Maria del Pi church, Guillem Abiell. The contrast is huge: Santa

tradition that a spring gushed forth from the spot), as well as the tiny strip with the final word to come from his lips: 'Iesus'. The tenth image is St Paul, glorified, sainted, and safely in heaven, just to the right of the door into the inner patio.

Llorenç Passolas was also the creator of the tiles around the inner patio. In the center, over the well, is a sculpture of St Paul, a copy of which is at the building's south-west corner on Carrer del Carme. The patio is a masterpiece of late 17th-century Barcelona architecture, with twice as many arches on the upper level, and a transparent section across from the entry through which a garden, dedicated to Catalan novelist Mercè

Maria del Pi is mysterious and penumbral. This space is open to the light of day and the light of science, not the spiritual illumination of religion. It was to this hospital that Antoni Gaudí was brought after he was struck by a trolley on June 7th, 1926. Among the library's collections are archives recording Gaudí's admittance and photographs of the infirmary and the private room where he died. The library's treasures and resources range from Renaissance silver book covers to illuminated manuscripts from the *Llibre Vermell* (Red Book), the Catalan early song book. Guided tours can be arranged at the main desk. *The library is open weekdays 9am-8pm; Sat 9am-2pm.*

Leaving through the wide doorway out to Carrer de l'Hospital, a look up to the right and left will reveal small grated windows with nearly completely disintegrated decorative sculptures, elements from the original 13th-century Hospital d'en Colom founded by canon Guillem Colom in 1219. From the far sidewalk you get a good view of the 16th-century Renaissance façade, with several 14th-century windows from the original hospital in the tower

A mother tends to her baby beneath the statue of Our Lady of Charity in the cloister of the medieval Hospital de la Santa Creu.

over the chapel on the right end, and its nine gargoyles, alternating between winged human faces and griffins. The heraldry over the main door includes, at the top, the bat, favorite emblem of Jaume I and the Crown of Aragon; the cross allusive to the hospital's official title, Hospital de la Santa Creu (Hospital of the Holy Cross), held by a pair of angels; and below, another brace of winged cherubim holding a coat of arms bearing the initials IHS, for *Iesus Hominum Salvator* (Jesus Savior of Mankind).

With the hospital behind you, turn left. At the corner of the street is the hospital's former chapel, now an art gallery. The little outdoor bar opposite serves a powerful espresso and impeccable beer and also serves the tables in the tiny Plaça Canonge Colom, a true crossroads between the Rambla and the Raval with a distinct North African atmosphere. The sculpture in the left-hand corner of this square commemorates the actress Margarida Xirgu (1888-1969). Barely legible beneath the pigeon deposits across the corner is the following dedication: '*La gran Margarita Xirgú, actriz de inmaculada historia artística, lumbrera del teatro español y admirable creadora. F. García Lorca.*' (To the great Margarida Xirgu, actress of immaculate artistic history, leading light of the Spanish theater, and

The jagged, unfinished façade of the 18th-century Església de Sant Agustí.

admirable creative artist. F. García Lorca). Lorca was murdered in Granada by local Fascists at the outbreak of the Spanish Civil War in 1936, though if Margarida Xirgu (the Catalan spelling of her name) had had her way, he would have been safe in Mexico with her. A close friend and probable lover, at least on a platonic level, of the poet and playwright, 'La Xirgu' had begged him to come with her to open his play *Yerma* in the Mexican capital. Look behind you across the square and you will see the **Teatre Romea**, founded in 1863 and considered the cradle of modern Catalan theater.

Return to the Rambla now, via Plaça Sant Agustí, which provides a look at the unfinished **Església de Sant Agustí**, a rough pile of stones with only the lower part of the main façade finished. Built in 1728, funding for the façade simply never materialized, and the church has been unfinished ever since. Every 22nd of May, the day of Santa Rita, patron saint of '*els impossibles*', lost causes and unfulfilled dreams, Rita devotees buy roses and come here to have them blessed by Santa Rita herself, whose chapel is at the east end of the church, to the right of the high altar. Long lines, almost all female, snake out across the square and down Carrer de l'Hospital. Once blessed, the roses are rubbed across the thighs of the crucifix in the rear of the church. The roses eventually dry, are crumbled to dust and stashed away until the following 22nd of May, when the crushed petals are burned and fresh roses are taken for blessing. Perhaps because Santa Rita is also the patron saint of unhappily married women, the right foot of the Christ is covered with a silver slipper to protect it from excessive erosion caused by the rubbing and kissing of hopeful supplicants.

Lunchtime scene along Passeig Joan de Borbó.

NEIGHBORHOOD ONE

BARCELONETA

A silty promontory jutting out to sea between the old harbor and present-day Port Olímpic, Barceloneta is the city's traditional fishermen's quarter. Originally composed of just over a dozen long, narrow streets, intersected by three cross-streets, the district is an early example of urban planning. It was built in the early 18th century to the designs of military engineer Juan Martín Cermeño as alternative housing for inhabitants of La Ribera, whose homes had been demolished to clear fields of fire for the Ciutadella fortress.

Barceloneta has always symbolized escape from the city's industrious bustle; an urban fishing village *barcelonins* sought out at weekends for paella on the beach and a stroll through an ambience more genuinely bohemian than the Rambla. With its history of seafarers, gypsies and other colorful characters, Barceloneta seems like a world apart, blending Mediterranean spontaneity with a pinch of the Andalusian picaresque.

Barceloneta's ancient fishing traditions depicted in ceramic tile.

THE TOUR

The following short route contains suggestions of places to eat and drink. For other ideas, plus telephone numbers and precise addresses, see the Barceloneta restaurants section on p. 246.

Barceloneta occupies a triangular peninsula, with the marina and waterfront restaurants of Passeig Joan de Borbó on the cityward side, and the sandy beaches of the Mediterranean on the other. One of the best streets to stroll along is Carrer de Sant Carles, which traverses the center of the peninsula, and where you will find a series of Barceloneta's most interesting buildings. To begin the tour, find your way to Plaça de la Barceloneta. This attractive square is dominated by the Baroque **church of Sant Miquel del Port** (1753-55). The façade boasts a replacement version of the winged archangel Michael, principal guardian of the Barcelona fishing fleet. The original statue was destroyed in the Civil War. The church has no tower. A military ruling passed when Barceloneta was

The church and square of St Miquel del Port, patron and protector of seafarers.

Tiny fisherman's cottage, one of the very few remaining in an area once filled with such structures.

built decreed that its buildings should not obstruct cannon fire from the Ciutadella's batteries. The cupola was only added in 1853. Even today the church makes do with a tiny bell, suspended from a frame.

Inside the church, look for the metopes, gilded bas-relief sculptures decorating the cornice. All are allegorical representations of the attributes of St Michael: the image of a boat and the inscription *iam in tuto* (now in safety), for example, allude to his protection against the perils of the high sea.

Step outside the church now, and turn left. The house immediately next door, at No. 41 Carrer de Sant Miquel, has a plaque dedicated to Ferdinand de Lesseps, who built the Panama and Suez canals, and who lived here while serving as French consul to Barcelona.

Continue down the street until you reach **Carrer de Sant Carles**, and turn left into it. On the right at No. 6 is one of the only completely original Cermeño-designed houses left in Barceloneta (there is another in Carrer de Sant Elm). Consisting of only two floors, a ground floor designed for boats and nets, and an upper floor used as living space, these diminutive structures were originally intended to house a single family. Overcrowding soon took its toll, however, and gradually fishermen and their families found themselves confined to a single floor, or even, at Barceloneta's lowest ebb, to a single room. In the mid-19th century the military ruling governing the height of buildings lapsed, and property owners took swift advantage of this; by the end of the century houses of four and five stories were towering over the original dwellings. This one dates from 1755.

Across the street at No. 7 is the **Farmacia Saim**, the successor of Barceloneta's first pharmacy,

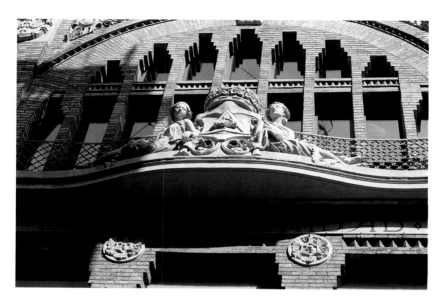

Barceloneta's only Modernist building, the 1918 workers' cooperative La Fraternitat.

occupying a stone house built in 1902 over an original Barceloneta structure. Like so many pharmacies in Barcelona, this one is as ornate as means would allow. Note the floral trim around the upper balconies and the griffins over the door. Despite these frivolous touches, however, Farmacia Saim is sturdily built. It was used as a bomb shelter during the Spanish Civil War, when bombs dropped on the Barcelona port in an effort to paralyze it sometimes misfired and hit Barceloneta instead.

Further down the street at No. 9 is the **Cooperativa Obrera La Fraternitat**, Barceloneta's only Modernist building, and a surprisingly elaborate one for a humble fishermen's quarter. It was built to house the workers' organization La Fraternitat, founded in 1879 (though the present building dates from 1918). The Fraternitat social services and community center supplied workers with affordable food and clothing and also doubled as a cultural and leisure center with a public library.

Walk all the way down Carrer de Sant Carles to the beach now. Just before you climb the steps to the beach-side boardwalk, stop to inspect the **Fuente de Carmen Amaya**. It does not look like much, but it is dedicated to an important daughter of Barceloneta, the gypsy flamenco dancer Carmen Amaya, born here in 1913, in the gypsy settlement of Somorrostro, which was part of Barceloneta until 1920. Amaya began her career before she reached her teens. International fame arrived at the age of 16, when she performed at Barcelona's 1929 International Exhibition. She went on to tour America, and made a number of movies over the course several decades, for example *La hija de Juan Simón* (1934) and *Los Tarantos* (1962). The fountain was placed here in 1959, and though sadly neglected

remains as a poignant reminder of Barceloneta's gypsy traditions. Much of that atmosphere disappeared forever when the last of the *chiringuitos* (ramshackle beach restaurants) were condemned and demolished shortly after the 1992 Olympics.

Climb the stairs beside the fountain and cross the Passeig Marítim to the walkway over the **beach**. From here, to your left, you will see the **Port Olímpic** and Frank Gehry's zeppelin-like goldfish, with Barcelona's twin skyscrapers, the Hotel Arts and the Mapfre office building looming overhead. The

Barceloneta's seashore, with the Port Olímpic in the background.

restaurant Agua, down to the left, is Barcelona's best dining available (10-minute risotto notwithstanding) closest to the Mediterranean.

Turn right up the walkway, which soon reaches beach level. At the beginning of Carrer de l'Almirall Aixada (No. 23) is **Can Majó**, one of Barceloneta's favorite seafood restaurants, popular with local-government functionaries. Watch them rolling up at lunchtime and having their cars valet-parked, while they commandeer the best tables. The restaurant opens at 1pm. If you arrive early, sit in the sun outside the tiny adjacent bar (marked 'Begudes'), which serves drinks and tapas, and offers a lovely view of the palm-fringed sea.

Cloister of the Monestir de Pedralbes.

NEIGHBORHOOD TWO

PEDRALBES & SARRIÀ

Pedralbes nestles in the Collserola foothills at Barcelona's north-western extremity. It is a tranquil neighborhood of villas and gardens scattered around the 14th-century Monestir de Pedralbes (Pedralbes Monastery), possibly the loveliest Gothic cloister in Catalonia, and home to an important collection of early paintings, part of the Thyssen-Bornemisza Collection.

Sarrià is a former village, once set amid farmland many leagues from Barcelona itself, but swallowed up over the centuries by the westward-encroaching metropolis. Today it is a lively residential suburb, still retaining much of its village atmosphere.

Points of interest near Sarrià include some of Gaudí's most memorable works: Finca Güell, Torre Bellesguard, and the Teresianes convent and school. All sights are marked on the map opposite.

14th-century depiction of the Nativity at Pedralbes, part of a mural covering the walls of the day cell of the convent's Mother Superior.

PRACTICAL NOTE

The Monestir de Pedralbes closes at 2pm, which means the best way to explore this part of town is to begin with the monastery (to be accurate, nunnery), exploring Sarrià at your leisure after that. Taxis from the center of town are reliable and good value. To get there by public transport, take the FF.CC. de la Generalitat train (U6 on the FGC, <u>not</u> the Metro) from Plaça Catalunya, and get off at Reina Elisenda. From there it's a 10-minute walk to the nunnery. (Don't walk along noisy Passeig Reina Elisenda; go one block uphill from the station, and turn left into Carrer Ramon Miquel i Planas. This takes you into the tranquil Carrer del Monestir, with its graceful mansions, high walls and laurel trees.)

MONESTIR DE PEDRALBES
Baixada del Monestir 9. Open Tues-Sun 10am-2pm.

This exquisite convent, still home to a small community of nuns, is one of Barcelona's best semi-hidden treasures. It was founded in 1326 by Queen Elisenda, fourth wife of Sovereign Count Jaume II, for nuns of the Franciscan

Tinkling fountains and calla lilies, to inspire the nuns to fluid purity of thought. Opposite: one of the day cells lining the nunnery cloister.

order of the Poor Clares, and as a retreat for herself when her royal husband died. His health was poor, and she knew that he would leave her a widow. Most of the nuns who lived here were of noble lineage, following St Clare's original model, which had consisted of herself, her mother and sisters and women from wealthy families, living lives of extreme austerity, dependent entirely on alms, and spending their days in devout contemplation. The convent's most famous feature - justly - is its cloister, an unusual, three-story structure, surrounding a beautiful garden of palms and orange trees. As you enter it, look straight ahead and you will see that the paving stones have been shattered along shallow grooves: these are the tracks made by French gun carriages, when Napoleon turned the nunnery into a barracks during his 1809 occupation of Barcelona. To the right of the entrance is the Cel.la de Sant Miquel, day cell of the Mother Superior, decorated with murals painted in 1346 by Catalan artist Ferrer Bassa. The cell is also famous for containing the earliest graffito in Barcelona. Look to your right, between the images of St Francis (bearing the stigmata) and St Clare (holding a book and a quill), and you will see a Gothic scrawl that reads '*Joan, no m'oblides*' (John, don't forget me!), a poignant reminder that not all of the novices were deposited in the monastery willingly, and some felt they were being dropped into an oubliette. It is surely no accident that the author of that heartfelt scribble should have chosen to place it between the two saints who founded the order which kept her prisoner.

You can also visit the nunnery's medieval living quarters, infirmary, wine cellars and refectory, with its hatch through to the kitchen, and admonitory sentences painted on the walls: '*Silentium! Audi tacens! Considera morientem!*' (Listen and be silent! Remember that you must die!).

The Thyssen-Bornemisza Collection

When the light is right, tombs of nuns who lived and died here can be seen through some of the iron grates in the walkway down to the painting exhibit. The collection is housed upstairs in what was once the dormitory. Surrounded by 14th-century windows and pointed arches, with views out to the cloister, these canvases by Italian and Spanish masters make up a rich artistic feast.

Where to Dine in Pedralbes

Walk down the cobblestone Baixada del Monestir alongside the sumptuously sculpted and sgraffito-covered El Conventet (Little Convent), named for an earlier Franciscan convent (one of the many luxurious private mansions in this district). Across the road at the bottom of the hill is the Mató de Pedralbes restaurant (named for the *mató*, or fresh curd cheese, for which the nuns of Pedralbes were once famous). Tel: 93/204-7962.

SARRIÀ

NB: Suggestions for where to dine in Sarrià are given on p. 248.

Sarrià was the last district formally to join the municipality of Barcelona. Not so very many years ago it was still a rural hamlet, a cluster of farms and merchants' houses overlooking Barcelona from the hills. Santa Eulàlia (*see p. 50*), the Barcelona saint martyred under Roman emperor Diocletian in the 4th century, is said to have been born here, 'the beautiful daughter of a wealthy Sarrià merchant'. Sarrià is now home to artists, writers and professionals, and is proud of its literary traditions. J.V. Foix, a Catalan poet who published in France throughout the Franco regime, is an honored Sarrià citizen, his descendants the proprietors of Sarrià's two Foix pastry shops. There are still a few old free-standing town houses scattered through the district, reminders of the days when it was even leafier and even more villagey than it is today.

THE TOUR

The best place to begin is **Plaça Sarrià**, the district's focal point. The main building on the square is the **parish church of Sant Vicenç** - the square was once its graveyard. It is a testimony to Sarrià's medieval agricultural and merchant wealth that the 14th-century church boasted an altarpiece by Jaume Huguet (*see p. 124*). That work (depicting St Vincent) is now part of the MNAC collection.

Plaça Sarrià is also home to one of Sarrià's two **Foix pastry shops** (No. 9-10). J.V. Foix (1893-1987), son of the store's founders, had absolutely no intention of going into the family business. His mind was set on higher things, and he went on to become one of the greatest Catalan poets of the 20th century, instrumental in keeping the Catalan language alive during the Franco years. The Plaça Sarrià shop sells delicious homemade ice cream, and has a bronze bust of the poet. (The other shop, the poet's birthplace, is at Carrer Major de Sarrià 57.)

Beside the church, on its left as you stand facing it, is the pretty **Placeta del Roser**, with benches and

Placeta del Roser, a quiet nook beside the church on Sarrià's main square.

a tinkling fountain. Cut through the little square to the elegant **Town Hall** in Plaça de la Vila, where a sculpture of Pomona, goddess of the harvest, stands outside to greet all comers - and again, to remind them of Sarrià's agricultural roots. From here go straight ahead into Carrer dels Paletes, looking up at the right-hand corner to see a miniature niche containing an effigy of St Anthony of Padua, patron saint of artisans, and in this case of bricklayers (*paletes*). The street takes you onto Major de Sarrià, the neighborhood's main thoroughfare, pedestrianized at this section. Turn right and then shortly left into Carrer

Vivid frontages on Plaça Sant Vicenç, dominated by a statue of Sarrià's patron saint.

has even been suggested that the doors are by the hand of none other than Gaudí.

Return to Cornet i Mas now, and continue down it until you reach **Plaça Sant Vicenç**, an attractive leafy square ringed by a jumble of old Sarrià houses, each one different. A statue of the district's patron, St Vincent, stands in the center, beside the millstone with which he was tossed into the Mediterranean after a brutal martyrdom in Valencia in 302. The millstone failed to sink him. His saintly body was washed ashore, and devotees buried it with full honor. For a cup of coffee to end your tour, look no further than **Can Pau**, where you'll be in good literary company. The place was once a favorite haunt of Gabriél García Márquez and Mario Vargas Llosa, who lived in Sarrià in the late 1960s and early 1970s.

Canet. Here you will see a uniform row of twelve small, two-story **artisans' cottages**, formerly workers' housing for a nearby factory, Can Canet, for which the street is named. Tiny dwellings at Nos. 15, 21, and 23 are examples of Sarrià's original village houses. Take a right at the first corner now, into Carrer Cornet i Mas, walking down it for two blocks until you reach Carrer Jaume Piquet. Duck down it to the left until you reach No. 30, a perfect, miniature **Modernist house**, thought to be the work of Domènech i Montaner (*see p. 91*). It

OTHER SIGHTS IN THE AREA

COL.LEGI DE LES TERESIANES

Carrer Ganduxer 85. For visits consult the Ruta del Modernisme, Casa Amatller, Passeig de Gràcia 41. Tel: 93/488-0139.

This building, still a functioning school, was built in 1889 for the Reverend Mothers of the Order of Santa Teresa, an order founded by a priest-friend of Gaudí. Gaudí was given little room to maneuver when he took over the project. The budget was scanty, timing was tight, and the building was already half complete. Looking at it, the contrast between Gaudí's top floor and the already extant bottom two floors is very marked. Gaudí's contribution crowns the building like a party hat, a zig-zag frill of slender peaks, picked out in crimson majolica, and with a tall pinnacle at each corner. The entrance porch is also Gaudí's work. Inside the building, the most striking and famous feature is the corridor on the second floor, where two rows of a dozen parabolic arches run the width of the building, each arch unique because, as Gaudí explained, nothing in nature is ever identical. The overall concept of the building owes much to Moorish or Mudéjar architecture. Austere on the outside, it is filled with light within, with inner courtyards full of plants.

Tapering crenellated brickwork on Gaudí's Col.legi de les Teresianes.

TORRE BELLESGUARD
Carrer Bellesguard 16-20. For visits consult the Ruta del Modernisme,
Casa Amatller, Passeig de Gràcia 41. Tel: 93/488-0139.

It took Gaudí almost a decade (1900-1909) to built this neo-medieval private residence. *Bell esguard* means 'beautiful view'. The house was constructed on high ground over the ruins of the summer palace of the last of Catalonia's sovereign counts, Martí I l'Humà (Martin the Humane, d. 1410) - and was clearly constructed with an image of the former palace in mind. Almost everything about Bellesguard is medieval in atmosphere. The front gate - a visitor's first encounter with the place - is composed of razor-sharp, barbed harpoons. It is almost a portcullis. The slender belfry, the gargoyles and the crenellated battlements are all inspired by Gothic models, often more ecclesiastical than secular. The house is built of rough slate from the Collserola Hills behind the site; doubtless the very same material from which King Martí's palace was constructed. As we have come to expect from Gaudí creations, there is nationalist and religious symbolism everywhere. The red and gold bars of the

Catalan banner spiral up the tower in colored ceramic. Over the front door is the inscription *'sens pecat fou concebuda'* (without sin was she conceived) referring to the Immaculate Conception. On either side of the front door are benches with *trencadís* mosaics of fish bearing the colors of the Catalan flag as well as a crown of Aragon, in reference to Catalonia's medieval maritime empire, when it was said that 'not even a fish dared swim the Mediterranean without the

Bellesguard, a Gaudí-designed private residence, towers above the trees at the city's edge.

Gaudí's ravening wrought-iron dragon on the gateway of Finca Güell.

Catalan colors'. Because Bellesguard is a private residence, the interior is rarely on public view, though the Càtedra Gaudí (*see below*) has photographs. For lunch overlooking Bellesguard, the Cafè Blau (*at Carrer de Roure 50*) is a sweet little restaurant, while a few blocks behind Bellesguard, La Balsa (*at Carrer Infanta Isabel 4, Tel: 93/211-8341, open for lunch Tue-Sat 2pm-3.30pm and for dinner Mon-Sat 9pm-1am*) is one of the top dining establishments in upper Barcelona.

FINCA GÜELL - CÀTEDRA GAUDÍ
Av. Pedralbes 7. Open weekdays 9am-2pm.

This little gatehouse sports one of the most famous Gaudí motifs in the world: the savage wrought-iron dragon, made by the master's own hand. The dragon itself is in chains, with claws outstretched. Originally there was a mechanism by which it would extend its limbs and open the gate. Its eyes were once inlaid with red glass. The park beyond belonged to the Güell family (*see p. 104*), hence the ornamental letter G on the gate-strut. The gatehouse is now home to the Càtedra Gaudí, a Gaudí library and study center open to the public. The former gardens still exist to a degree, though much was lost when the final extension of the Diagonal was constructed in 1924.

PALAU REIAL DE PEDRALBES
(ROYAL PALACE OF PEDRALBES)
Av. Diagonal 686. Open 10am-3pm every day.

In 1910 Eusebi Güell (*see p. 104*) was created Count Güell. He chose the motto 'Shepherd today, gentleman tomorrow' for his coat of arms - certainly an apposite slogan for a man whose father had been the son of a poor fisherman, and whose fortune had come from the sweat of his own brow. The Palau Reial de Pedralbes stands on the site of an 18th-century house, inherited by Count Güell from his father, where the family would retreat for tranquil country holidays in what was then an area of farms and forests. Eusebi Güell died in 1918. The following year the house and its parkland were given to the Spanish royal family, who had the old building demolished, replacing it with the palace that stands here today. Members of the royal family used it as their residence during the 1929 International Exhibition. During the Second Spanish Republic (1931-1936) the palace became the property of the municipality and was turned into a decorative arts museum, which is its function still. It houses both the Museu de les Arts Decoratives and the Museu de la Ceràmica. The collections include furniture and ornaments from the 15th through 20th centuries, and ceramics from all over Spain, from the 12th century to the present.

Gràcia, one of the few places on the planet that still believes in a Red Revolution.

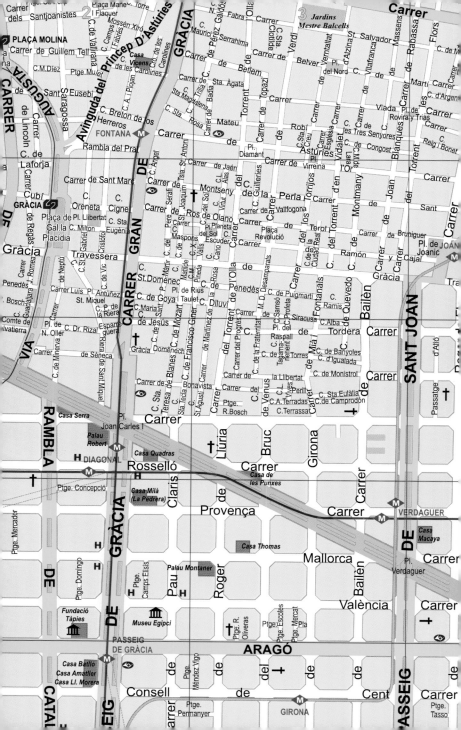

GRÀCIA

Gràcia is more an idea - or an ideal - than a reality. What you see is a Barcelona district like any other. What you might not realize is that in fact you have stumbled into a hotbed of anarchism and dissent, a fermentation tank of protest and rebellion that has twice declared itself independent - in 1821 and 1850 - and which eventually joined the municipality of Barcelona only under duress. Street-names like Llibertat, Fraternitat and Progrès give a clear idea of the ideological history of this fierce little nucleus of trades-union sentiment. Gràcia was the site of Barcelona's first manufacturing collective; its working-class credentials are impeccable.

But Gràcia can be charming as well as confrontational, and it is probably as famous for its architecture as it is for its politics. It is home to Gaudí's Casa Vicens, as well as to a number of creations by Francesc Berenguer, Gaudí's protégé

Ironwork and stained-glass detail of a window by Francesc Berenguer, from one of the handful of Modernist buildings that line Gràcia's main thoroughfare.

and assistant, who built a succession of apartment buildings for aspiring members of the petit bourgeoisie, who couldn't afford the Eixample, but who didn't want to go too far from the center. The best of these are given below.

NB: Suggestions for where to dine in Gràcia can be found on p. 247.

NB: Suggestions for where to dine in Gràcia can be found on p. 247.

CASA VICENS
Carrer de les Carolines 24-26.
For visits, consult the Ruta del Modernisme, Casa Amatller, Passeig de Gràcia 41. Tel: 93/488-0139.

This private residence was the young Antoni Gaudí's first important commission. Work began in 1883 and and was completed two years later. The straight lines and angles of the façade - not a parabolic arch in sight - clearly mark this out as an early work. Gaudí is still basing his designs on traditional architectural canons, embellishing them with extravagant and original touches, but as yet not daring to depart from them altogether. The early Art Nouveau movement was eclectic in its borrowings from other artistic traditions. Casa Vicens makes marked use of Orientalist themes and Mudéjar motifs. Manuel Vicens, the man who commissioned this building, is thought to have been a ceramics manufacturer, which explains the use of the green and white majolica that gives the exterior - Barcelona's first polychrome façade - its striking appearance, and effectively turns the house into a gigantic billboard for its owner's wares. The palmetto leaves decorating the gate and surrounding railings are believed to be the work of Gaudí's assistant Francesc Berenguer.

Wrought-iron palmetto leaves on the Casa Vicens railings. The house was designed by Gaudí, and the railings are thought to be the work of his assistant, Berenguer.

Berenguer - Carrer Gran de Gràcia

Berenguer (*see also p. 95*) was known as a master of the semi-detached or terraced apartment building: most of his known works line Carrer Gran de Gràcia. Unfortunately the road is narrow and noisy, which makes viewing the buildings a less than tranquil experience. The Modernist building at No. 81, over the excellent Galician seafood restaurant Botafumeiro, is one of his creations, while at Carrer Ros de Olano 9 (just above Botafumeiro to the right) is his Centre Moral Instructiu de Gràcia, a neo-Mudéjar façade of exposed brick, created in 1904 for the YMCA-like institution of which he was a president. Walking down Gran de Gràcia from here, Nos. 77, 61, 23, 15, and 7 - visible from the left side of the street heading down - are all amply endowed with Modernist techniques. Many of these buildings are by Berenguer, though all are signed by different architects, as Berenguer never took his architect's diploma and was thus never officially licensed. No. 77 is officially credited to Berenguer, as is No. 15, over the Colmena pastry shop, with its twin stained glass galleries.

A Tour of Gràcia

Plaça Rius i Taulet, also known Plaça del Rellotge (Square of the Clock) is the historic and administrative center of Gràcia, named for Barcelona mayor Francesc de Paula Rius i Taulet (1853-1889), the man who brought the 1888 World Exhibition to Barcelona (and died a year later). At the lower end of the square, the cobalt blue façade of the **Casa de la Vila** (Town Hall), punctuated only by its jet-black, wrought-iron sculptures, is one of the many Gràcia works by architect Francesc Berenguer, Gaudí's 'right hand' (*see above*). The square is dominated by its 33-meter **clock tower**, built by Antoni Rovira i Trias in 1864, in a witty, stylized version of Catalan Gothic. It was badly damaged in 1870 during a local uprising over military conscription. Perennial symbol of Gràcia's belligerently independent spirit, the clock tower was bombarded by federal troops when the town mothers burned the files in order to keep their sons out of the draft that was sending Catalan youth off to fight colonial wars in North Africa and Cuba. A full-scale assault by Spanish troops ensued, with mortalities,

Gràcia's clock tower in Plaça Rius i Taulet, the heart of the district.

executions, and bloody reprisals on both sides before law and order was re-established. Today, mercifully, everything has gone quiet, and sidewalk cafés prosper under the leafy, yellow-flowering acacias. The clock tower itself, which can be visited on Saturdays (*Tel: 93/285-0357 to reserve a slot*), has coats of arms on four sides representing the Spanish crown, Barcelona, Gràcia and Catalonia, while above a dozen medallions representing the months of the year encircle it. The architect, Rovira i Trias, is interesting. In fact his story has a tale to tell about

Barcelona's eternal struggle with Madrid. In a square named after him, to the north-east of here, his statue sits on a bench with, at its feet, a map of Barcelona showing what the city might have looked like if Madrid had not rejected his designs for the Eixample (designs which Barcelona had approved) and foisted Ildefons Cerdà on the city instead. Whether Rovira i Trias's Eixample would have been better we shall never know. But we can admire his town-planning skills in Gràcia, where the short streets always lead sooner or later into a leafy square.

Leaving Plaça Rius i Taulet on Carrer Diluvi to the left facing the cerulean façade of the Town Hall, the 123-year-old **Farmàcia Gras** occupies a low, two story, original Gràcia town house dating from the middle of the 19th century. The colorful advertisement for its own trademarked *callicida* (corn remover) has been there for over 80 years - not counting, the pharmacist will point out, when it was ordered redone in 1939 to replace the Catalan version with a Spanish translation, after Franco's *Movimiento Nacional* had taken charge and set about homogenizing the Iberian peninsula's bothersome separate cultures and languages. Catalans of the 1940s were hectored by signs in official places reading '¡*No ladres! Habla el idioma del Imperio Español*' (Don't bark. Speak the language of the Spanish Empire) or with admonitions such as '¡*Habla en Cristiano!*' (Speak Christian) from impatient Spanish officials, patriots, and nationalists.

Carrer Diluvi leads past a tiny flower-covered original Gràcia house, now home of Sucumbios, a shop selling wares and curios from North Africa, past a solid two-story town house with six urns and the date 1899 topping the façade (No. 3). One block farther, a jag right across Torrent de l'Olla takes you into Carrer de Siracusa, past Carrers Progrès and Fraternitat. The brick smokestack of the Puigmartí textile factory, Gràcia's **Vapor Nou** (new factory), founded in 1839, is straight ahead in Plaça del Poble Romaní, a square dedicated to the gypsy culture and language long established in this corner of Gràcia. A turn down Carrer Samsó drops into shady little Plaça Raspall, traditional hub for Gràcia's gypsy community, a cosmopolitan and urbanized society known to include bankers, car salesmen, and the full range of bourgeois pursuits. Bar Resolis, at the corner of Carrer Tordera, is the

Typical Gràcia apartment buildings, tall and slender, once the home of the minor bourgeoisie.

traditional hangout for the gypsy families of the neighborhood. A right on Carrer Tordera leads past a diminutive, overgrown original house at No. 16 on the left, with a leafy wisteria arbor covering an interior yard. At the corner of Carrer Fraternitat, with the tiny Sant Roch shrine over the intersection, a look left reveals a row of two-story **workers' quarters**, built by the Puigmartí factory.

Two blocks up Carrer Fraternitat past the corner herbalist, Herbodiética de las Maravillas, the roofing protecting the greengrocers around the Mercat de la Revolució, founded in 1892, now officially called the Abaceria Central, becomes visible. At the far right

corner, **Cafeteria Trébol**, named for the cloverleaf, is the place for a coffee, wedged between the cooling and fragrant fish display and the lingering melodies of Billy McHenry and Ben Waltzer, Manhattan jazz greats who spent a few years here during Barcelona's roaring (nineteen) nineties.

A cut back across the market takes you up into **Plaça de la Revolució de Setembre de 1868**, named for the revolution leading to the abdication of Isabella II and the short-lived constitutional monarchy that placed Amadeus, of the anticlerical House of Savoy, on the Spanish throne from 1870 to 1873. The tiles in the pavement refer to the *Xarranca de la Festa Major*, a traditional game and dance, while running up the left side of the square are the letters R-E-V-O-L-U-C-I-O, an ever-popular Gràcia concept.

Continue straight ahead up Carrer Verdi past the Egyptian restaurant at No.2. At No. 7 on the left is the curious pre-Modernist **Casa de los Animales**, with birds, beetles, butterflies, turtles, frogs and fish stenciled up the façade. The houses at Nos. 29 and and 39 both have striking façades with neo-Gothic details. A right on Carrer de l'Or, one of many Gràcia streets named for precious metals (in this case gold) as the result of a 19th-century jeweler-mayor, leads over to **Plaça de la Virreina**.

This square was laid out in 1878 on land that had belonged to La Virreina, Maria Francisca Fivaller, child widow of the Spanish Viceroy in Peru. The Viceroy had married her after his nephew jilted her at the altar (*see pp. 39-40*). When he himself died only three years later, La Virreina spent the rest of her life honoring his memory and charitably administering his fortune. The **statue of Ruth** - Old

Ruth with her sheaf of wheat, placed here to commemorate La Virreina, who remained faithful to the memory of her husband.

Testament paradigm of wifely faithfulness - in the center of the square was erected in her memory. The parish church of Sant Joan de Gràcia at the top of the square is of little architectural interest, having been used as a barracks by Napoleonic troops and sacked and destroyed repeatedly, including during the *Setmana Tràgica* of 1909 (*see p. 23*), after which Berenguer attempted to put it back together again. Just across the street at Carrer de l'Or 44, the raspberry-colored **Casa Rubinat** is another Berenguer building (1909), an Art Nouveau apartment house, and one of his finest achievements: an exercise in verticality, with pinnacles at the stress lines over layers of wrought-iron balconies. The large town house on the right side of Carrer Torrijos is typical of the mansions constructed by textile barons and *indianos* (Catalans who had become wealthy in the New World) in the late 19th and early 20th centuries.

Through the shady tunnel of Carrer d'Astúries, **Plaça del Diamant** is just a minute's walk away. This unfortunately restored square, one of Barcelona's always controversial *places dures* ('hard squares') is, nevertheless, of great sentimental importance in Barcelona as the site of the opening and closing scenes in Mercè Rodoreda's acclaimed 1962 novel *Plaça del Diamant* (translated into English by the late American poet David Rosenthal as *The Time of the Doves*). A bronze sculpture in the square portrays **Colometa**, the novel's protagonist, a young woman whose youth and first love are lost to the Spanish Civil War.

PART IV

FOOD & DRINK

DINING IN BARCELONA

WHAT'S ON OFFER

Barcelona's culinary offering is vast but need not be overwhelming. There are four basic choices: Catalan gourmet, Mediterranean rice and seafood, Basque cuisine, and itinerant wine-tasting and tapa grazing.

Each formula has its advantages. Barcelona has a growing fleet of world-famous chefs, all twinkling in the reflected light of media darling and high priest of experimental cuisine Ferran Adrià ('the foam guy', famed for his foam of smoke and, more recently, rabbit-ear chips) from northern Catalonia's El Bullí. Inspired by his lead, other Catalan *maîtres de cuisine* are producing ever more superlative dining. Santi Santamaria has as many Michelin stars as Adrià; Fermí Puig of Drolma (in the Hotel Majestic, see p. 266) is closing fast; Carles Gaig

Sitting out with a beer and the daily news in the Barri Gòtic's Plaça del Pi.

(*see p. 244*) is perennially perfect; Isidre Gironés of Ca l'Isidre (*see p. 245*) is a quiet master, but everyone has always known that he's peerless. All of these options share one unfortunate drawback (some more, some less): dining is expensive, and a little too ceremonious. Another, more relaxed, tier of Catalan gourmet dining would include Tram-Tram, Vivanda, Casa Leopoldo, Comerç 24, Folquer, Casa Calvet, and L'Olivé. All feature in the listings below.

The seafood and rice emporiums, all of them on the waterfront, are led by Can Majó and include Els Pescadors and, on the budget end, Can Manel la Puda. All are uproarious, popular and fun, and food is ample and excellent. The Basque contingent, always a force to be taken into account when it comes to food, offers fine dining, though the cuisine can be a little heavy for the Mediterranean, especially in summer. For a listing of the leading choices, see Pintxo Bars below.

Finally, the wandering picnic concept offers some of the best cuisine in town in small portions that can be walked off between servings, infinite variety, a changing cast of characters, and good value. Six of the city's finest tapas bars are given on pp. 231-2.

CATALAN CUISINE

The restoration of democracy after 1975 brought a late 20th-century cultural renaissance to Catalonia. Catalans are celebrating a reunion with their traditional identity, and this confidence has embraced cuisine as well. For centuries Barcelona was under the thumb of Madrid, and true Catalan cooking was a rural phenomenon. Now all that has changed. Barcelona has rediscovered its gastronomic heritage and has brought it back to town. Inventive chefs are giving traditional dishes a metropolitan finesse that is propelling the city toward the forefront of world cuisine.

Catalonia is also fortunate in its diet. Olive oil, seafood, vegetables, garlic and red wine have become an international fashion and health statement, and Catalonia is well-placed to make the most of this. The combination of the sea, a fertile hinterland, and the lush Pyrenees to provide dairy produce, also means that the offering is more varied than in other parts of the Iberian peninsula. That variety comes from Catalonia's patchwork heritage as well, producing a culinary style has been influenced by Moorish cooking from the Balearic Islands (seen in subtle combinations of sweet and savory, as exampled by *espinacas a la catalana*, spinach cooked with raisins and pine nuts), by Italy, which in medieval times was closer by water than Madrid was by land, and by nearby France (the Catalans love a good sauce). Indeed, Catalonia's sauces say much about the idiosyncrasies and sensibilities of the Catalan palate. *Allioli*, for example, is an emulsion of garlic and olive oil, beaten to a mayonnaise-like consistency and used to accompany anything from fish and lamb to potatoes and chick-peas. *Romesco* (olive oil, garlic, almonds and red pepper) is another Catalan favorite used for fish. A similar concoction called *salbitxada* is used on the long-stemmed spring onions, *calçots*,

Dining outside in early spring with a view of the blue Mediterranean.

charcoal-grilled and a staple of late winter feasts in the south-western reaches of the province.

Traditional Catalan favorites include *escudella* (a thick vegetable and sausage stew with pasta and, often, chicken added), *esqueixada* (raw cod with peppers and onions), and *escalivada*, peppers cooked over wood coals. Look for combinations such *cigrons amb chipirones* (chick-peas with baby octopi) or *ànec amb peres* (duck with pears). Bread is drizzled with olive oil and tomato squeezings to make *pa amb tomàquet*. Using fish, vegetables, rabbit, duck, lamb, game, and natural ingredients from the Pyrenees or the Mediterranean, local chefs frequently favor the *mar i muntanya*, ('sea and mountain'), combinations of seafood with inland products - meatballs and cuttlefish, for example. For more on the subject, Colman Andrews's *Catalan Cuisine-Europe's Last Culinary Secret* brilliantly tells the story of Catalan cooking and much more about the geography, history and culture behind it.

TAPAS & PINTXOS

Walking, sipping, grazing and conversing is arguably Spain's greatest contribution to world culture (not forgetting the guitar, flamenco or Tomás Luís de Victoria). Even Barcelona, not traditionally known for its tapas (they are a Castilian phenomenon), has developed into a leading tapa environment over the last twenty years. Following (literally) your nose through the Boqueria, the Barri Gòtic, the Eixample or La Ribera will reveal an ever-evolving variety of taverns and bars where wines, beers and cava accompany morsels of cheese, sausage, fish, peppers, wild mushrooms, or the ubiquitous Spanish potato omelet. Whether for whetting an appetite or for an ambulatory dinner, prowling the streets of El Born or Barceloneta in search of the perfect prawn or the ideal green pepper is an experience not to be missed.

In general, a tapas bar serves small portions (*raciones*) of morsels ranging from olives to baby octopi, either on view at the counter for you to choose from, or listed on a menu. Many bars have everything at the counter under glass, so

Around midday the cafés and bars of La Ribera and Passeig del Born begin to set out tables. Lunch is not usually served until a good hour later.

you can view and choose. One universal rule: if you're serving yourself at the bar, you are expected to stay at the bar. Table service is slightly more expensive. If you're serving yourself at the bar and a table opens up and you feel the need to sit down, by all means do. Usually a gesture to the barman will suffice for permission, and they may charge you table rates.

WHERE TO GO

The area around Santa Maria del Mar, including the Passeig del Born and Plaça de les Olles are paradigmatic *tapeo* (tapa-tasting) theaters. Gràcia is good at night. The Eixample, particularly along Rambla de Catalunya and over to Carrer Muntaner, is rich in wine-tasting and tapas emporiums. Passeig de Gràcia and Rambla tapas offerings should be regarded warily; microwaved vacuum-packed fare is the rule. The Port Olímpic is over-populous and mediocre.

TOP TAPAS BARS

NB: Map references refer you to the section of the street where the bar is located. Where relevant, for bars in the Eixample, a cross-street is also given.

LA BODEGUETA (Eixample)
Go down steps in winter to a traditional narrow tapas bar with tiny individual tables at the end and a bar at the front. In summer sit out in the central zone of the Rambla de Catalunya and feed on acorn-fed ham (*jamón ibérico bellota*) and fresh marinated anchovies (*boquerones*). *Rambla de Catalunya 100 - corner of Provença. Open 7am-2am every day. Tel: 93/215-4894.* Map p. 284, D2

CAL PEP (La Ribera)
Genial Pep Manubens personally serves excellent fresh tapas, cooked across the counter and served piping-hot in a consistently ecstatic environment. Trust Pep on seating; waiting is worth it. Ask for wine while you wait for a place at the counter. If he's offering chick-peas (*cigrons*) with spinach, served with or without blood sausage, don't miss it. *Plaça de les Olles 8. Tel: 93/319-6183. Open Tues-Sat 1pm-4pm & 8pm-midnight; Mon 8pm-midnight.* Map p. 287, D4

CERVESERIA LA CATALANA (Eixample)
This wide entryway is always booming, filled with color and

hilarity, a crossroads for night owls gathering strength for the early hours ahead. The *chipirones* (baby octopi) and the *pimientos de piquillo* (sweet red peppers stuffed with cod) are house favorites, along with the miniature *solomillo* (filet mignon).
Mallorca 236. Tel: 93/216-0368. Open daily 8am-1.30 am. Map p. 284, D2

CIUDAD CONDAL (Eixample)
Always nicely humming just a block uphill from Plaça Catalunya, this is an excellent place to begin or end an evening, or both. *Escamarlans* (jumbo shrimp) are standouts here, along with sublime steak canapés.
Rambla de Catalunya 18. Tel: 93/318-1997. Open daily 7.30am-1.30am. Map p. 286, A3

LA ESTRELLA DE PLATA (La Ribera)
The gourmet tapas here are original and inventive with combinations of ingredients such as quail eggs and sea snails sharing canapé space with truffles and foie gras. The ambience is less uproarious than most tapas emporiums, but the food is excellent.
Pla del Palau 9. Tel: 93/319-6007. Open Mon-Sat 10am-2am. Map p. 287, D4

SANTA MARIA (La Ribera)
From frogs' legs to coca-cola pudding with pop rocks, this is an exciting post-modern dining experience with a clearly discernible flair in both cuisine and decor.
Comerç 17. Tel: 93/315-1227. Open Tues-Sat 1.30pm-3.30pm & 8.30pm-12.30. Map p. 287, C4

TOP PINTXO BARS

Pintxos are a strain of tapa, slightly smaller directly accessible on top of the bar, mounted on a piece of bread, and skewered with a toothpick. Their name comes from the Spanish verb *pinchar*, meaning 'to prick, stick, poke, impale'. The 'tx' spelling is a Basque derivation, for pintxos are most at home in the Basque country, though in Barcelona they have gained an enthusiastic following. Most pintxo bars operate the following policy: arrive at the bar, order whatever you want to drink, and ask for a plate. When you finish each pintxo, put the used toothpick on the plate, and let them mount up there as a tally of how many you have had.

NB: Map references refer you to the section of the street where the bar is located. Where relevant, for bars in the Eixample, a cross-street is also given.

The Basque bar Sagardi in La Ribera. The huge barrel itself is false, but the cider spurts from it in a true stream. Freshly-made pintxos are laid out on the counter.

SAGARDI (La Ribera)

Part of a chain - but a very good one. This attractive cider house is about as near to the real thing as you will get in Barcelona. Cider spurts from a huge (faux) barrel. The selection of fresh pintxos is continuously replenished, and the restaurant area at the back does good beef.
Carrer Argenteria 62. Tel: 93/319-9993. Open daily 1.30pm-3.30 pm; 8pm-midnight. Map p. 287, D4

EUSKAL ETXEA (La Ribera)

The tapas and canapés are distinguished at this Basque restaurant and cultural center at the Santa Maria del Mar end of Carrer Montcada. *Placeta de Montcada 13 - where Carrer Montcada joins Pg. del Born. Tel: 93/310-2185. Open Mon-Sat 9am-1am; Sun 9am-4.30pm.* Map p. 287, D4

TAKTIKA BERRI (Eixample)

This revered family operation serves superbly hot and fresh tapas straight from the kitchen along with *txakolí*, the young Basque white wine, or a good Rioja crianza (aged three years). Reserving a table can take weeks, but the bar is always open and the pintxos of fish, *chistorra* (spicy Basque

sausage), or *morcilla* (blood sausage) are the best in Barcelona.
Carrer València 169. Tel: 93/453-4759. Open Mon-Fri 1pm-4pm; 7pm-11pm; Sat 1pm-4pm. Map p. 284, D1

QUIMET-QUIMET (Poble Sec)
This extraordinary canapé artist is out on the far side of Avinguda Paral.lel, and it may well be crammed with devout foodies. Not strictly a pintxo bar, but if you can squeeze in and let Quimet build you a creation with *torta del casar* (a creamy sheep cheese from Extremadura), or anything else he might dream up, you'll quickly understand why this tavern is so respected by Barcelona's culinary cognoscenti.
Carrer del Poeta Cabanyés 25. Tel: 93/442-3142. Open Tue-Sat 1pm-4pm; 7pm-10pm. Map p. 121, C3

WINE & CAVA BARS

ATENEU (Barri Gòtic)
A quiet restaurant and wine bar across from the Town Hall on the site of the former Roman baths. The wine selection is encyclopedic, and the food is carefully purchased and prepared.
Plaça de Sant Miquel 2 bis . Tel: 93/302-1198. Open Tues-Sat 1.30pm-3.30pm & 8.30pm-12.30am. Map p. 286, D3

CATA 1.81 (Eixample)
Cutting edge design and cuisine are available at this chic spot - and they know their wines as well. Smallish portions feature precious ingredients from foie gras to truffles, while the new Priorats, Jumillas, Riojas, and Ribera del Dueros are well represented on the wine list.

València 181. Tel: 93/323-6818. Open Mon-Sat 6pm-1am. Map p. 284, D1

REINA (Eixample)
Wine and pâté are co-stars at this corner tavern ideal for small tables for two in a cozy ambience. Always buzzing yet quiet enough for a tranquil tête-à-tête.
València 202. Tel: 93/452-6450. Open Mon-Sat 10am-midnight. Map p. 284, D1

LA TINAJA (La Ribera)
A rustic cavern, La Tinaja offers an interesting selection of wines from all Spain's wine-growing regions, plus cheeses, and acorn-fed Iberian ham (*jamón bellota*). La Tinajilla next door is equally recommendable.

Carrer L'Esparteria 9. Tel: 93/310-2250. Open Tues-Sat noon-4pm & 6.30pm-midnight. Map p. 287, D4

La Vinya del Senyor wine bar.

VA DE VI (La Ribera)

Va de Vi - 'it's all about wine' - which this place definitely is, as well as some delicious hams and cheeses on the side. This is a rustic and ancient setting, in what was once the stables of a medieval palace.

Banys Vells 16 . Tel: 93/319-2900. Open daily 6pm-2am. Map p. 287, D4

LA VINATERIA DEL CALL (Barri Gòtic)

In the heart of the medieval Jewish Quarter, this dark grotto with flickering candles serves carefully selected wines and tapas.

Sant Domènec del Call 9. Tel: 93/302-6092. Open Mon-Sat 6pm-1am (from 8pm in summer). Map p. 286, C3

LA VINYA DEL SENYOR (La Ribera)

'The Lord's Vineyard', directly across from the church of Santa Maria del Mar, has an international wine-by-the-glass list and delicious, albeit miniature, tapas.

Pl. Sta. Maria 5. Tel: 93/310-3379. Open Tues-Sun noon-1am. Map p. 287, D4

EL XAMPANYET (La Ribera)

One of Barcelona's prettiest *xampanyerias* and usually full of revelers. Flutes of cava and slabs of *pa amb tomàquet* are served on marble-top tables. If the cava is too sweet for your liking, go for draft beer or cider.

Montcada 22. Tel: 93/319-7003. Open Tues-Sat noon-4pm & 6.30pm-midnight; Sun noon-4pm. Map p. 287, D4

XAMPÚ XAMPANY (Eixample)

It's best to arrive early at this popular den, before the crowds descend. When relatively peaceful it makes a good place to do a comparative tasting of different cavas.

Gran Via 702 - corner of Bailèn. Tel: 93/265-0483. Open daily 6pm-2am. Map p. 287, A4

CATALAN WINE

The Penedès region south-west of Barcelona, with its *méthode champenoise* sparkling wine (cava), has held Catalonia's viticultural center stage ever since Josep Raventós, owner of Codorníu, opened the first bottle in 1872. Though the phylloxera louse decimated Catalan winemaking not many years later, the industry refused to die altogether. Presently, there are ten Denominations of Origin in Catalonia: Empordà-Costa Brava, Pla de Bages and Alella (north of Barcelona); Costers del Segre to the west; the Penedès; and Conca de Barberà, Tarragona, Priorat, Terra Alta and Montsant to the south.

Traditional grape types such as Parellada, Garnatxa, Ull de Llebre (Tempranillo), Xarel.lo, Macabeu and Cariñena have been joined by noble varieties including Chardonnay, Merlot, Cabernet Sauvignon and Pinot Noir. Exciting new wines are emerging from Priorat, Costers del Segre, and Empordà-Costa Brava, while the cava industry grows daily. Most Catalan cava is still produced in the Penedès, with giants Codorníu and Freixenet joined by smaller, often better, names such as Agustí Torelló (especially his amfora-shaped Kripta Brut Nature), Gran Caus, Albet i Noya, Lacrima Baccus, Gramona III Lustros and Juvé & Camps. Distinguished non-cava wines from the Penedès begin with the Can Rafols dels Caus winery, with their aromatic reds, whites and rosés. Albet i Noya, Cellers Puig Roca's Avgvstvs wines, the Colet reds, and the Miguel Torres Gran Viña Sol Chardonnay, Coronas Tempranillo, and Gran Coronas Cabernet Sauvignon are other top selections.

The ancient Priorat is now one of Spain's most exciting wine stories. From the 5th to the 11th centuries, when the region's booming Roman wine industry had been abandoned by non wine-drinking Visigoths and, later, Moors, it was only the Bacchic monks of the Catalan uplands who managed to keep any vines alive at all. Their legacy lives on, with winemakers such as Álvaro Palacios vinifying powerful, fruity reds - Finca Dofí, L'Ermita, and Les Terrasses - using old Garnatxa, Cabernet Sauvignon and Cariñena vines in the shaly licorella soil once cultivated by the Carthusian monks of Scala Dei. Other leading Priorats include Clos Mogador, an intense, complex, inky red wine fragrant with dark fruits; Clos de L'Obac, a simpler, finer brew; or the powerful, full-bodied Morlanda Crianza.

Other leading wineries in Catalonia include the Costers del Segre Raimat wines (Tempranillo, Pinot Noir and Cabernet Sauvignon) and the Castell del Remei reds and whites. In the Empordà-Costa Brava DO, Celler Oliver Conti is an ascendant star, with the Oliver Conti Negre 1998 (Cabernet Sauvignon, Merlot, Cabernet Franc) rated one of the top red wines in Catalonia, and the Oliver Conti Blanc 2000 (Gewürtztraminer, Sauvignon Blanc) a regular on wine lists in Barcelona's top gourmet restaurants.

CAFÉS

Barcelona may be business-minded, but this is still a culture where it is important to show that you are a man or woman of leisure. Cafés abound, and serve an important multiple function: safety valve, outdoor living room, meeting place. Combining the Vienna coffee-house ethos (alone but in company) with a native southern European instinct for improvised gregariousness, Barcelona has hundreds of intimate-yet-hyperactive nooks, ideal for lovers seeking anonymity or large groups of friends seeking a boisterous good time.

Spain is also a country that proudly challenges Italian hegemony where coffee is concerned. Of course you can ask for espresso and cappuccino, but it's not the native way of doing things. The main ways to drink your coffee are black (*café solo*, merely *cafè* in Catalan); with milk (*café con leche*, *cafè amb llet*); *cortado* (*tallat* - strong coffee muted by a dash of milk; ask for it '*largo de leche*' if you prefer a milkier version) or *carajillo* (with a shot of brandy). Other popular drinks are hot chocolate, which comes thick and rich, preferably eaten with sugared dough-worms (*churros*). *Horchata* (*orxata*) is sweet tiger-nut milk, available in the summer time. For a soft drink that isn't cola or Fanta, there is Bitter Kas, a vivid red brew with a taste reminiscent of strong Campari.

An old monastic wine-cellar in the Barri Gòtic - Philippus, on Carrer Banys Nous - makes an atmospheric space for a drink, a coffee or a light meal.

Selected Cafés & Bars

ALMIRALL (Raval)
Barcelona was once full of Modernist bars. This is one of the few surviving. Quiet, dimly-lit and evocative, with an atmosphere of clandestine romance. *Carrer de Joaquim Costa 33. Open noon-2am daily. Map p. 286, B2*

EL BORN (La Ribera)
Once a codfish shop (hence the marble salting basins), this is now a haven for coffee or something stronger. *Passeig del Born 26. Open Tues-Sat noon-2am. Map p. 287, D4*

CAFÈ DE L'ÒPERA (Rambla)
Age-worn and charming, with a smoke-stained interior that has welcomed passing Rambla traffic for more than 100 years. Late at night it feels like the place for absinthe. *Rambla 74. Open daily 9.30am-2.15am. Map p. 32*

CAFÉ PARIS (Eixample)
Café Paris is always there when you need it, whether for coffee in the morning or something sedative late at night. Spanish omelet, *patatas bravas* (potatoes and hot sauce) and beer have begun or ended many a lost weekend here. *Carrer Aribau 184 - corner of Paris. Open daily 6am-2 am. Map p. 284, C1*

DULCINEA, LA PALLARESA (Barri Gòtic)
Both preserve the décor of a bygone age (mid 20th century). Both serve excellent hot chocolate. *Carrer Petritxol 2 & 11. Open 9am-1pm & 4pm-9pm Mon-Fri; 9am-1pm & 5pm-9.30pm Sat-Sun. Map p. 286, C3*

ESPAI BARROC (La Ribera)
Baroque-theme café in Carrer Montcada's most beautiful courtyard, that of the 15th-century Palau Dalmases. *Carrer Montcada 20. Open Tues-Sun 8pm-2am. Map p. 287, D4*

Pastry and dairy confections in the display window of Granja La Pallaresa.

RESTAURANTS, DISTRICT BY DISTRICT

The red numbers beside the restaurants below correspond to the numbers on the restaurant locator map on pp. 242-243. To find the exact street location, use the map references given after the restaurant name. Note that two restaurants are beyond the scope of the map, but included here because they are worth the trip.

NB: Unless otherwise stated, restaurants are open 1pm-4pm & 8pm-11pm.

BARRI GÒTIC

1 CAFÈ DE L'ACADÈMIA Map p. 287, D3
Delicious Mediterranean fare in a good-looking *rus in urbe* setting. Officials from both the city and Catalan governments frequent this spot for lunch, when a *menú del día* is on offer, so advance booking is recommended. In summer the dining spills outside into pretty Plaça Sant Just.
Carrer Lledó 1. Tel: 93/315-0026. Closed weekends.

2 AGUT Map p. 287, D3
Simple Catalan fare and great value have made this a Barcelona favorite ever since the place opened in 1924. A family enterprise from the start, the warmth is palpable the minute you step through the door.
Gignàs 16. Tel: 93/315-1709. Closed Mon and July. No dinner Sun.

3 CAN CULLERETES Map p. 286, C2
This traditional dining favorite, founded in 1786, is a family-operated standard. Centuries of happy diners seem to contribute to the atmosphere of the place. The traditional Catalan cuisine ranges from *escudelles* (thick meat, bean, and vegetable stews) in winter to refreshing *esqueixada* (raw salt cod vinaigrette).
Carrer Quintana 5. Tel: 93/317-6485. Closed Sun night and Mon.

4 COMETACINC Map p. 287, D3
In a little-known and up-and-coming area of the old town, this restaurant is a perfect example of how modern design is adapting itself to ancient spaces. Note the lovely floor-to-ceiling wooden shutters. The design theme carries over into the food as well, on a menu that offers new and interesting takes on traditional dishes.

Carrer Cometa 5. Tel: 93/310-1558.
Open 8pm-1am. Closed Tues.

5 Casa Martí/Els Quatre Gats
Map p. 287, B3

First a caveat: Els Quatre Gats is okay for a coffee or the odd lunch, but, in general, the cuisine is far from good and the place doesn't get much local clientèle. Because of its artistic associations, though, it is a landmark, perfect for a beer and a bite - even then you're likely to get bossed around by the staff. Don't let their attitude put you off. Built by Josep Puig i Cadafalch in 1896 for the Martí family, this Modernist house once

served coffee to Picasso, among others. The interior is cluttered with portraits of famous denizens and reproductions of some of their works, including the poster-art scene (by Ramon Casas) of himself (the stout one, cigar-in-pipe) and Pere Romeu (the entrepreneur who set up Els Quatre Gats, grinning toothily) teamed up on a tandem bicycle. Picasso had his first opening here on February 1st, 1900, and Antoni Gaudí hung out with Modernist painters Casas, Rusiñol and Nonell - the artistic resonances should still be palpable. Pere Romeu, sadly, was no businessman. Els Quatre Gats went

Evening scene in Senyor Parellada.

into liquidation in 1903. Today's enterprise is more hard-nosed.
Montsió 3 bis. Tel: 93/302-4140. Open daily 9am-2am. Closed first two wks Aug.

6 LA TAXIDERMISTA Map p. 286, D2
Once a natural-science museum and taxidermy shop, this is the best restaurant in Plaça Reial. The interior preserves the original beams and steel columns. You can choose whether to sit in or out - though outside remains an option even in winter, when the midday sun pours into Plaça Reial.
Plaça Reial 8. Tel: 93/412-4536. Closed Mon.

LA RIBERA

7 COMERÇ 24 Map p. 287, C4
Chef Carles Abellan is an artist for all seasons, combining minimalist design and original cuisine. Traditional Catalan favorites all appear to be on the menu, but they've all been subtly - or not so subtly - streamlined. The *tortilla de patata* (potato omelet) redux is a case in point.
Carrer Comerç 24. Tel: 93/319-2102. Closed Sun.

8 MEY HOFMANN Map p. 287, D4
This upstairs dining room near Santa Maria del Mar is a good place to come for Mediterranean cooking with an international flare. Hofmann is also a cooking school, and the food is classic but with innovative, nouvelle twists. The waiters and waitresses are chefs-in-training themselves - don't hesitate to ask their advice.
Argenteria 74-78. Tel: 93/319-5889. Closed weekends.

9 PASSADIS DEL PEP Map p. 287, D4
A narrow passageway conceals a popular and authentic eatery serving freshly-prepared seafood. Nearly before you're seated, food and drink appears before you. You can either stick with the tapas or move on to a main course. Fish is the best option.
Pla del Palau 2. Tel: 93/310-1021. Closed Sun and last 2 weeks of Aug.

10 SENYOR PARELLADA Map p. 287, D3
Basic Catalan standards served in a graceful space arranged around a central patio. Selections include a wide variety of seafood and meat dishes that vary with markets and seasons. NB: It's best to reserve a ground floor or patio railing table for the best views and ventilation.
Argenteria 37. Tel: 93/268-3157. Open daily 1pm-4pm; 7pm-11pm.

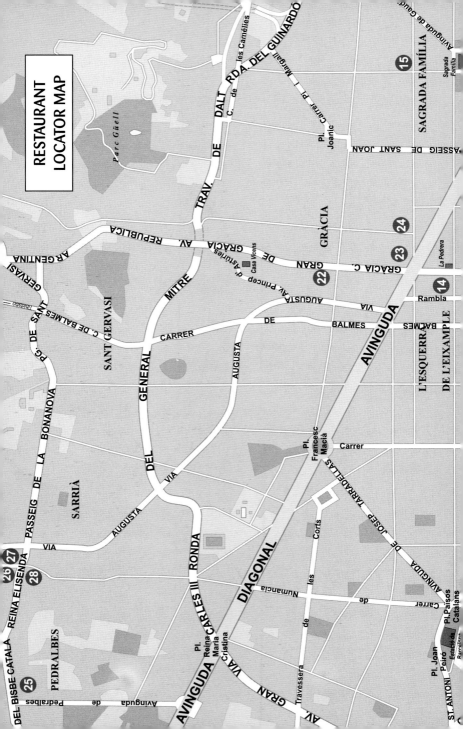

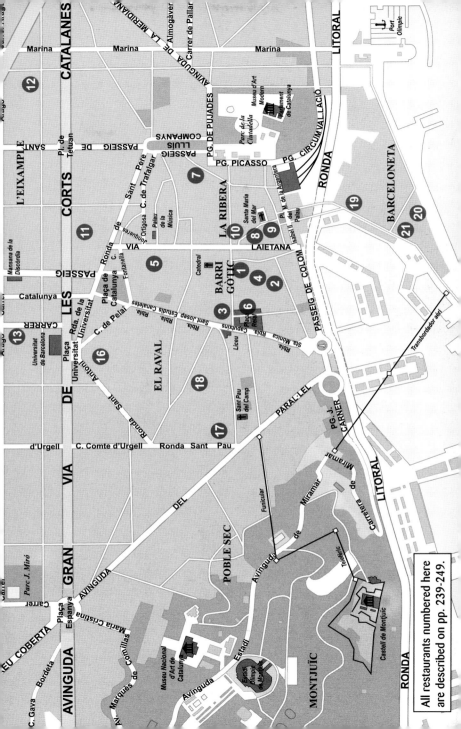

All restaurants numbered here are described on pp. 239–249.

EIXAMPLE

⑪ CASA CALVET Map p. 287, A4
Dining in a Gaudí creation is an experience not to be missed. The dining room is located in what were once the offices of textile manufacturer Andreu Calvet. The decorative details are either original Gaudí or Gaudí-inspired. The menu is light and contemporary, and the presentation echoes the architecture. The wood pigeon and the *lubina* (sea bass) are unbeatable.
Casp 48. Tel: 93/ 412-4012. Closed Sun and last 2 wks of Aug.

CAN GAIG (Beyond the map)
Carles Gaig is one of Barcelona's established, pre-Ferran Adrià master chefs. His restaurant at the northern edge of the Eixample is infallibly excellent, and the place to come for experimental yet traditional preparation of market-fresh produce. Game, meats, and seafood, all sourced locally and in season, are peerless here. Truffle canneloni and woodcock are two wintertime favorites.
Passeig de Maragall 402. Tel: 93/429-

Tranquil scene under the plane trees in Gràcia. At night the area is home to some of Barcelona's liveliest tapas bars.

1017. Closed Mon, Holy Week, and Aug.

⑫ GORRÍA Map p. 285, E4
A second-generation family business, Gorría offers some of the best Basque cooking in Barcelona. Thick stews, hunks of beef, fresh bread. The wine list ranges from traditional selections to the new Rioja brews such as Roda I or Viña Artadi. Try the *alubias de Sangüesa* (white beans stewed with tomato, onions and Iberian ham).
Diputació 421. Tel: 93/245-1164. Closed Sun.

⑬ L'OLIVÉ Map p. 284, E2
This sleek and stylish restaurant is always filled to the brim with savvy diners having a great time, confident that they're in the right spot. Traditional Catalan fare cooked flawlessly using carefully chosen produce is the house trademark. Get a table with a view into the kitchen for the full experience, and try the *llenguado a la catalana* (sole cooked in raisins and pine nuts).
Balmes 47 - corner of Consell de Cent. Tel: 93/452-1990. No dinner Sun.

⑭ EL TRAGALUZ Map p. 284, D2
A sliding roof (*tragaluz* means 'skylight') opens to the heavens in good weather over fixtures and fittings by Javier Mariscal, the designer who gave Barcelona its 1992 Olympic mascot. Light, innovative Mediterranean cuisine.
Passatge de la Concepció 5. Tel: 93/487-0196. No lunch Mon.

⑮ YIA YIA AMELIA Map p. 285, C4
A few steps from the Sagrada Família. In a rustic atmosphere reminiscent of village restaurants, La Yaya serves Basque cuisine as well as Catalan favorites such as *mel i mató* (curd cheese with honey).
Sardenya 364 - corner of Còrsega. Tel: 93/456-4573.

EL RAVAL

⑯ CA L'ESTEVET Map p. 286, B2
A popular, unpretentious little place, serving fine Catalan cuisine on tables set with homey gingham cloths. The prices are hard to beat, and the clientèle tends to be local. The house wine is light and inexpensive.
Valdonzella 46. Tel: 93/302-4186. Closed Sun.

⑰ CA L'ISIDRE Map p. 286, C1
Isidre Gironés has been a favorite with Barcelona's art crowd for the past 30 years, as the paintings and

engravings by Dalí, Miró, Tàpies and others amply attest. Freshly-prepared, traditional Catalan cooking is expertly teamed with wines, usually novelties from all over the Iberian Peninsula. The simplest dishes here are superb, the *foie gras* is always handled perfectly, and the partridges Isidre serves are usually wild birds he has shot himself. Location is a slight downside. If you come here at night, it's best to take a taxi. *Carrer de les Flors 12. Tel: 93/441-1139. Closed Sun, Holy Week, and mid-July-mid-Aug.*

18 **Casa Leopoldo** Map p. 286, C2
This well-known Barcelona favorite a five-minute walk from the Rambla serves fine seafood and general Catalan fare, none of it elaborate, but all of it home-cooked and delicious. If you're unsure what to choose, owner Rosa Gil will be happy to invent a menu for you, and select the wine as well. You won't be disappointed.
Carrer Sant Rafael 24. Tel: 93/441-6942. Closed Mon. No dinner Sun.

Barceloneta & Port

19 **Antiga Casa Solé** Map p. 198, B2
A traditional Sunday lunch favorite occupying an original two-story Barceloneta house and serving fresh, beautifully cooked seafood. The *arròs caldosos* (succulent rice dishes with lobster or fish) and *sepietes al forn amb tomàquet* (roast cuttlefish with tomato) are house specialties.
Sant Carles 4. Tel: 93/221-5012. Closed Mon. and last 2 wks of Aug. No dinner Sun.

20 **Can Majó** Map p. 198, B2
With a terrace outside on the beach, Can Majó is a solid Barcelona favorite

where you might easily run into the Mayor showing off the city's finest waterfront restaurant. House favorites begin with *caldero de bogavante* (a rice and lobster bouillabaisse). Iberian ham and *chipirones* (baby squid) combine nicely with an Albariño white wine from Galicia.
Almirall Aixada 23. Tel: 93/221-5455. Closed Mon.

21 **Can Manel la Puda** Map p. 198, B2
Sit out in the winter or early spring sunshine and watch the world go by at this top-value, often oversubscribed

terrace on the main street into Barceloneta. The atmosphere is relaxed and the lunch-hour is long, lasting until 4 o'clock. A variety of traditional rice-based paellas are served. Try the *fideuà* (a noodle paella).
Passeig Joan de Borbó 60. Tel: 93/221-5013. Closed Mon.

Els Pescadors (Beyond the map) With an early 20th-century café-style dining room and a charming terrace under a low awning, this seafood specialist just past the Olympic Port in Poblenou is off the beaten path, but worth the trip. Paellas, *fideuà*, and fresh fish prepared *a la sal* (encased in salt), or as a *suquet* (stewed in its own juices) are all excellent.
Plaça de Prim 1. Tel: 225-2018. Closed Mon.

Just before opening time Can Majó is empty. Minutes later it will be packed.

GRÀCIA

22 Botafumeiro Map p. 284, B2 The fleets of waiters swarming around this Galician restaurant give the place an ever-present hum. Botafumeiro looks excited and exciting and always feels busy and thriving. The *Mariscada Botafumeiro* seafood medley is a tour de force. Half rations at the bar (at which a seat can be reserved in advance) are another option for fine food, good service, and great value.

Gran de Gràcia 81. Tel: 93/218-4230. Open 1pm-1am every day.

23 Jean-Luc Figueras Map p. 284, C2
Ask a local to tell you his favorite restaurant, and this one will probably be on his list. Fine Catalan cuisine with a French touch is the order of the day - appropriate for a place housed in the former salon of haute

couturier Balenciaga. Innovative interpretations such as the *mar i muntanya* of tripe and seasnails or anything Jean-Luc does with fresh foie are foolproof.

Carrer Santa Teresa 10. Tel: 93/415-2877. Closed Sun. No lunch Sat.

24 **FOLQUER** Map p. 284, C3

An understated little enclave offering superb sampler menus: innovative, small-format combinations using impeccable ingredients and traditional yet original techniques..

Torrent de l'Olla 3. Tel: 93/217-4395. Closed Sun and last 2 wks of Aug. No lunch Sat.

PEDRALBES & SARRIÀ

25 **EL MATÓ DE PEDRALBES** Map p. 206, B1

Authentically Catalan and good value, this tastefully decorated space -

named for the *mató* (fresh cheese) prepared by the nuns of the Monestir de Pedralbes - is a perfect postscript to a tour of the convent. The menu often

El Mató de Pedralbes, just downhill from the medieval convent.

includes game (redleg partridge or wild rabbit), and there is often *trinxat*, a Pyrenean dish of cabbage, potato, and bacon.
Bisbe Català 1. Tel: 93/204-7962. Closed Sun evening.

26 **TRAM-TRAM** Map p. 206, B2
Isidre Soler's modern yet classical Catalan cooking using contemporary techniques and tastes have made Tram-Tram an upper Barcelona institution. Isidre's wife Reyes, maître and dessert chef, is charming and helpful, while the little garden out back is a leafy retreat (unless the kindergarten next door is having recess). Ask for the round table in the back room to get the most rustic feel of the house.
Major de Sarrià 121. Tel: 93/204-8518. Closed Sun and late Dec-early Jan. No lunch Sat.

27 **VIVANDA** Map p. 206, B3
This lush green garden just above the Plaça de Sarrià is a cooling place for lunch in spring and summer, though the inside decor is slightly chilly. Catalan standards and classic dishes are presented in a relaxed atmosphere.
Carrer Major de Sarrià 134. Tel: 93/203-1918. Closed Sun.

Traditional Catalan architecture in Sarrià's Plaça de la Vila, home to the Vell Sarrià restaurant.

28 **VELL SARRIÀ** Map p. 206, B2
Fine rice dishes with game, seafood, or wild mushrooms are standout offerings here. This 17th-century Catalan farmhouse is a key Sarrià sight as well as a place to dine, especially at Sunday lunchtime, when nearly everyplace else nearby is closed.
Carrer Major de Sarrià/Plaça de la Vila. Tel: 93/204-5710. No dinner Sun.

PART V

PRACTICALITIES

Buying roses on the Diada de Sant Jordi.

PRACTICALITIES

FIESTAS & HOLIDAYS

The Catalan year is punctuated with festivals, some Christian, some pagan, some mythical in origin. The result is that whenever you visit Barcelona, there is likely to be a fiesta either looming or in progress. The main celebrations are given below:

The first major festival of the year is **Epiphany (January 6th)**, when the *Cavalcada dels Reis* celebrates the three kings' arrival. **February 10th** brings the *Festes de Santa Eulàlia*, in honor of Barcelona's second patroness (second to Our Lady of Mercy). The **April 23rd *Diada de Sant Jordi*** celebrates St George, patron saint of Catalonia, who saved a princess from the dragon's jaws somewhere south of Barcelona. The dragon's blood turned into a rosebush, hence the traditional Rose Festival, celebrated in Barcelona since medieval times in honor of chivalry and courtly love. In 1923, the Rose Festival merged with International Book Day, held in honor of Cervantes and Shakespeare, who both

died on April 23rd, 1616. Flower stands and book stalls set up all over town, men give their inamoratas roses, while the women respond with books. Widely considered Catalonia's true national day, though not even an official holiday, it is the best day of the year to be in Barcelona. **May 11th** brings the *Fira de Sant Ponç* to the Raval: beekeepers, herbalists and artisans bring their wares to Carrer Hospital and other outdoor city markets. **Corpus Christi**, a moveable feast held in June, on the Thursday after Trinity Sunday, is another beloved unofficial festive day. Floral displays surround the *ou com balla* (the dancing egg), an egg balancing magically on the fountains of the best

Fleeing from the flames of a correfoc through the streets of the Barri Gòtic.

patios of the Gothic Quarter. The Barcelona Town Hall, the Generalitat, and the City History Museum open their doors to the public and the dancing egg, a pagan symbol of fertility, balances hypnotically in the cathedral cloister, the Casa de l'Ardiaca, the Ateneu Barcelonès, Palau del Lloctinent, and the Acadèmia de les Bones Lletres on Carrer Bisbe Caçador, just off Plaça Sant Just. The **June 23rd** *Verbena de Sant Joan* celebrates Midsummer's Eve with bonfires, fireworks, and beach parties that last until dawn. Descended from pagan tradition surrounding the summer solstice, the bonfires are meant to extend the light of day through the abbreviated hours of darkness. An erotic and fiery explosion of joy coinciding with the end of school and the beginning of summer vacation, bonfires are stacked for days with old furniture and flammable throwaways. The tradition includes sweet wine and *coca* (sugared bread) and jumping through the bonfire for good luck and, for lovers, *amour éternel*. In some villages the oldest couple in town is honored with the final jump over the fire's dying embers. All the districts of Barcelona celebrate *Festa Major* on the day of their patron saint. **Gràcia's *Festa Major*** is one of the most spectacular, beginning on **August 15th** and lasting for a week, with concerts and dances and long tables set out for neighborhood street dinners. Catalonia celebrates its **national day** on **September 11th**, in defiant commemoration of the 1714 defeat by Felipe V, when the Bourbon claimant gained the Spanish throne and brought Catalonia under Madrid's jurisdiction. Barcelona's own *Festa Major* is **September 24th**, *Festa de la Mercè*, honoring Our Lady of Mercy, the city's main patron saint. For four days there are open air concerts, street dances, sardanas, *castellers*, and, most spectacularly, *correfocs*, processions through the streets involving fire-breathing dragons and devils. Meanwhile *piro musical*, a music and pyrotechnical display explodes on Montjuïc.

SHOPPING

Barcelona is stuffed to the gills with retail opportunities. Here is a selection of some of the city's best: the kind of places you won't find anywhere else in the world.
NB: Larger stores and touristic boutiques are always open, but most other stores take a lunch break between 1.30-3.30 or 4pm.

BOOKS

ALTAÏR Map p. 286, A3
Barcelona's major travel bookstore has many titles in English.
Gran Via de les Corts 616 (Eixample).

LA CENTRAL Map p. 284, D2
Barcelona's best bookstore has a seriously bookish feel and piles of recent publications, with many titles in English. The new branch in the former chapel of the Casa de la Misericòrdia at No. 6 Carrer Elisabets

More hiking guides than you can shake a stick at in the Llibreria Quera.

(Raval) is equally atmospheric.
Mallorca 237 (Eixample).

LLIBRERIA QUERA Map p. 286, C3
For hikers and mountaineers, this is the place for maps, guides, charts and all the information you will need to navigate the Iberian highlands.
Petritxol 2 (Barri Gòtic).

LLIBRERIA SANT JORDI Map p. 286, C3
Tiled floor and wooden Modernist fittings. A total jumble with books stacked on the ground, but Barcelona's prettiest bookstore without question.
Ferran 41 (Barri Gòtic).

SALA DE ARTE CANUDA Map p. 286, B3
One of the best second-hand bookstores in the world. Some foreign-language titles, but if you speak Spanish a real treasure trove, good for hours of browsing.
Canuda 4 (Barri Gòtic).

CERAMICS

ART ESCUDELLERS Map p. 286, D2
A cavernous ceramics center with work from all over Spain and Catalonia, with scores of artisans represented and maps showing where the work is from. Downstairs is a wine, cheese and Iberian ham tasting bar. *Escudellers 23-25 (just off the Lower Rambla).*

ITACA Map p. 286, D3
Piled high with ceramics of all kinds. Particularly strong on *azulejos*, decorative hand-painted tiles.
Ferran 26 (off the Lower Rambla).

MOLSA Map p. 286, C3
Ceramics, textiles and diverse crafts.
Pl. Sant Josep Oriol 1 (Barri Gòtic).

DESIGN

ATALANTA MANUFACTURA Map p. 287, D4
This master artisan sells beautiful handpainted and silk-screened shawls and scarves. They will also make to order.
Passeig del Born 10 (La Ribera).

bd Map p. 284, D3
bd (the initials stand for 'Barcelona Design') is a warehouse-style designer home-furnishing store in a Modernist gem, Domènech i Montaner's Casa Thomas (*see p. 98*).
Mallorca 291-293 (Eixample).

GIMENO Map p. 284, C2

A range of design from salt cellars to the latest in interior design concepts. Its sister store diagonally opposite is a lovely old space selling pipes, cigar cutters, cigarette lighters, fountain pens and other accouterments.
Passeig de Gràcia 102 & 101 (Eixample).

VINÇON Map p. 284, D2

Probably Barcelona's most famous store, a design emporium next to Gaudí's Casa Milà, which has expanded its premises through a rambling Modernist house that was once the home of poet-artist Santiago Rusiñol and the studio of Ramon Casas (*see p. 116*). Everything from handsome kitchenware to lamps and furniture has attitude here. If for nothing else, come here to see the molded ceilings and spectacular Modernist fireplace, with its enormous stylized face, a sort of cast-iron Vulcan. The wide roof terrace affords a rear-end view of La Pedrera, and gives a feel for how oases of cool quiet - even with a garden atmosphere - were created in the helter-skelter Eixample.
Passeig de Gràcia 96 (Eixample).

Roof terrace of Vinçon, with designer bench and good views of the back of Gaudí's La Pedrera.

FOOD, WINES & SPICES

LA BARCELONESA Map p. 287, D4
Spices, teas and saffrons make this aromatic grocer's store a must. *Comerç 27 - below the Born market (La Ribera).*

CAELUM Map p. 286, C3
Handicrafts and artisanal foods such as honey and preserves, made in convents and monasteries all over Spain.
Carrer de la Palla 8 (Barri Gòtic).

LA CASA DEL BACALAO Map p. 287, B3
Just off Portal del Àngel, this unique store sells only one thing: salt cod, plus books of recipes.
Comtal 8 (Barri Gòtic).

CASA GISPERT Map p. 287, D4
A picturesque old-fashioned grocer's that has been in service since 1851, selling home-ground spices, saffron, candies and nuts.
Sombrerers 23 (La Ribera).

CHOCOLATE AMATLLER Map p. 284, E2
A variety of chocolates, traditionally or novelty-wrapped, available in

Casa Amatller, once home to Barcelona's premier chocolate manufacturer. NB: Some of it is cooking chocolate, so check before you buy.
Passeig de Gràcia 41 (Eixample).

JOBAL Map p. 287, C4
This fragrant shop carries pungent saffron and spices by the burlap sack.
Princesa 38 (above La Ribera).

MANTEQUERIA RAVELL Map p. 285, D3
This superb foodstuffs expert brings

Olive oil glimmers viscous and delicious in Casa Gispert.

in Spain and Europe's very finest produce, from anchovies from L'Estartit to the best Idiazabal sheep cheese from the Basque Country to acorn-fed Iberian hams from Extremadura. The long table in the back of the store is open and available for tastings on a first-come-first-served basis from 10 in the morning until 10 at night.
Carrer d'Aragó 313 (Eixample).

TOT FORMATGE Map p. 287, D4
Cheeses from all over Spain and the world.
Passeig del Born 13 (La Ribera).

VILA VINITECA Map p. 287, D4
Barcelona's best wine shop with wine-tastings and world wines. The Vila grocery store across the way sells the top cheeses from around Spain.
Agullers 7 (La Ribera).

JEWELRY & FASHION

Barcelona has thousands of clothing stores. For a sample browse, try the Rambla de Catalunya for high-street fashion (Zara) and one-off boutiques hosting the creations of Spanish fashion designers. Barcelona's well-known department store, El Corte Inglés on Plaça Catalunya, has brand-names by the rail-full.

JOAQUIM BERAO Map p. 284, D2
One of Barcelona's leading jewelry designers.
Rambla de Catalunya 74 - corner of València (Eixample).

CANDELA Map p. 287, D4
Next to Santa Maria del Mar in a superb 17th-century house, young designers show their work.
Santa Maria 6 (La Ribera).

GROC Map p. 284, D2
Toni Miró's two shops have the latest look for men, women, and children.

Carrer Muntaner 382 and Rambla de Catalunya 100 - corner of Provença (Eixample).

DAVID VALLS Map p. 284, D2
This fashion designer is representative of new, young Barcelona trends.
València 235 (Eixample).

SOLÉ Map p. 286, D3
This small shoe shop near the Plaça de la Mercè offers its own hand-made selections, plus a host of others from shoemakers worldwide.
Ample 7 (La Mercè).

Cereria Subirà.

ODDS & ENDS

CERERIA SUBIRÀ Map p. 287, C3
This candle shop founded in 1761 is considered Barcelona's oldest store, even though the Subirà waxworks didn't move here until 1909. The twin stairways and ornate décor are from the mid 19th century when a dressmaker's occupied the space.
Baixada de la Llibreteria 7 - continuation of Carrer Llibreteria (Barri Gòtic).

GANIVETERIA ROCA Map p. 286, C3
Directly opposite the giant rose window of the Santa Maria del Pi church, this legendary knife store offers a century of nonpareil cutlery culture. Scissors, penknives, tweezers, shaving tackle: if it's made of steel, they have almost certainly got it.
Plaça del Pi 3 (Barri Gòtic).

GUANTERIA COMPLEMENTS ALONSO
Map p. 286, B3
Pretty Modernist façade and fittings, and stacks of delicate hand-made fans brought out of little drawers for you to inspect and select. Evening bags and étuis also a specialty.
Santa Anna 27 (Barri Gòtic).

LA HERBORISTERÍA DEL REY Map p. 286, D2
This herbal remedy specialist is an olfactory oasis not to miss. The paintings on the wooden drawers, and the hand-blown glass window panes are priceless gems. Presently selling anything from lime blossom tea, *hierbaluisa*, and camomile, to ginseng and guaraná, just a breath or two here will cure you of ills you didn't even know you had.
Carrer del Vidre 1 - corner of Carrer Heures (Barri Gòtic).

Window display at Guanteria Complements Alonso, an old-fashioned shop selling old-fashioned accessories.

Scissors for all seasons, at the Ganiveteria Roca on Plaça del Pi.

LA MANUAL ALPARGATERA   Map p. 286, D3
This shop and studio just off Carrer Ferran specializes in handmade rope-sole sandals and espadrilles, once standard Catalan footwear, and still used in traditional sardana-dancing. *Avinyó 7 (Barri Gòtic).*

SOMBRERERIA OBACH   Map p. 286, C3
A handsome storefront heralds a 75 year-old hat store at the edge of the old Jewish quarter. A Barcelona classic. *Carrer del Call 2 (Barri Gòtic).*

PAPIRUM   Map p. 287, C3
A minuscule shop selling exquisite hand-printed notepaper, marbled blank journals, and writing implements. *Baixada de la Llibreteria 2 - continuation of Carrer Llibreteria (Barri Gòtic).*

Right: Exterior of the Hotel Jardí, a recently renovated center-of-town refuge on Plaça del Pi.

HOTELS & ACCOMMODATION

Barcelona has hundreds of hotels. The following is not an exhaustive list, but a personal selection, covering all styles and price ranges. Prices or price ranges are rack rates for a double room in high season, excluding taxes.

CIUTAT VELLA (OLD CITY)

HOTEL BANYS ORIENTALS Map p. 287, D3
Fashionable design hotel above the Senyor Parellada restaurant (Catalan cuisine) - very good value, close to Santa Maria del Mar and the lively bars and restaurants of the Born.
43 rooms. € 89.
Carrer de l'Argenteria 37 (La Ribera). Tel: 93/268-8460.
www.hotelbanysorientals.com

COLÓN Map p. 287, C3
Comfort, ambience and old-fashioned style make this one of the best hotels in Barcelona. Directly across the square from the cathedral, its location could hardly be bettered. Rooms and service are irreproachable.
147 rooms. € 229.
Restaurant, in-room data ports, minibars, cable TV, bar, baby-sitting, meeting room, travel services.

Av. Catedral 7 (Barri Gòtic). Tel: 93/301-1404.
www.hotelcolon.es

CONTINENTAL Map p. 286, B3
At the very top of the Rambla, this is a perfect jumping-off point for both the old town and the Eixample. Rooms are small but cozy. George Orwell stayed here in 1937, hiding from a Stalinist purge and recovering from a bullet wound in the throat.
35 rooms. €75.
Rambla 138. Tel: 93/301-2570
www.hotelcontinental.com

JARDÍ Map p. 286, C3
The perfect choice if you want to stay in the heart of the Barri Gòtic. Plaça del Pi and Plaça Sant Josep Oriol are lively hangouts day and night. The rooms have simple furnishings and small but spotless bathrooms.
40 rooms. €80.
Pl. Sant Josep Oriol 1 (Barri Gòtic). Tel: 93/301-5900.
www.hoteljardi.com

LE MERIDIEN Map p. 286, B2
The premier hotel in the Rambla area, home to opera stars and rock artists, accommodations here are light and spacious. Computer hookups are ubiquitous. Rooms over the Rambla are spectacular (and soundproofed).
206 rooms. €270-360.
Restaurant, bar, baby-sitting, business services, parking (fee).
Rambla 111. Tel: 93/318-6200.
www.meridienbarcelona.com

PARK HOTEL Map p. 287, D4
50's minimalist gem. The entryway, lobby and stairs are splendid survivals. Rooms are functional: good, clean 3-star quality. The Park is known around town for its style and its

Reception area of the minimalist Hotel Park in La Ribera.

fashionable restaurant, Abac. Rooms at the front can be noisy.
91 rooms. €142.
Av. Marquès de l'Argentera, 11 (La Ribera). Tel: 93/319-6000.
www.parkhotelbarcelona.com

RACÓ DEL PI Map p. 286, C3
This sleek space on a lively Gothic Quarter street offers cheerful service and flawless accommodations. Equidistant from the cathedral, the Boqueria market, Plaça Catalunya and the Palau de la Música, this cozy *racó* (corner) is as practical as it is spotless.
37 rooms. €180.
Bar, breakfast room, minibars, cable TV.
Carrer del Pi 7 (Rambla). Tel: 93/342-6190.
www.h10.es

Room with sun terrace in Le Méridien, one of the premier hotels overlooking the busy Rambla.

EIXAMPLE

CLARIS Map p. 284, D2
Barcelona's best, offering a counterpoint of contemporary design and classical furnishings in the former Vedruna palace. Lamps and chairs with attitude, a Japanese water garden, the gourmet East 47 restaurant, and an archeological museum combined with polished service make the Claris a standout.
80 rooms, 40 suites. €372.
2 restaurants, pool, gym, sauna, bar, meeting rooms, parking (fee).
Carrer Pau Claris 150 - corner of València. Tel: 93/487-6262.
www.derbyhotels.es

CONDES DE BARCELONA Map p. 284, D2
Excellently located for exploring the Modernist Eixample, this refurbished townhouse is all new behind the marble entrance and stairway from the original 1891 building. The best rooms have hot tubs and terraces overlooking interior

gardens. The annex across the street is somewhat less festive, but rooms are comfortable and modern.

183 rooms. €205.

Restaurant, pool, gym, hot tub, piano bar, business services, meeting room, parking (fee).

Passeig de Gràcia 73 & 75 - corner of Mallorca. Tel: 93/467-4780.

www.condesdebarcelona.com

CONTINENTAL PALACETE Map p. 284, E2

Small hotel in a grand, late 19th-century Eixample town house on the corner of Barcelona's nicest promenade, Rambla de Catalunya.

The sumptuous stairway and public rooms make you feel to the manor born. The rooms are full of fabrics and frills - no minimalism here.

19 rooms. €120-295.

Rambla de Catalunya 30 - corner of Diputació. Tel: 93/445-7657.

www.hotelcontinental.com

GRAN VIA Map p. 287, A3

This 19th-century town house is a Modernist enclave, with an original chapel, a hall-of-mirrors breakfast room, an Art Nouveau staircase, and belle époque phone booths. Guest rooms are less remarkable, with bottle-green carpets and Regency-

The lobby of the Hotel Claris, adorned with pieces of Roman sculpture.

style furniture.
53 rooms. €110.
Minibar, parking (fee).
Gran Via 642. Tel: 93/318-1900.
www.nnhotels.es

MAJESTIC Map p. 284, D2
A family operation run by one of
Barcelona's finest clans, the personal
touch is palpable here, from the front
desk to the chic rooms, the bustling
hotel bar, or the gourmet enclave
Drolma, where master chef Fermí
Puig experiments with culinary
traditions and fine products. A nerve
center for business and the arts alike,
this impeccably comfortable hotel is
an exciting spot, with all the
confident effervescence a big-city
hotel ought to have.
273 rooms, 30 suites. €330.
2 restaurants, in-room data ports,
minibars, cable TV, pool, health club,
bar, parking (fee).
Passeig de Gràcia 70 - corner of
València. Tel: 93/488-1717.
www.hotelmajestic.es

PASEO DE GRÀCIA Map p. 284, C2
This budget choice offers small
but comfortable rooms. High
over Barcelona's major shopping
boulevard and surrounded by
Modernist architecture, the top
balconies even have views over the
Collserola Hills behind the city. The

The Hotel Majestic at dusk.

pivotal location is convenient for
exploring all of Barcelona on foot: a
45-minute hike will get you to
Barceloneta, Pedralbes, the Sagrada
Família, or Montjuïc.
33 rooms. €68.
Passeig de Gràcia 102 - corner of
Rosselló. Tel: 93/215-5828.
hotelpdg@terra.es

RITZ Map p. 287, A4
This classic Barcelona hotel founded
in 1919 by Caesar Ritz, was restored
to its former splendor in the mid-
1990s. The rambling lobby is at once
imperial and informal, while the
rooms contain Regency furniture and
faux-Roman baths and mosaics. The
restaurant, Diana, is Francophile and
phenomenal.
122 rooms. €361.

Lobby of the Ritz.

Restaurant, coffee shop, gym, sauna, baby-sitting, business services, meeting rooms.

Gran Via 668 - corner of Roger de Llúria. Tel: 93/318-5200.
www.ritzbcn.com

BARCELONETA & PORT OLÍMPIC

HOTEL ARTS Map p. 198, B4
A ten-minute taxi ride from the center of the city, this Ritz-Carlton skyscraper has little to do with Barcelona. Nevertheless, it is a chic and splendid universe of its own, with three restaurants, an outdoor pool, and the beach nearby. Impeccably comfortable, with falling water and Frank Gehry's goldfish out front, the Arts hovers over the nearby Olympic Port, offering a studiedly manufactured ambience.
397 rooms, 59 suites, 27 apartments.
€350-450.
3 restaurants, pool, hair salon.

Carrer de la Marina 19-21 (Port Olímpic). Tel: 93/221-1000.
www.harts.es

MARINA FOLCH Map p. 198, B3
This little Barceloneta secret over the Peru restaurant offers views over the harbor and the beach a five-minute walk away. The wonderful family that runs the hotel and the restaurant will take good care of you. The rooms are small but clean and modern.
7 rooms. €55.
Restaurant.
Carrer del Mar 16 pral. (Barceloneta). Tel: 93/310-3709.

TIBIDABO

GRAN HOTEL LA FLORIDA (Beyond the map)

Spectacular Barcelona views from Tibidabo and state-of-the-art technology and comfort are the main features of David Stein's latest creation in this mountaintop retreat, first opened in 1925. Gardens, waterfalls, pools, massage therapy, the gourmet L'Orangerie restaurant: this is a spa city of its own, just twenty minutes by taxi from the heart of the Barri Gòtic.

74 rooms and suites. €310-410.
Restaurants, pool, garden, fitness center, massage therapy, parking.
Ctra. Vallvidrera-Tibidabo 83-93. Tel: 93/259-3000.
www.granhotellaflorida.com

APARTMENT RENTALS

There are various possibilities for renting apartments. For a selection of centrally-located (Barri Gòtic) and sympathetically-furnished apartments in historic buildings try Barcelona Rentals at bcnrentals@mindspring.com
http://www.atlanta-ads.com

The two buildings of the Condes de Barcelona (see p. 263).

PRACTICAL TIPS

WHEN TO VISIT

August is holiday month in Spain, which means that some of the things you have come to see might not be open. Everyone goes away, and the city shuts down. Restaurants close, the Liceu suspends performances - Barcelona is only half itself. April to June are probably the nicest months to visit, though winter time has a charm all its own too.

TRANSPORT

The metro system is easy to use and reliable: by far the cheapest and fastest way to get around town. Tickets cost the same no matter the distance you travel. If you know you are going to be using the metro more than once, it's best to buy

Barcelona, winter city. Publicity poster from the turn of the last century.

The black and yellow Barcelona taxis are easily identifiable and good value.

a 'Targeta T10', which gives you ten rides. It is valid on the metro, on the FGC (the line which runs from Plaça Catalunya to Sarrià), the Montjuïc funicular and the Tramvía Blau, which runs from Av. Tibidabo up to the summit.

Taxis are good value and easy to find. Either hail one in the street (they are black and yellow and easy to spot) or phone for one on 93/387-1000, 93/490-2222 or 93/357-7755.

TOURIST OFFICES

There are information centers on Plaça Catalunya and Plaça Sant Jaume (in the Barri Gòtic). The main tourist information center is the Palau Robert at Passeig de Gràcia 107, Tel: 93/238-8091. Map p. 284 C2.

CITY TOURS

The Bus Turístic runs from 9.30am to 7.30pm, every 10 to 30 minutes, depending on whether it's high or low season. There are two routes, passing all Barcelona's main sights. You buy a day pass on the bus: the ticket includes the Montjuïc funicular, the cable car across the port, and the Tramvía Blau up to the summit of Tibidabo. Buses leave from Plaça Catalunya, and operate on a hop-on, hop-off basis. (NB: Tibidabo offers a funfair - good for entertaining children - and spectacular views over the city, particularly good when the air is crisp and clear, which it almost never is. Apart from the funfair there are no sights as such to see. If your time in Barcelona is limited, don't make it a priority. If you want to admire the neo-Gothic church of the Sacred Heart (Sagrat Cor) and Sir

Tibidabo and the Torre de Collserola reflected in the doors of the MNAC.

Norman Foster's Torre de Collserola communications tower, you get as good a view as any from the summit of Montjuïc.)

TELEPHONE NUMBERS

All telephone numbers in this book should be prefixed (00 34) for calls from outside Spain; To make calls from within Barcelona, just dial the number as given. Likewise for calls to Barcelona from elsewhere in Spain.

PERSONAL SAFETY

Just as in any big city, it pays to be careful. The jostle of the Rambla offers myriad opportunity to pickpockets; the streets branching off it, at the lower end towards the port, lead into areas of town where you might feel uneasy, particularly at night. A broad spectrum of humanity inhabits Barcelona: you are likely to see a number of things to make your eyes widen. Most of it, on the whole, is unthreatening.

Yes, but is it art? A graffiti artist at work in the Raval.

GEGANTS I GEGANTES
BARCELONA'S CEREMONIAL GIANTS

The tradition of parading giant figures through the streets of Catalonia goes back at least to the 14th century, when official records confirm the presence of two giants in Barcelona's Corpus Christi procession. One represented Goliath, while the other was Christopher, the saint usually portrayed as a giant who, carrying a child across a river, suddenly felt the weight of the whole world on his shoulders, as the child turned out to be Jesus. These early *gegants* caused such a sensation that no procession or festivity afterwards was complete without giants and, subsequently, *capsgròssos* (literally 'big heads'), oversized heads paraded along with the giants. Little by little, the early

figures became more numerous and were not limited to the Bible. Moors and Christians were a universal theme for giants up until the 17th century. In 1564 municipal files recorded that, on the occasion of the entrance of King Felipe II into Barcelona, the ropemakers' guild carried male and female giants. Competition between guilds led to a general proliferation of giants, with different parishes and neighborhoods creating their own variations on this theme. For years *gegantes*, giantesses, served as runway models for the year's fashions and hair styles. Today

each of Barcelona's ten municipal districts has its own giants, while there are *penyes* (clubs) with giants, and even families with *capsgròssos*, *nans* (dwarves), or *dracs* (dragons) brought out for neighborhood fiestas and processions. Different giants represent neighborhood-specific traditions: Barceloneta's giants, for example, are a fisherman and his wife. Barcelona's official giants, Jaume and Violant, representing King Jaume I el Conqueridor (*see p. 15*) and his wife Violant of Hungary, are on display at the Palau de la Virreina (La Rambla 99), along with the Barcelona eagle, representing independence and justice, and the *gegantona Laia* (little giant Laia), representing Eulàlia, Barcelona's second patron saint (*see p. 50*).

INDEX

Numbers in italics refer to illustrations. Numbers in bold are major references.

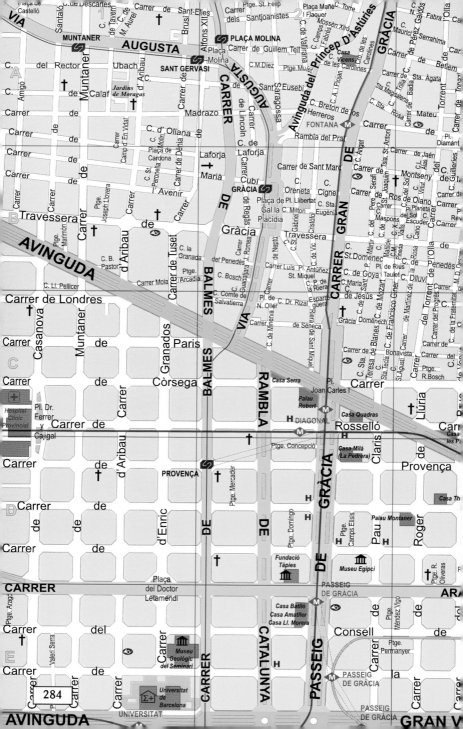

THE EIXAMPLE &
UPPER BARCELONA

285

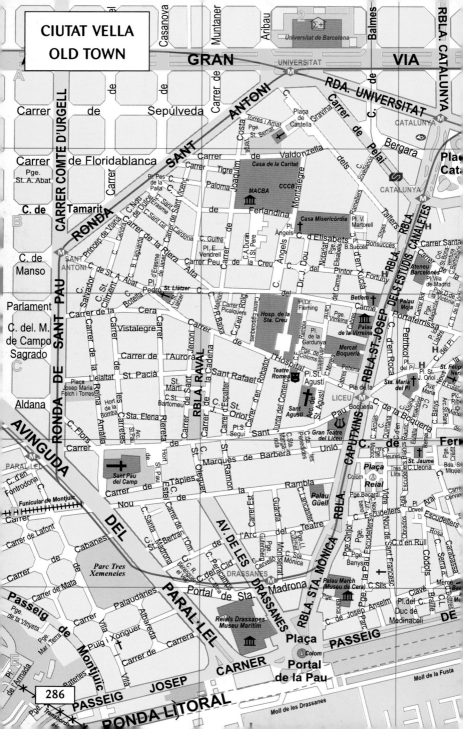

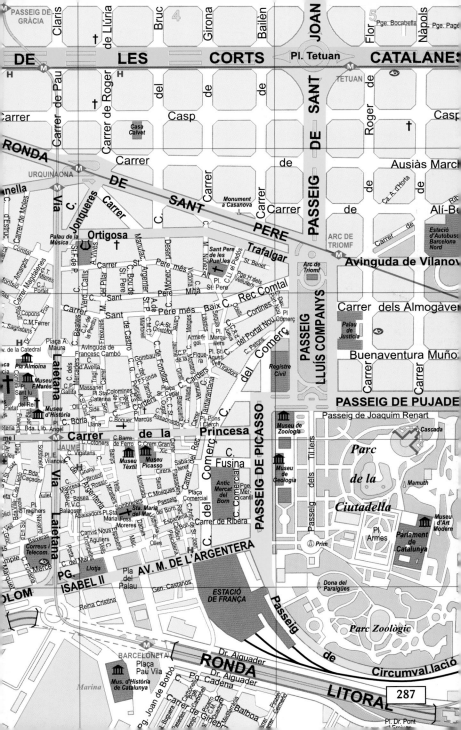

SOMERSET LIMITED
Lövőház utca 39, 1024 Budapest, Hungary
Felelős kiadó: Ruszin Zsolt, a Somerset Kft. igazgatója
Repro studio: *Timp Kft.*
Set in Berkeley Book 9.8pt and Barmeno
Printed by: *Novoprint Rt. Attila Miseje, Director*
ISBN 963 206 323 6